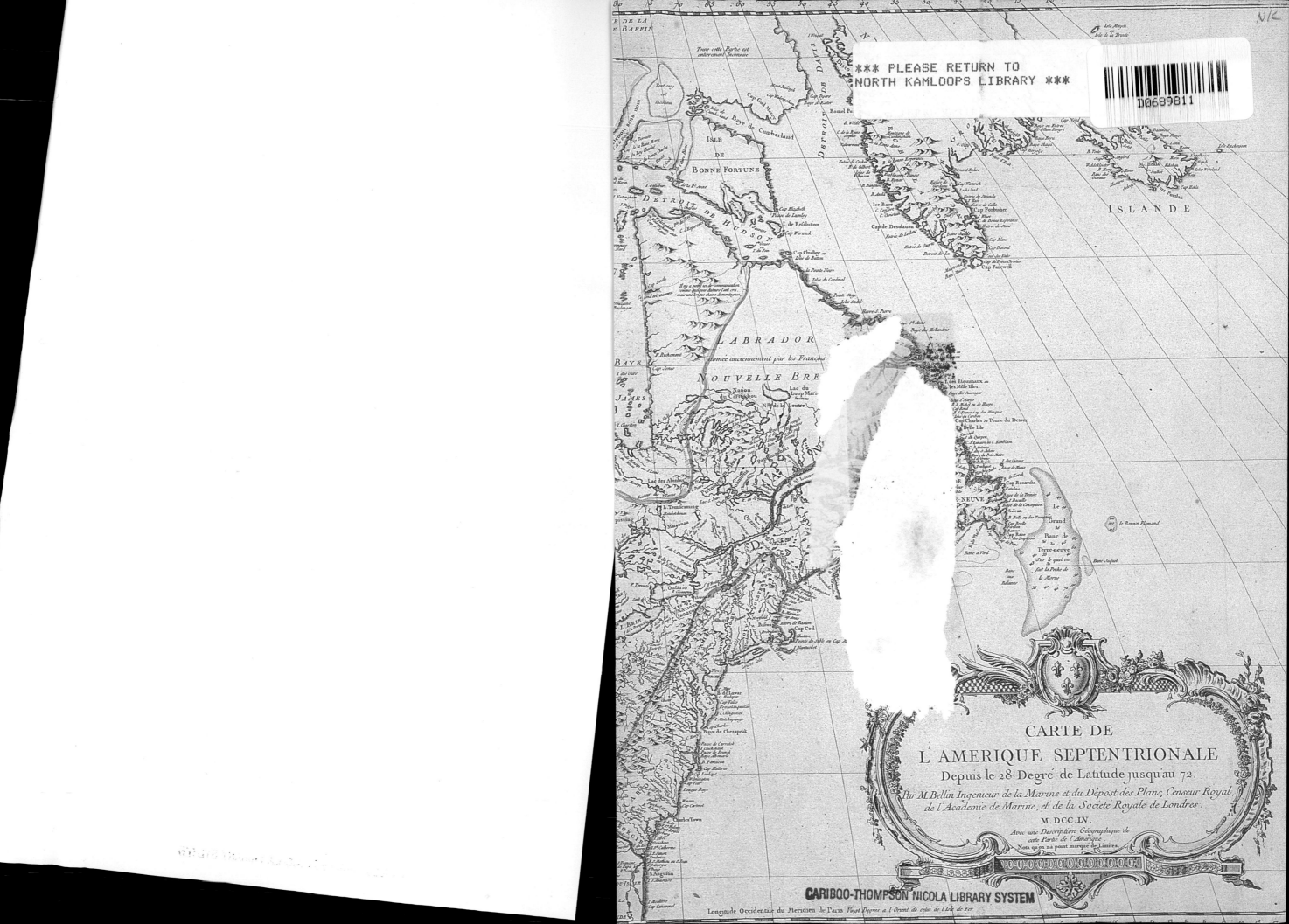

CARTE DE

L'AMERIQUE SEPTENTRIONALE

Depuis le 28 Degré de Latitude jusqu'au 72.

Par M. Bellin Ingenieur de la Marine et du Dépost des Plans, Censeur Royal,
de l'Academie de Marine, et de la Societé Royale de Londres.

M. DCC. LV.

Avec une Description Géographique de
cette Partie de l'Amerique
Nota qu'on n'a point marqué de Limites

Longitude Occidentale du Meridien de Paris Vingt Degrés a l'Orient de celui de l'Isle de Fer

Taking Root

Records of Our History

Taking Root
Canada from 1700 to 1760

André Vachon, M.R.S.C.,
with the assistance of
Victorin Chabot and André Desrosiers

 Public Archives   Archives publiques
Canada   Canada

©Minister of Supply and Services Canada
1985
English translation ©1985
by John F. Flinn

Available in Canada through authorized
bookstore agents and other bookstores or
by mail from
Canadian Government Publishing Centre
Supply and Services Canada
Ottawa, Canada K1A 0S9

Catalogue No. SA2-129/2-1985E
ISBN 0-660-11895-5
Canada: $34.95
Other countries: $41.95
Price subject to change without notice

Canadian Cataloguing in Publication Data
Vachon, André, 1933-
    Taking Root : Canada from 1700 to 1760
(Records of our History)

    Issued also in French under title: L'enracinement.
    Includes index.
    DSS Cat. no. SA2-129/2-1985E (bound)
    DSS Cat. no. SA2-129/2-1985-1E (pbk.)
    ISBN 0-660-11895-5 (bound). - ISBN 0-660-11896-3 (pbk.)
    1. Canada—History—1663-1713 (New France)—Sources.
    2. Canada—History—1713-1763 (New France)—Sources.
    I. Chabot, Victorin. II. Desrosiers, André. III.
Public Archives Canada. IV. Title. V. Series.
FC350.V313 1985   971.01′8   C85-097-007-5
F1030.V313 1985

Table of Contents

v

Foreword

Taking Root, like its predecessor *Dreams of Empire*, provides the reader with a rich and carefully chosen array of beautiful reproductions of archival records. Both historians and the general public will enjoy this privileged look at our past: landscapes and rural scenes; cities and buildings; political, military and religious figures, and ordinary Canadians. Using manuscripts, other written material and pictures, this book gives us an intimate understanding of the thinking, interests and concerns of the men and women who — though we sometimes tend to forget this — were as much alive as we are today.

As the minister responsible for the Public Archives of Canada, and consequently for the conservation and optimum use of a large part of Canada's archival heritage, I am very pleased to welcome this second volume, which is an excellent tool for fulfilling the PAC's mission of serving as the collective memory of the Canadian people. The major exhibition, also called *Taking Root*, has the same theme and uses about half the archival records that appear in the book. Like the book, the exhibition will make this period of our history more accessible and understandable to the general public. The past has great significance for the present, but it is very difficult to bridge the gap created by the years.

Taking Root deals not only with geography, population, government, economy, and social and religious life, but also with the fact that the people living in the St. Lawrence River valley in the early eighteenth century had their own way of life and way of thinking. They were conscious of their distinct traditions and history, and were becoming very firmly rooted as Canadians. The following statement by a group of inhabitants around 1719 to the political authorities in France clearly illustrates this new identity:

"Notice if you will, milords, that the residents of this colony have been here for up to four generations, or have recently settled here; that their families, many of which are large, are with them; that they were the first to help found this colony; that they cleared and cultivated the land . . . built churches and fine homes, helped fortify the settlements, supported the war effort . . . ."

As the colony along the St. Lawrence was developing, British colonies were being established in Nova Scotia, in Newfoundland and around Hudson's Bay. A great many immigrants had settled in Canada and had no desire to return to their countries of origin.

These settlers were the ancestors of a large part of Canada's present population. Their descendants will no doubt be pleased to find a wealth of information in this book about the activities and way of life of their forebears. Those people who came to Canada more recently, in particular those of various origins who settled and cultivated the West from the Prairies to the Pacific, will gain a better understanding of their fellow Canadians through this book by learning about the political and social organization and the economic and artistic development of the first settlers from the Atlantic countries, and by comparing these things with the culture of their own ancestors, who came from Central Europe, Asia or elsewhere.

This book can be used as a reference tool, and can also be read at various levels. It is my sincere hope that many people will have the opportunity to enjoy it, and that *Taking Root* will fulfil the objectives of the Public Archives of Canada by increasing Canadians' awareness and understanding of their past, and by bringing the past to life for them, using the authentic records of our history.

Marcel Masse
Minister of Communications

Preface

Taking Root is the second volume published by the Public Archives of Canada in its series *Records of Our History*. This series, which is intended for both students and the general public, gives an overview of the many facets of Canada's development and presents reproductions of the main archival records — evidence from the past — that researchers consult when writing the history of our country. As a celebration and illustration of Canada's history, the volumes of this series, which contain many hitherto unpublished and little-known records from the Public Archives and other Canadian and foreign institutions, give readers a wonderful opportunity to expand their knowledge of the past, and they will make a student's first experience with original sources a pleasant one.

Whereas *Dreams of Empire* covered the period from the discovery of Canada to 1700, *Taking Root* reviews Canada's history from 1700 to 1760. It begins with a brief summary of the period being examined. The text is illustrated with 207 reproductions of archival records — maps, engravings, paintings, seals, medals, manuscripts and printed materials — from 38 Canadian, American and European institutions. These records are divided into themes and sub-themes prefaced by short introductions. Each record is accompanied by a description, giving the technical details, background, origin and occasionally major excerpts.

The book is designed to enable readers to browse through it, and if an illustration catches their eye, they can find the description and historical background close by. Of course, they can also read the book from cover to cover, and refer to the records that illustrate, support and explain the text.

André Vachon, historian, editor and a member of the Royal Society of Canada, was responsible for the content of the book. He wrote the summary of the period and the introductions to the themes and sub-themes. Victorin Chabot and André Desrosiers of the French Archives Section at the Public Archives participated in the project as well. André Desrosiers researched the manuscripts and many of the other records; he assisted André Vachon in his research, joined in the final selection of items and wrote the descriptions. Victorin Chabot co-ordinated the project by overseeing all stages, providing liaison between the various units involved and communicating with outside institutions. We should also thank the following people for their help: Gilles Langelier, maps; Marc Lebel and Auguste Vachon, pictures; and Yves Marcoux, printed material. All these persons participated in the preliminary selection of records and the preparation of the technical descriptions. Raymonde Litalien, head of our Paris office, was responsible for locating and reproducing a number of records conserved in France. Aline Brunet typed the texts.

Photography Services reproduced the records. Graphic design was by Wawa Design based on a concept by Eiko Emori. The Publications Division edited the texts and produced the book.

The original volume was written in French under the title *L'enracinement*. It was translated into English by John F. Flinn, professor at the University of Toronto.

In addition, an exhibition was prepared of many of the items reproduced in the book. This exhibition will travel around Canada and to other countries during the next few years.

We would like to express our sincere thanks to André Vachon and all those who worked on the preparation of this book, especially the institutions that allowed us to reproduce originals for this publication and the exhibition.

Bernard Weilbrenner
Assistant Dominion Archivist

Provenance of Documents

Canada

Archives des soeurs grises, Montréal
Archives nationales du Québec, Centre d'archives de Québec
Archives nationales du Québec, Centre régional de Montréal
Hudson's Bay Company Archives, Provincial Archives of Manitoba, Winnipeg
McCord Museum, Montréal
Monastère des augustines de l'Hôpital-Général de Québec
Monastère des augustines de l'Hôtel-Dieu de Québec
Musée de l'île Sainte-Hélène, Montréal
Musée du château Ramezay, Montréal
Musée du Québec, Québec
Musée historial, Basilique de Sainte-Anne-de-Beaupré
Musée régional de Vaudreuil-Soulanges
National Currency Collection, Bank of Canada, Ottawa
National Gallery of Canada, Ottawa
National Library of Canada, Ottawa
Parks Canada, Fortress of Louisbourg
Parks Canada, Ottawa
Public Archives of Canada, Ottawa
Queen's University Archives, Kingston
Société du Musée du Séminaire de Québec

Other Countries
Archives du ministère des Affaires étrangères, Paris
Archives municipales, Rochefort, France
Archives nationales, Paris
Archives nationales, Paris: Section Outre-Mer
Bibliothèque de l'Inspection du Génie, Paris
Bibliothèque nationale, Paris
British Library, London
Musée de la Marine, Paris
Museum of Art, Carnegie Institute, Pittsburgh
Newberry Library, Chicago
Peabody Museum, Harvard University, Cambridge, Massachusetts
Public Record Office, London
Royal Library, Windsor Castle, England
Séminaire des Missions étrangères, Paris
Service historique de l'Armée, Vincennes, France
Service historique de la Marine, Vincennes, France

Private Collections
Collection Le Moyne de Martigny, Rubelles, France
Private collection, France

During the eighteenth century, New France experienced considerable growth, despite losing Hudson's Bay, Newfoundland and Nova Scotia in 1713. The rapidly increasing population spread out into new territory, including Louisiana and Île Royale. The residents of New France multiplied their industrial and commercial ventures, established social institutions, and developed their own customs, values and characteristics. Attachment to the land, strong family ties and community life characterized French-Canadian society more and more as time passed.

Several thousand English and Irish immigrants settled in Newfoundland between 1700 and 1760. Nova Scotia remained populated almost exclusively by Acadians until 1749, when England began sending over many English, German and Swiss colonists, who brought with them diverse customs and religious beliefs.

Although the Indians maintained their traditional way of life, they could not escape the white man's influence, and adopted some of his values and habits.

Introduction

When the eighteenth century began, New France was officially at peace with her neighbours to the south, but no one in the colony had any illusions about the stability of the situation. The signing of the Treaty of Ryswick in 1697 was of much more consequence for Europe than for America. On this side of the Atlantic the ambition that had consumed both sides since the 1680s had not become any less intense, fuelled as it was by the same motives that had kindled the first conflagration. Consequently, far from forgetting their quarrel, the rivals took advantage of what was in effect only a truce to strengthen their positions and furbish their aims.

On the political level, for example, Louis XIV took two very important decisions in rapid succession: to found Louisiana in 1700 and Detroit in 1701, with a view to containing the thrust by the English towards the Mississippi and the Great Lakes, which would have brought them closer to the Spanish colonies. Governor General de Callière would have much preferred that the western posts be reopened and trading licences, which had been abolished in 1696, be re-established; his counsels were not heeded, and the king gave his approval to the purely military conception — albeit a defensive one — of the planned establishments. In this way the royal determination to assert French dominion and maintain it over the part of the continent west of the Appalachians was made clear.

On the diplomatic level Callière undertook a task in this period that had perhaps had no parallel up until then. During this time there were almost incessant wars that stirred up several of the tribes allied with the French against one another. Some of these tribes, moreover, were attacking the Iroquois themselves, which risked at any moment setting the West ablaze or plunging the colony into a new Franco-Iroquois war. In the face of this turmoil, Callière undertook the almost impossible task of pacifying these tribes, some thirty in number, and inducing them to sign a general peace treaty to which the French and the Iroquois would themselves subscribe.

He was a skillful negotiator, and on 4 August 1701 he brought his task to a successful conclusion; from then on people referred to the Great Peace of Montréal. It is true that circumstances had aided the governor: as the English, who nevertheless pretended to consider the Iroquois to be British subjects, had failed to come to their aid when they were attacked on their own territory, the Five Nations had felt freer to parley directly with the French and reach an understanding with them. The French had won a signal victory: the Iroquois had in fact pledged their word to remain neutral in the event of a conflict between France and England.

The War of the Spanish Succession

Five years after the Treaty of Ryswick a new European war, the War of the Spanish Succession, was the signal for the resumption of hostilities in North America. Callière, who died soon after, decided on his own to avoid any action that by giving offence to the Iroquois might have nullified the effects of the 1701 treaty. This time the minister agreed with him, and Governor de Vaudreuil, who had been appointed Callière's successor in 1703, applied himself very zealously and intelligently to implementing a strategy that would respect that policy. He viewed New France as being made up of three distinct parts, each of which he should approach differently. First, Canada (the heart of the French empire in America) had to be protected against a third Iroquois war; consequently he had to refrain from any sort of action against the Five Nations, or even against their English allies in the colony of New York. He was very successful in this, at least to begin with, and the New Yorkers themselves abstained from any warlike acts against the French until 1709. Secondly, in the East, Acadia, a buffer zone between the English and the Canadian colony, had to be retained, and to do so Vaudreuil had to keep the Abenakis — formidable warriors — from going over to the side of the English; that was why he had to immediately compromise them by launching them against Massachusetts and what is now Maine before they switched their allegiance. Finally, on a third front, the West, it was of supreme importance, in order to retain that immense region, to be able to count upon the loyalty and support of the allied tribes and to prevent them by all possible means from warring among themselves.

In the West the situation was very difficult, as Callière had foreseen when Detroit was founded. In the western posts it was customary to carry on trade and diplomacy side by side: excellent diplomatic relations with the various tribes assured the French of a good harvest of furs, and the inverse was equally true. But, as a result of the markets being glutted, France had, to all intents and purposes, closed posts such as Michillimakinac by forbidding all trade there: being deprived of their means of subsistence, the garrisons had withdrawn. Consequently the personnel of the posts was no longer there to keep an eye on the tribes and exert an influence upon them — particularly to keep them from quarrelling among themselves — and to keep them in the French trade network. Furthermore, the Five Nations, who had never allowed those tribes to cross their territory in order to take their pelts to Albany, began to give them permission after 1701 to do so. The Iroquois, who had been very much weakened by their wars in the seventeenth century, were in fact seeking to prevent the nations from resuming hostilities against them. Finally, at the new post of Detroit, which had been built amidst the Iroquois hunting grounds, a few tribes (Hurons and Ottawas for example) came to settle, and they did not fail to trade with the Iroquois and the English, which in the long run could only put their loyalty to the French in peril.

The minister's policy, therefore, risked seriously endangering the Canadian economy and diplomacy in the West. But the governor general had requested in vain that the posts be reopened and the system of trading licences re-established, measures without which, in his opinion, disaster lay straight ahead. He was not entirely wrong.

The war was, then, confined to the eastern fronts. In Newfoundland, French and English multiplied their raids and ravaged one another's settlements and harbour installations. The most outstanding successes were the capture by the French of Bonavista in 1705 and St. John's in 1709.

It was, nevertheless, Acadia that was really at stake in this war — Acadia, which since 1613 had never known a period when it was not subject to attack, taken, retaken and constantly coveted. It has been written that whoever held it was in possession of "the key to the St. Lawrence." Acadia was also the only French position in New France that directly threatened the English settlements on the Atlantic coast. That was why it was the scene of so many military actions and surprise attacks in the seventeenth century; and that was also why, during the War of the Spanish Succession, almost all military activity was concentrated there. At the beginning of the century the Acadians were very few in number (about 1,200), hence the importance of the Abenakis. Although they were very early courted by the English and were at first tempted to join them, they finally allowed themselves to be persuaded by the French to switch allegiance. With a few Frenchmen at their head they carried out terror raids: they killed wantonly, took prisoners and destroyed everything in their path. The riposte from the English was swift and Acadia took as much as it gave. But that was only a matter of reprisals: what the English wanted was possession of the very heart of Acadia — the capital, Port-Royal; in 1704 and 1705 they tried to take it unsuccessfully.

Harassing and ravaging Massachusetts and Maine to keep the Abenakis loyal to their allegiance with the French was perhaps not a bad idea. But in 1708, just when the French were completing the pacification of the tribes that, having come together at Detroit, had been warring with one another since 1706 — which Callière had once more foreseen — a *rapprochement* took place between the English in New York and the Iroquois on the one hand and the New England settlers on the other. With the support of reinforcements from England, who had been called to the rescue, they would deliver the final blow to New France.

This determination to be done with the enemy to the north was marked by an initial success: in 1710 Port-Royal fell. The following year Admiral Walker, commanding an imposing fleet, was sailing for Québec, while land troops, accompanied by some 700 Iroquois, were preparing to invade Canada by way of Lake Champlain and the Richelieu River. On a foggy night eight of Walker's ships were shattered on the reefs of Île aux Oeufs. The admiral turned about; the invasion plan had failed. New France, one may well believe, had had a narrow escape.

Vaudreuil was not, for all that, at the end of his difficulties. The following year (1712), war broke out at Detroit, where several tribes, supported by the French garrison, attacked the Foxes and Mascoutens. By having Michillimakinac reoccupied immediately and sending emissaries to dissuade the Miamis and Illinois from joining the belligerents, the governor general narrowly prevented a wide-spread conflagration in the West.

The beaver crisis

The War of the Spanish Succession had been fought out entirely at a time when the colony was plagued by unprecedented economic problems. It had all started towards the end of the seventeenth century. After the expansion of the fur trade, which had been brought on by the obligation requiring the lessee of the Domaine d'Occident holding the trading concession to take all the beaver at a set price, and by the ill-considered policy followed by Frontenac, who used the pretext of military operations to launch big trading operations, France found herself with an enormous surplus of beaver pelts that no market could absorb rapidly. It was a matter of extreme urgency to reduce radically the shipments of beaver to the mother country, and, in order to do that, to cut down the production of pelts at their main source. In 1696 the king did away with the twenty-five fur-trading licences granted each year, shut down the western posts and ordered the coureurs de bois to return home. The measure seemed excessive to the Québec authorities: would their alliances with the western tribes survive the departure of the French? For, as Vaudreuil wrote in 1713, "the Indians' hearts are retained only by supplying them with what they need," and "they always take the side of those with whom they are trading." Now, there was good reason to wager that henceforth they would trade with the English. From Versailles the minister agreed to maintain a few posts in the West, but he refused to re-establish the trading licences. This settled nothing.

In Canada the merchants and leading citizens, upset by the crisis that had just burst upon them and that threatened them with ruin in short order, would not comply with the request of the French holders of the monopoly on pelts that they accept a lower price for their beaver furs or reduce production considerably. The unanimity that marked their refusal, the community of interests that motivated them and the attitude of the king himself, who seemed not to be at all opposed to their representations, led them to form the Compagnie du Canada, better known as the Compagnie de la Colonie, which was essentially an enterprise for exporting Canadian furs. In leaving management of pelts to them Versailles was hoping that they would very quickly impose upon themselves the restrictions made necessary by the saturation of the European market. Be that as it may, under the conventions signed by Pascaud in the name of the Canadian settlers, the lessee of the Domaine d'Occident sold the Canadians his surplus stock of beaver pelts and granted them the monopoly of the sale of beaver in France and Holland, and at the same time all the rights attached to the Domaine d'Occident (duties on the colony's imports and exports, benefits

4

from the exploitation of the Domaine du Roi, and domanial duties). In return the Canadians agreed to pay the tax-farmer Guigues the sum of 170,000 *livres* a year and to discharge the statement of charges (payment of certain salaries, pensions and subsidies in the colony). This contract was solemnly ratified at Québec on 10 October 1700.

In reality the company could not have come into being at a worse juncture. In Europe it proceeded to purchase an enormous quantity of unsold beaver skins at a time when the latest fashion decreed that less use be made of the fur in hat-making. In America, since the abolition of the trading licences and the closing of the western posts, smuggling was growing at an alarming rate: western furs were rerouted to the factories at Schenectady and Albany. The founding of Louisiana in 1700 provided a place of refuge for many coureurs de bois who, rather than comply with the repeated orders from the king and the Québec authorities, preferred to carry on their trade there, bringing to it a new form of contraband, the profits from which, however, did not benefit Canada. The founding of Detroit in 1701, followed soon after by the authorizations granted the western tribes by the Iroquois to cross their territory in order to trade at Albany, greatly encouraged the illegal trading.

Scarcely had it been formed when the Compagnie de la Colonie was confronted with serious problems: since it had no capital, it had to borrow in Paris, where money-lenders soon imposed conditions that were distinctly unfavourable; in Canada it suffered considerable losses at certain posts at a time when the return from the dues paid to the Domaine did not allow it to discharge the statement of charges; in short, because of the weak demand for beaver on the European markets, the company's financial charges, increased by the high cost of interest and steep management costs, proved to be much too heavy when compared with much too slender returns. It was a complete impasse: in 1704, being unable to meet its obligations, the company sought the king's help, but in vain. Matters went from bad to worse, and in 1706 the company went bankrupt: the beaver monopoly was transferred to the French firm of Aubert, Néret, et Gayot. This bankruptcy must be attributed essentially to the saturation of the market in Europe and to the shareholders' lack of capital in Canada.

The new holders of the monopoly could not work miracles: they were willing to buy annually up to 80,000 pounds of beaver, but at the price of only thirty *sols* a pound. In addition, until 1712 they refused to take *castor gras*. The Canadian merchants considered this proposition unacceptable: never had the price for beaver been so low, and never had the cost of barter goods been so high. The solution: illegal trade. And thus, from 1706 until 1712 a double policy was pursued in the beaver trade: it was one of limited purchases at an extremely low price on the part of the holders of the monopoly, and one of smuggling on the part of the Canadian traders.

Without the complicity of Albany, motivated by self-interest, the Canadian merchants would have been utterly ruined before long. Furthermore, without the trade goods obtained in the colony of New York, the French would never have been able to retain the allegiance of the allied tribes. And that was the reason why the colonial authorities tolerated this trade. That was in no way the least paradoxical aspect of a particularly troubled period, when France, which was at a very low ebb financially, perhaps owed the survival of her American colony to the very people who were bitterly disputing its possession with her!

Until 1713 the government in Versailles, ruined by the War of the Spanish Succession, did not take into account in the slightest the increase in expenditures caused by the military operations in America; on the contrary, it asked the colony to reduce its expenditures, refused to reimburse them entirely and even resorted to delaying its payments. Being unable to meet all the everyday needs (goods and services), the colonial authorities were forced to put into circulation more and more playing-card money, redeemable theoretically through bills of exchange drawn on the treasurers-general of the Marine. But soon even these bills of exchange were no longer honoured in France, except sometimes in the form of treasury notes convertible into cash at only half their value. This monetary crisis, combined with the staggering rise in shipping costs in wartime, brought on uncontrollable inflation, disastrous for trade, in Canada. In the period 1714–1720 this crisis was little by little resolved from within, after the State had decided to pay its debts in the colony by redeeming the playing-card money — but at only half its face value.

The Treaty of Utrecht

In America, France had come out of the War of the Spanish Succession the victor everywhere, except in Acadia. It was New France, however, that bore nearly all the cost of the war, which was disastrous for the mother country on the European battlefields. The Treaty of Utrecht, which put an end to the conflict, was so unfavourable to New France that it could be feared that she would not survive the amputations inflicted upon her or the political disorders she was threatened with in that same year, 1713.

Newfoundland, where the French occupied a few posts, including Plaisance, was ceded to England, although France retained fishing and occupation rights on the Grand Banks and on the north shore of the island, which were essential to her to supply herself with fish as well as to train some of the men needed for her navy.

Again in the East, Acadia came under British rule. By Acadia (or Nova Scotia) the British meant not only the peninsula of present-day Nova Scotia but also, by claiming the territory according to "its former frontiers," present-day New Brunswick and even the Gaspé peninsula. The French succeeded in retaining Île du Cap-Breton (Cape Breton Island) and Île Saint-Jean (Prince Edward Island), and in actual fact they considered New Brunswick to be French territory, even extending their claims as far south as the Kennebec River in the region inhabited by their Abenaki allies. A commission was supposed to be set up to examine the "boundaries" of Acadia, but the question was not settled until the Treaty of Paris in 1763.

In the North, Hudson Bay and its hydrographic system were also ceded to the British: the French abandoned Fort Bourbon and left the Hudson's Bay Company in complete control of the region. It was not so much the loss of the bay itself that was disturbing, since French trade there had never been very profitable — although, according to Vaudreuil and Bégon, the finest pelts on the continent were harvested there — but rather the prospect that, thanks to the river system that emptied into it, the English were going to establish themselves inland, to the west, among tribes that were suppliers of furs.

In reality, up until that time France's losses, although considerable, were not fatal, insofar as her fishing rights were guaranteed; possession of Île du Cap-Breton could assure her, in theory at least, of freedom of navigation up to Québec; and finally, the presence of the Abenakis between the English colonies to the south and Canada created a security zone for Canada. The real danger was in the West, and everyone realized that.

In recognizing the Iroquois as British subjects, the Treaty of Utrecht in fact gave the British direct access to the Great Lakes region. In addition, by giving the French and the British equal rights to trade with the western Indians, it suddenly threatened the alliances on which rested French trade and France's dominance in the West. In the event of a thrust by the English of New York and Pennsylvania, with the complicity of the Iroquois and some of her former allies, the possibility was foreseen that Canada would soon be cut off from the Great Lakes region at Lake Ontario, and the Illinois country, the Mississippi and Louisiana isolated at the same time.

Finally, the treaty was silent about the Ohio, Wabash and Mississippi region. It would, however, be one of the hot points in the next war. Indeed, in the West, for traders from Virginia and Pennsylvania the only passage through the Appalachians was the Monongahela, a tributary of the Ohio.

Consequently, as soon as the treaty was signed, there was great danger that Canada would be smothered within a space that was too confined, and that the very base of her economy would be swept away. Still, at first sight it might seem that the fate of the colony depended more on the Indians than on the French themselves. That is the interpretation that must be given Vaudreuil's remark in 1714 when he wrote: "With regard to the Indians, the war with the English was more favourable to us than is the peace."

Remedial measures

In the north-east corner of the continent, where at all costs she had to maintain her fisheries and provide a port of call for her ships, France decided to fortify Île du Cap-Breton, renamed Île Royale. The garrison and the inhabitants of Plaisance were transferred there and established at Hâvre-à-l'Anglais, a port that offered the advantage of being open all year long. And in 1719 construction was begun there on the fortress of Louisbourg, at a cost of thirty million *livres*. As soon as the treaty had been signed, the Acadians had been urged to settle there: very few, however, agreed to do so, as most of them considered the island unsuitable for growing wheat and raising livestock, from which almost all of them gained their livelihood.

Île Saint-Jean took on little by little, under the circumstances, great importance: it was seen eventually as the granary of Île Royale, a place of refuge for the Acadians, and in time a point from which to repulse "the English fishermen who might come to these parts to interfere with ours." That was the reason why Île Saint-Jean and

Île Miscou, which had similar features, were granted in 1719 to the Comte de Saint-Pierre, who was charged with their settlement and development. The experiment was inconclusive, and in 1730 the two islands were returned to the Crown.

For several years Louisbourg was considered an impregnable fortress. In any case it became a very active trading centre, a sort of hub between Québec and the West Indies in particular. Great fortunes were built up there, particularly within certain families that were closely connected with the military administration. Fishing and cabotage were also great sources of wealth.

Thanks to the thirty years of peace that followed the Treaty of Utrecht, Louisbourg and a few other settlements on Île Royale were able to develop in a fairly normal fashion. The colony was given civil and religious institutions that were sufficient for a population that in 1726 still counted only 3,131 inhabitants. This facility was due in large part to the fact that the British were in no haste to establish themselves on the Nova Scotia peninsula, being satisfied with maintaining a few small garrisons there.

In reality the English were casting their covetous glances in another direction, towards the Kennebec River. After having tried in vain to win over the Abenakis, they actually began to overrun their territory, first by setting up trading posts, then small communities, and by gaining ground little by little towards the northwest, that is to say in the direction of Canada. In 1716 hundreds of settlers had already established themselves in the Abenaki country and were protected by forts, five of them on the Kennebec itself.

There was a danger that this expansionist movement might weaken the French positions in the East by allowing the English to keep on getting a little closer to Canada. Now, to ward off this threat the French could count solely on the Abenakis, whom they aided secretly by supplying them with arms and ammunition and kept in their alliance by handing out presents.

In the West the situation was more dangerous still, and more urgent. Scarcely had the Treaty of Utrecht been signed than the English traders rushed to the shores of Lake Ontario in an effort to establish trading relations with the Indians who owed allegiance to France. A fort was soon built in Mohawk territory to serve as a staging point between Albany and Lake Ontario, and there was talk of building a second one still closer to the French zone of influence, in Onondaga territory. Fortunately, just at that point and following upon the death in 1715 of Louis XIV, changes made in the administrative machinery in the mother country were in harmony with a policy favoured by Vaudreuil, who immediately obtained ample powers for himself.

Vaudreuil had begun to put this new policy, which was completely expansionist, into effect in 1712, by having Michillimakinac reoccupied. The presence of French garrisons and coureurs de bois in the West was necessary on the one hand to pacify the tribes, which were often warring among themselves, and on the other to strengthen their loyalty to France. And as soon as the European markets had opened up and demanded beaver again, the trading licences were speedily re-established. The trade recovered some of its vigour, and the annual shipments of pelts poured once more into Montréal. In 1717 a company called the Compagnie d'Occident, which became the Compagnie des Indes in 1719, took on the responsibility of exporting beaver.

Two measures initiated by Vaudreuil facilitated the revival of trading in the West: first, in 1716 he forced the Foxes, who had once more dug up the hatchet, to sign a peace treaty; then he ordered some posts to be built in the western Great Lakes region (Lakes Michigan and Superior) — at Baie des Puants (Green Bay) in particular — and on the Upper Mississippi. These posts presented several advantages: they would serve as bases for future exploration expeditions, and (at least some of them) would shut off the Indians' routes to Hudson Bay while at the same time protecting the routes to the Sioux country, which was rich in furs; furthermore they would keep peace among the Indians and prevent some of them — the Miamis and Weas in particular — from coming together with the British traders.

Next, in view of the thrust by the English towards Lake Ontario, Vaudreuil, who had received permission to build the forts and posts needed to stop them, had three built in 1720 and the following years: Niagara, Rouillé (Toronto) and Kenté (Quinte). Fort Niagara, which was rebuilt in stone in 1726–27, was very well situated on a portage that almost all the western Indians took to go to either Montréal or Albany. The English retaliated by building the post of Oswego in 1725 and despatching a garrison to it in 1727.

If, by putting up forts and trading posts on Lake Ontario, the English and the French could apparently compete on an equal basis, the French were in actual fact at a distinct disadvantage. The English were offering the Indians goods of much higher quality for their furs and at a lower price than were the French: consequently many of the Indians avoided the French posts and traded as far away as Albany. Partly to compensate for the losses incurred in that area, and partly to forestall the influence of the Hudson's Bay Company in the Northwest, in 1717 the governor general, with the enthusiastic support of the Conseil de Marine, set himself a new task: the search for the Mer de l'Ouest — the Western Sea — which would be conducted mainly by La Vérendrye and his sons.

There remained the formidable Foxes, the perpetual trouble-makers in the West, who periodically attacked the French both in Canada and Louisiana. In 1721 they had again gone on the warpath. Even in Versailles people had begun to speak of exterminating them to the last man. Vaudreuil adopted another tactic, making peace with them, but without including in the terms of the treaty Louisiana, which continued to be a favourite target for those fierce warriors and to which the Illinois country had been annexed in 1717, much against the wishes of Vaudreuil and the Canadians.

Competition and diplomacy

In 1726 the Marquis de Beauharnois arrived to replace Governor General de Vaudreuil, who had died in October 1725. Throughout a term of office that lasted until 1747, he would oppose the determined expansionist policy of the English, who were spurred on by commercial aims certainly, but also by the desire to open up, with the aid of land companies, new centres for settlement in the interior. Since by virtue of the Treaty of Utrecht there could be no question of resorting to arms directly against the English colonies — although one could attack their Indian allies — Beauharnois had to find other solutions for containing this advance: first, replying to competition with competition by offering the Indians more barter goods in the French posts, authorizing trade in spirits, and returning to the practice of selling trading licences with a view to stimulating trade; next, by tightening or re-establishing the alliances through a sustained diplomatic action, while at the same time launching the Indians who owed allegiance to the French against the English traders who encroached upon French territory or against their Indian allies; and finally, owing to a network of posts, by retaining at all costs the loyalty of the Indian allies while making clear to the English the limits beyond which their ambitions could not extend.

In the middle of a period of peace a veritable diplomatic war was fought in North America. To begin with, no one on either side, neither the English in New York or Pennsylvania nor the French in Canada, had anything to gain by offending the Iroquois. The latter, caught between the two great rivals, applied themselves with increasing success to maintaining between the two great powers an equilibrium that would be advantageous to them, at the same time gaining through certain concessions the good will of the tribes that traditionally had been hostile to them. If they gave permission for Niagara to be built on their territory, they granted the British permission to do the same at Oswego. By preventing either of the two nations from dominating the other, they were above all seeking to maintain their independence, but also to play a certain role as middlemen in the fur trade between the western tribes and the English.

When Beauharnois arrived in the colony, his task seemed as difficult as it was delicate. In October 1727 he and Intendant Dupuy were already painting a very sombre picture of the situation in the West. They wrote the minister that the English, envious of the trade the French were carrying on with the Indians, were using every means possible to take it away from them. The English had won over many Indians to their side, thanks to the generous gifts they gave them daily; they had even sent "colliers souterrains" (secret wampum belts) to all the tribes on whose territory the French were established to incite them to get rid of them and to "massacre the garrisons." For their part the Foxes had stated that they would not allow any more Frenchmen on their territory. In reality, the French could scarcely count on the stability of their alliances in the West, so harmful had been the effect on the various tribes of English diplomacy and trade.

The Foxes, in addition to hurting French trade, constituted a permanent threat to the fragile network of French alliances through their intrigues and hostile behaviour. Occupying the trade routes between the Sioux to the north and the tribes in the Upper Mississippi region, and considering themselves the middlemen as a matter of course in the fur trade between the two centres, they did not hesitate to war upon the French themselves, whether they were from Canada or Louisiana, in order to retain that advantage. If the English were thinking of blocking the route to the West at Lake Ontario, the Foxes would perhaps be successful in doing the same thing at Lake Michigan, where they held an extremely strategic region. The danger became more imminent when the English, who had reached the Wabash, became more insistent still to have the Foxes join with other tribes and apply themselves to driving the French to the last man out of the West.

It so happened that in 1728 the Foxes went on the warpath again, this time against the Illinois. Lignery, who had been sent by Beauharnois at the head of a force of 1,500 men to bring these troublemakers to their senses, was unable to confront them; they had fled towards the West. In 1730 the French tried again: attacked by 1,400 men, hundreds of Foxes were killed and a great many more were reduced to slavery and distributed among several tribes. The failure in 1728 had damaged France's prestige among the western tribes; paradoxically, the victory in 1730 had a similar result. The Indians pitied the unfortunate Foxes to such an extent that they freed them, with the result that a new French expedition against "this accursed tribe" ended in 1735 in a new failure — due in large part, it is true, to causes other than the military might of the enemy, who had finally been crushed in 1730.

Meanwhile in Louisiana an attempt was being made to exterminate the Natchez, who had massacred the French at Fort Rosalie in 1729. Then in 1736 began a long war against the Chickasaws, who with the help of the traders from Carolina were trying to ruin French trade and their alliances in that colony.

In the Northwest the situation was just as bad. In the 1730s La Vérendrye, whose activity was essential for the expansion and protection of French trade, simply had to count on the loyalty of tribes such as the Monsonis, the Crees and the Assiniboines; now, all these tribes were almost permanently at war with the Sioux, who as a result turned against the French. In 1736 the Sioux — the new terror of the West — massacred the Jesuit Aulneau and twenty Canadians at Lac des Bois (Lake of the Woods).

Besides the posts with which he covered the West and which were, so to speak, the "high places" of French diplomacy, it was through handing out presents, gratuities and medals with rather princely largess that Beauharnois finally succeeded, as Vaudreuil had with the Abenakis, in winning over most of the tribes, and that he established relative peace in the West just on the eve of the War of the Austrian Succession. In 1742 alone he had allocated 76,000 *livres* to the "diplomatic" effort!

Economy and society

While in the West the nature of the stakes was becoming clearer and the two great imperialist powers were constantly increasing their bets, in Canada an attempt was being made to consolidate and diversify the colonial economy.

In the first decade of the century, the merchants, having been cut off from part of the traditional fur trade profits as a result of the abolition of the trading licences and the closing of certain of the western posts, were naturally led into other sectors of activity. There resulted a modest diversification of the economy: at Madame de Repentigny's insistence, a textile industry was created in Montréal; a brewery was reactivated at Québec; the manufacture of tar was resumed, particularly at Baie Saint-Paul; tanneries were established at Québec, Lévis and Montréal; the exportation of hay and various kinds of flours and meals increased; fisheries were established; in short, one might have thought that one was back in the time of Jean Talon, who had dreams of such small industries and commercial ventures. In fact, Canada was bent on producing at home whatever inflation, brought on by the war, prevented it from obtaining from France.

The security guaranteed by the Iroquois peace of 1701 was put to advantage to stimulate development of the land, and was further encouraged by a certain increase in manpower resulting from the return to the colony of a rather large number of coureurs de bois who had been recalled from the West. Now, after the founding of Louisbourg, Île Royale soon provided an outlet for the surplus of agricultural products. The same was true of the French West Indies, to which flour and cod, but also various other kinds of fish and lumber, began to be exported in 1708. Later (this trade would reach its peak after 1730), new exports would be added to the list: "vegetables and other small eatables," for example. It is true, as already mentioned, that most of the ships coming from Québec unloaded their cargoes at Louisbourg, whence they were shipped to the West Indies by the local merchants, who pocketed the lion's share of the profits. This sea-going trade was nonetheless a blessing for the colony in that above all it triggered the creation or the development of a whole series of industries, including lumbering and shipbuilding, without mentioning the tars, cordage and sails needed by the latter. And up to a certain point it encouraged a number of the farmers to produce more.

It must be recognized, however, that although it did exist, the large-scale three-sided trade (Canada–West Indies–France) was almost entirely in the hands of French people in the mother country who, being better equipped than the Canadians and having greater capital resources, retained most of the income from the trade, as they did in other areas. Indeed, because of its distance and severe climate, Canada did not attract much capital, any more than it did immigrants from the mother country (only slightly more than 5,000 in sixty years). Those were the two major obstacles to her economic progress, to which must be added the high costs of shipping and local labour, which prevented Canadian products from being competitive on French markets. Now, those markets were themselves far from being certain, since Canada produced almost nothing that France could not obtain at home or more cheaply elsewhere, and although it was applied with greater flexibility, Colbert's mercantilist system had been put into practice again by Maurepas: "The colony of Canada is of value only insofar as it can be useful to the kingdom."

None of that prevented tile and slate works and sawmills from being set up and the Forges du Saint-Maurice (Saint-Maurice ironworks) from being created in Canada. However, at grips with a chronic lack of capital and specialized workers in a colony where cash was extremely scarce, and confronted, besides, with almost insuperable problems of transport, the Canadian merchants failed in many of their enterprises. Many of them stuck with the fur trade, which required less capital and labour and which more or less guaranteed a profit. This attitude went against the policy of diversifying the economy that was being preached by the mother country, but Intendant Hocquart could not change it. In the countryside, because of the instability of the markets, aggravated by the low prices offered for products until about 1740, the habitants had little inclination to produce much more than they needed for themselves.

Despite some incipient diversification, during the period of peace that followed the Treaty of Utrecht the Canadian economy remained centred upon its great natural resources: furs, agriculture and fishing. In addition to the obstacles already mentioned (scarcity and high cost of labour and lack of capital), Canada suffered from the absence of any infrastructure, as well as from the incompetence of many of her civil officials. Hocquart nevertheless gave a rather good boost to trade and industry, but on the eve of the wars that would override everything else, Canada was economically still an underdeveloped country. The State injected large sums of money into public works, roads and defence works, without, however, making any great change in the situation. It even paid subsidies to entrepreneurs, even though it was counting ultimately on the initiative of private individuals, but without much success.

In this century, as in the previous one, nearly a quarter of the population of Canada lived in the towns. Here one found the merchants, who, all things considered, formed perhaps the most prestigious class: bourgeois for the most part, they were often connected, directly or indirectly, with the fur trade; the nobility, who almost completely monopolized the officers' ranks in the colonial regular troops, took advantage of the periods they spent in distant garrisons to also engage in the fur trade. The nobility and the bourgeoisie had access to various administrative posts, although the ones at the top of the hierarchy were generally filled by Frenchmen from the mother country, as was the practice in the administration of the Church of Canada.

The nobles often owned seigneuries, but many commoners were also seigneurs, without for all that being ennobled. However, they did not draw large incomes from their lands, at least not until they were heavily populated. For their part the country people worked their farms with their families and rarely sought outside help. As soon as they became self-sufficient, most of them had little inclination to go any further; on the other hand they were not much drawn to the fur trade — an activity embraced mostly by young men from the towns, and particularly from Montréal, and they were not much affected by it. If they left their farms, it was to go to live in town, where, accustomed to being their own masters, they formed a working class that was not easily managed nor much disposed to team-work.

In this society in which people lived comfortably but not opulently, the military and aristocratic values inherited from Old France were carried on, chiefly by the nobility. But it seems that around 1740 the "merchant-bourgeois" class, located in Montréal and Québec, was considered the most dynamic social class. In any case it is striking to note that at the beginning of the century the Canadian merchants, united in a sort of common front, elaborated for New France a general policy and precise strategies that were different from those followed in France but for which they finally won acceptance on almost all points by their determination and their deep knowledge of Canadian reality. Through these original views, of course, they incurred, as did the working-class people in the rural areas and the members of the lower clergy, who were equally aware of their status as Canadians, many reprimands on the part of the French authorities, both in the mother country and in the colony. They were often accused of being very headstrong, of cultivating a harmful "spirit of independence," and of carrying insubordination to the point of open rebellion.

13

This seems a clear sign that what had begun as an off-shoot of Old France had now taken root as a new nation in America.

The War of the Austrian Succession

A new war in Europe, which would again have its counterpart in America, broke out after the death of Charles VI, emperor of Austria, who had died without leaving a male heir. On 15 March 1744, France declared war on Great Britain. As soon as Louisbourg was informed of this, it was decided to retake Nova Scotia. An initial success marked this attempt when François Du Pont Duvivier seized Canso, whose garrison surrendered on 24 May 1744, almost without striking a blow. In September and October Duvivier's second effort was directed to reducing Annapolis Royal (formerly Port-Royal): the Acadians did not depart from their neutrality, and the expedition was a failure.

To the French, as to the English in Massachusetts and New England, Louisbourg seemed almost invincible. However, the prisoners who had been brought from Canso in May 1744 and spent some time in Louisbourg discovered that such was not the case. Returning to Boston that year, they convinced their fellow citizens of this, and the latter decided to conquer the fortress. In May 1745 the ships carrying the militiamen from the English colonies, under the orders of the commander-in-chief William Pepperrell, and the British naval force that had joined it under the command of Admiral Peter Warren, attacked the fortress. The British disposed of 8,000 men, the French of about 1,300. The siege lasted 47 days, and Du Pont Duchambon finally surrendered on 27 June.

The news of this, which was received with enthusiasm in the English colonies, was shattering for the authorities in Versailles. Maurepas, who particularly wanted to protect the French fisheries in the gulf, immediately had a large expedition fitted out, to recapture not only Louisbourg but also Newfoundland and Nova Scotia. Under the command of the Duc d'Anville, 54 ships and 7,000 men would sail. But they were going to meet with failure: considerable delays in setting off, a late arrival in Chebucto Bay (Halifax), lack of drinking water, and diseases that carried off several hundred men, including the Duc d'Anville himself, who died of apoplexy. The Marquis de La Jonquière, the new governor general of New France, took command of operations and wanted at least to attack Annapolis Royal: unfavourable winds carried his ships off course, preventing him from doing so. A costly undertaking for no results whatsoever.

As usual, however, war parties had been sent against the English colonies with the cooperation of the Abenakis and Micmacs. Once more everything was put to fire and sword and a certain number of prisoners were brought back. The terror that was spread through the English settlements along the Atlantic coast by the Canadians and their Indian allies from 1745 to 1748 contributed greatly to strengthening the determination among the enemy populations to seize all of New France as quickly as possible.

The opportunity to do so would soon be at hand. But for the time being, a peace treaty signed at Aix-la-Chapelle in October 1748 put an end to the conflict and re-established the pre-war situation. On 23 July 1749 France officially regained possession of Louisbourg.

The Ohio question

Before the outbreak of the War of the Austrian Succession, which in America was fought entirely on the eastern fronts, various defensive works had been built in Canada, among them Fort Saint-Frédéric on Lake Champlain in 1731, which was intended to close the invasion route along the Richelieu River to the enemy. But in the period of peace that followed the Treaty of Utrecht a good many of the posts dotted about the western territories were to play a role that was as much an economic as a strategic one.

Shortly after 1713 the traders from Virginia and Pennsylvania had begun to spill over into the Ohio region and had finally established some small trading posts there. Although they were aware of the danger that these posed to the Indian alliances and to the very survival of Louisiana, the French had reacted weakly to this expansion, being content to put up a few small posts a little farther west (on the Wabash River, for example), in order to keep some tribes, such as the Miamis and the Weas, away from the British as much as possible. The latter had greatly increased their trade in the region during the 1740s, and several tribes were in league with them. The French had to recognize that their dominion over the region was just about over, and that the Indians, from south of Lake Erie to the Ohio River, had to all intents and purposes forsaken their alliance with them.

Actually, by depriving the French posts in the Ohio valley and the West of trade goods, which, when there were any to be found, reached astronomical prices, the War of the Austrian Succession precipitated the events. Not only were the French unable to maintain the fragile alliances that they had safeguarded until then, but in 1747 they were threatened with a general uprising of the tribes, who were talking of destroying all the French establishments in the West. Meanwhile, land companies in Pennsylvania and Virginia were getting ready to open up immense stretches of the Ohio valley to English settlement.

Once more a desperate attempt had to be made to recover lost ground. When peace returned, there was a rush to supply the posts with trade goods, which were sold at more reasonable prices. Then, while refraining from any warlike acts, the French sent Céloron de Blainville to the Ohio valley in 1749: he had the official mission of laying claim to it in France's name by burying some lead plaques, but was also to map the region with the help of the Jesuit de Bonnécamps. Céloron firmly requested that the English traders whom he encountered return whence they came. As for the Indians — Miamis, Shawnees and Senecas — he could only observe that they had gone over completely to the side of the English. Céloron's expedition had been of little diplomatic value, whereas the information that he brought back deeply perturbed the authorities in Québec.

In 1752 Mouet de Langlade received the mission of attacking the English post of Pickawillany; in the absence of most of the Miamis who normally stayed there, his force, made up of 300 French and Indians, seized it. The following year Governor General Duquesne sent Marin de La Malgue to fortify the area south of Lake Erie and to build a road, with forts spread out along it, between the lake and the Ohio River, as Céloron de Blainville had suggested. La Malgue, who also had the task of expelling the English from those regions, carried out his mission at top speed and with ruthless determination. He died before completing it.

It was Pécaudy de Contrecoeur who in 1754 was finally to carry out Céloron's plan. At the head of a considerable force he seized a fort that the English were building at the mouth of the Monongahela. He expelled the English, after buying their tools, and completed the work. This fort, named Fort Duquesne (Pittsburgh), finally ensured control of the region for France.

An undeclared war

For the French, in any case, there could be no question of giving the Ohio country over to the English, who, according to La Galissonière "would find even more opportunity there than at Chouaguen to lead astray the Indian nations" of the West: in addition "they would find it easier to cut Canada off from communication with Louisiana."

Since each side had its own interests, and since no one would give way, it was inevitable that sooner or later there would be open warfare in the region. It came the very year that Fort Duquesne was built, in 1754. Virginia militiamen under command of George Washington attacked a French party under Jumonville, who was killed in the ambush. Although France and Britain were at peace, this incident set off hostilities in the Ohio valley. On 3 July Jumonville's brother forced Washington to surrender at Fort Necessity. From then on the Ohio valley was rid of the English, and all the Indian tribes there then leaned towards the side of the French. During the years 1755–57 many parties made up of Frenchmen and Indians went to devastate the settlements in Pennsylvania, Virginia and Carolina.

In 1755, on 9 July, the French won a brilliant victory against the 1,800 men from both the regular army and the militia who, under Major-General Braddock's command, had been assigned to capture Fort Duquesne. Braddock lost his life in the battle, and the victory of the "Mal-Engueulée" (the Monongahela) was celebrated in all of Canada. But the conflict was already tending to spread: in two days, 16 and 17 June, the French had lost Fort Beauséjour and Fort Gaspereau, which, situated in the south of present-day New Brunswick, were intended to contain the English advance towards Canada. And in September, after winning an initial success at Lake Saint-Sacrement (Lake George) against Colonel Johnson's troops, Baron Dieskau did not succeed in capturing the fortified position of William Henry and, seriously wounded, was himself taken prisoner.

The deportation of the Acadians also began in 1755 and went on until 1762. In the autumn of 1755 alone, more than 6,000 out of a population of some 13,000 were deported to various English colonies, and some of them to England. The very few who escaped deportation — the "grand dérangement" — did so by fleeing to Canada or hiding in the woods. This small community that had long been left to its own devices had, after 1713, chosen its leaders and adopted a policy for itself, one of neutrality. Therefore it had steadfastly given a collective refusal to take the oath of allegiance to Great Britain, and that was the pretext that the British authorities used to seize it after they had decided to settle Nova Scotia with British subjects.

Such, then, was the mock peace that had set in in North America in 1755 and that, in the event of a war in Europe that would once more set France against Great Britain, foreshadowed a fight to the finish.

The crowning effort

In the spring of 1756 the Seven Years' War began in Europe. At that time the American colonies had a population of about 1,500,000, and New France, including Louisiana, some 85,000. But the French could throw into the fray seasoned militia-men, whose bravery was recognized and who had nothing but contempt "for the English in the new world." The English colonies, on the contrary, did not have at their disposal any experienced or even properly organized provincial troops, and those that they did have were not used to colonial warfare, which was very much different from classic wars on the European model. In this regard the superiority of the English colonials was far from being assured. The difference in this war would come from the superiority of the regular troops that Britain would send to America in large numbers over the regulars whom France would send by driblets.

But it was the determination of William Pitt of England to win the war in America, and that of France to be victorious on the battlefields of Europe, that sealed the destiny of New France. From 1757 on Pitt devoted fabulous sums to realize his great aim: he furnished troops, material and supplies to the colonies with a sort of prodigality: he left nothing undone to reach his goals. At the same time France stinted on everything, and from 1755 until 1758 the quality of her troops and armaments declined greatly, while Canada was in the grip of famine.

Unlike the previous ones, the Seven Years' War was not just a struggle between English and French settlers. It was a gigantic combat between the two imperialist powers for trading supremacy in the world, for which France had contended seriously with Britain in peacetime. The navies of the two rival nations were consequently going to play a capital role on several seas, while the decisive struggle, which had been expected since 1713, would take place in the colonies.

In America, the French were the first to go on the attack. In the summer of 1756 they besieged Oswego, on Lake Ontario. The fortress surrendered in August and the fortifications were razed. The English colonials, who were planning to take Fort Saint-Frédéric, were disconcerted by the news of this defeat and immediately abandoned their plan. Throughout the autumn and winter the French launched murderous raids as usual against the English settlements in order to sow terror among them, but also to create confusion and thus keep the enemy at home by preventing him from getting organized.

In 1757 Montcalm, who had taken part in the final assault against Oswego the previous year, took Fort William Henry, on Lake Saint-Sacrement, without any difficulty on 9 August. But despite Governor General de Vaudreuil's wish, he refused to march on Fort Edward, situated on the Hudson River. This was the only outstanding event of the campaign in America. But in London, William Pitt took the firm decision in that year of 1757 to take Louisbourg and Québec, since he was convinced that that would crush New France.

In 1758 Montcalm had time to win the defensive battle of Carillon, in the Lake Champlain region, and that despite the disproportion between the forces facing each other: 15,000 on the British side, 3,500 on the French. The victory was gained in six hours on 8 July; Abercromby lost 2,000 men, killed and wounded, in the battle, and his incompetence was the main cause of his defeat.

But the siege of Louisbourg was already under way. Amherst, who was in command on the British side, had 27,000 men under his orders. On the French side Drucour had 8,000 at the most, in a crumbling fortress. The French held out for 60 days, but on 26 July the fortress surrendered. From that moment Québec had cause to tremble: the way was wide open to the enemy — and since 1756 the French navy had suffered such losses that one could not hope for much help there.

On 27 August Fort Frontenac, on Lake Ontario, surrendered to the enemy. And off in the Ohio country, in the face of the risk that it might fall into the hands of the British, Fort Duquesne, which had been the keystone of the French defensive system in the region, was blown up. Then on 25 July 1759 Fort Niagara, which protected communications between Montréal and the Far West, surrendered to Sir William Johnson, leading to the abandonment by the French of other forts: Presqu'île, Venango, Le Boeuf. In 1758 and 1759 the whole West was collapsing.

After his victory at Louisbourg Amherst was supposed to sail for Québec, which he was to besiege, but he considered it to be too late in the season, therefore the project was postponed until the following year. In 1759 it was Admiral Charles Saunders who sailed for Québec at the head of an imposing fleet; for his part, James Wolfe had military command of the expedition. On 23 June the first ships anchored a little below the town. Wolfe landed on the Île d'Orléans. Later, he installed his quarters at Montmorency. From Pointe-Lévy (Lauzon), batteries were trained on the capital. On the evening of 12 July the bombardment of Québec began.

Meanwhile the French, who to all intents and purposes had lost the West, also lost almost all of the Lake Champlain region. Amherst was marching on Fort Carillon: it, along with Fort Saint-Frédéric, were blown up one after the other, on 26 and 31 July, and the troops withdrew to the northern tip of Lake Champlain, to Île aux Noix. Amherst then decided to put off action with his 12,000 men until he received news from Québec.

While the British shelling continued to devastate Québec, Wolfe ordered the destruction of the French communities on both shores of the St. Lawrence, especially to the east of the capital. In the face of the French refusal to budge, he tried an attack to the west of Montmorency and suffered a stinging reverse. The tactic used by the French was, in fact, not to expose themselves, and their hope was that, as time went by, the season would force the British to sail off. It was not a bad calculation, but it was upset by events.

During the night of 12–13 September, following a path that he had discovered leading up the cliff a little west of Québec, Wolfe sent up nearly 5,000 soldiers, whom he drew up in battle formation on the Plains of Abraham. The town, which was well fortified on that side, could have held out until Bougainville's troops arrived. But in the morning Montcalm, who had not budged until then — a tactic that had served him well — hurried out from behind the town fortifications to confront the enemy forces. In thirty minutes the British had gained the victory: Wolfe was killed on the battlefield, and Montcalm, who had been mortally wounded, died shortly afterwards.

It was a bitter defeat for the French, but the town could still put up a resistance. Without waiting for the forces led by Bougainville and Lévis, however, Ramezay in turn acted hastily and surrendered on 18 September. In the spring of 1760 Lévis was victorious at Sainte-Foy, west of Québec, in a glorious but futile feat of arms — the last by the French in Canada. They withdrew to Montréal, on which three armies converged during the summer from Québec, Lake Champlain and Lake Ontario. The colony had been overwhelmed and was reeling from total exhaustion. On 8 September Vaudreuil capitulated, surrendering Montréal and all of New France to the British.

The terms of surrender gave the Canadians a certain number of guarantees, but it left them many causes for anxiety, especially concerning the practice of their religion. In reality these sons of France were suddenly being plunged into the unknown, and a long period of uncertainty was beginning for them.

Exploration and Discovery

At the very beginning of the eighteenth century, Governor General Louis-Hector de Callière and Intendant Jean Bochart de Champigny had set themselves two objectives in the West: ensuring that France received the furs from those vast regions, and, to that end, maintaining the alliances with the Indian tribes living there. But to be entirely successful in those aims it would have been necessary to re-establish the trading licences that had been abolished by the king in May 1696 and to reopen certain trading posts whose garrisons had been removed at that time, and which had been more or less abandoned. These were requests that Callière and his successor, Philippe de Rigaud de Vaudreuil, made in vain. Under these conditions, and taking into account furthermore the fact that life in the woods had been declared illegal, there could be no question of exploring the West, where Jacques de Noyon had spent the winter of 1688–89, in the Assiniboine country around Rainy Lake.

What was impossible for the colony of Canada to do, newly-created Louisiana was going to carry out. In 1700–01 Louis Juchereau de Saint-Denis explored the territory between the Red River in Louisiana and the Wichita River in Oklahoma; later he would cross Texas and in 1714 get as far as San Juan Bautista in Mexico. Canada was even more impressed by the expedition led by Pierre-Charles Le Sueur, who, on the pretext of seeking and exploiting mineral resources, went more than 600 leagues up the Mississippi in 1700 and, continuing along the Rivière Saint-Pierre (Minnesota River), stopped at the Rivière Verte (Blue Earth River) in the Sioux country (Minnesota), where he built Fort L'Huillier. In the spring of 1701 he came back down with a cargo of beaver pelts, angering the merchants and authorities in Canada, in particular Callière.

The Treaty of Utrecht in 1713 and the ceding of Hudson Bay to England the following year brought about a change in the situation. In 1715, in fact, William Stuart, an employee of the Hudson's Bay Company, was designated by James Knight, the governor of Fort York, to travel to the West with the aim, among other things, of estimating the resources in furs to be found in the interior, and probably to urge the Indians to go to trade at the bay. Stuart, who was the first white man to cross the Barren Grounds, got back to Hudson Bay in 1716. He had suffered innumerable hardships but had reached the region to the south of Great Slave Lake in the Northwest Territories.

The loss of Hudson Bay had an immediate effect upon the Canadian fur traders, who were determined to keep the Western Indians from taking their furs to the Hudson's Bay Company posts. With the same idea in mind, Vaudreuil and Intendant Michel Bégon proposed in 1716 that an attempt be made to discover the Mer de l'Ouest — the Western Sea — as a means of extending French trade by opening up a sea route to China and Japan. In 1717 the Conseil de Marine, which had just restored the system of fur-trading licences, adopted the views of the colonial authorities; in particular it suggested that the establishment of posts along the routes to the northwest would "dissuade the Indians from taking their pelts to the English at Hudson Bay . . . , which might force them to give up that post, where they have no trade other than with the Indians."

The task of carrying out this policy was entrusted to Zacharie Robutel de La Noue, who started out by canoe in July 1717 with the order to found three posts: one on the Kanastigoya (Kaministiquia) River, "to the north of Lake Superior," another at Takamamiouon (Rainy Lake) and the third at Lac des Assiniboines (or Lac des Bois). Unfortunately the Conseil de Marine had decided "to have these establishments built without any cost to the king, seeing that trade was to reimburse those who built them." Robutel was held back by the Indians' hostility and did not go beyond Kaministiquia. At the same time as the Conseil de Marine launched this first attempt at discovering the Western Sea, it charged the Jesuit François-Xavier de Charlevoix with the task of gathering information about it and the routes leading to it. After travelling from Montréal to Michillimakinac and then from that post to Louisiana in 1721, Charlevoix unfortunately recommended that the searches be conducted in the region between 40° and 50° latitude, with the Upper Missouri being taken as the point of departure.

Correcting this error in orientation would fall to Pierre Gaultier de La Vérendrye, who, having been charged officially with discovering the Western Sea, would send his sons and partners off in 1731 to explore in the direction of the Missouri and also the lakes in the Northwest. The building in 1731 of Fort Saint-Pierre on Rainy Lake and of Fort Saint-Charles, which he made his headquarters, on Lake of the Woods in 1732, assured him control of the border lakes. In 1734 Fort Maurepas was built on the Red River in Manitoba. In 1737 Lake Ouinipigon (Winnipeg) had been explored and two possible routes toward the Western Sea noted—the Saskatchewan River and the region southwest of the Mandan country. In 1738 La Vérendrye himself visited these Indians in North Dakota, on the way building Fort La Reine (Portage-la-Prairie), his new headquarters, on the route that the Assiniboines followed to go to Hudson Bay. His son Louis-Joseph, who pushed on farther, failed to appreciate the southeast orientation of the Missouri; it was not until Louis-Joseph made a new expedition in 1742–43 that the error attributable to Charlevoix became apparent.

Meanwhile La Vérendrye's men were establishing three more forts on the threshold of the prairies: Fort Dauphin, near Lake Winnipegosis, Fort Bourbon, northwest of Lake Ouinipigon, and Fort Paskoya, on the Saskatchewan River. But obliged, like Robutel, to finance his own undertakings, La Vérendrye, according to the minister, was too much absorbed with trade and not enough with exploration. Foreseeing his impending disgrace, he resigned in 1744. He died before he could return to the West.

In the Northwest the French from Canada settled in under La Vérendrye's two successors, Jacques Le Gardeur de Saint-Pierre and Louis de La Corne, in Saskatchewan — at Fort La Jonquière, which was built in 1751 in the Nipawin region, and farther west still, at Fort Saint-Louis, built in 1754 near the forks of the Saskatchewan. In the Southwest, since the expeditions by Le Sueur and Juchereau de Saint-Denis, exploration had gone on without a stop, spreading from Louisiana into the surrounding territories: in 1714 Étienne Véniard de Bourgmond had gone up the Missouri as far as the present-day state of Nebraska; then around 1720 Jean-Baptiste Bénard de La Harpe and Claude-Charles Dutisné explored Oklahoma, and Dutisné also travelled across Kansas. But with the failure of the sea voyages of exploration led by James Knight (1719), John Scroggs (1722), Christopher Middleton (1742) and William Moor (1747) in the search for the Northwest Passage, it was one of the Hudson's Bay Company's men, Anthony Henday, who, travelling overland in 1754, was the first European to tread the soil of Alberta, getting as far as the present-day city of Edmonton — a proud response by the English company to the fierce competition waged by the French since La Vérendrye's period.

A break-through by the Hudson's Bay Company

William Stuart, an employee of the Hudson's Bay Company, was stationed at Fort York, on the Hayes River at Hudson Bay, when he left for the West on 27 June 1715. He had been given the mission of making an inventory of the fur resources of the interior and of restoring peace between two Indian tribes that supplied furs.

Like his predecessor, Henry Kelsey, another Company employee who had reached the Western Plains in 1691 and had probably gone as far as southern Saskatchewan, Stuart was also to concern himself with minerals. James Knight, the governor of York, on whose orders he was making his trip, was thinking of copper, and still more of gold; he even made the search for those products the principal aim of the exploration trip.

The first European to push as far as the Great Slave Lake region, Stuart was successful in pacifying the Crees and Chipewyans, so that in 1717 Knight was able to keep his promise to the latter to found a post on the Churchill River.

However, Stuart had experienced so many difficulties on his trip that Knight became convinced that it was better to continue exploration in this direction by sea: the Company gave him permission to set out in 1719 by ship to look for a Northwest passage by way of the Strait of Anian. His two ships were wrecked on Marble Island and their crews vanished.

Indians hunting for beaver. James Isham (circa 1716–1761). Watercolour and ink on paper, 1743.

The desire to increase the trade in furs with the Indians pushed Hudson's Bay Company men such as James Isham to favour exploration in the West.

Archives of the Hudson's Bay Company, Provincial Archives of Manitoba, Winnipeg.

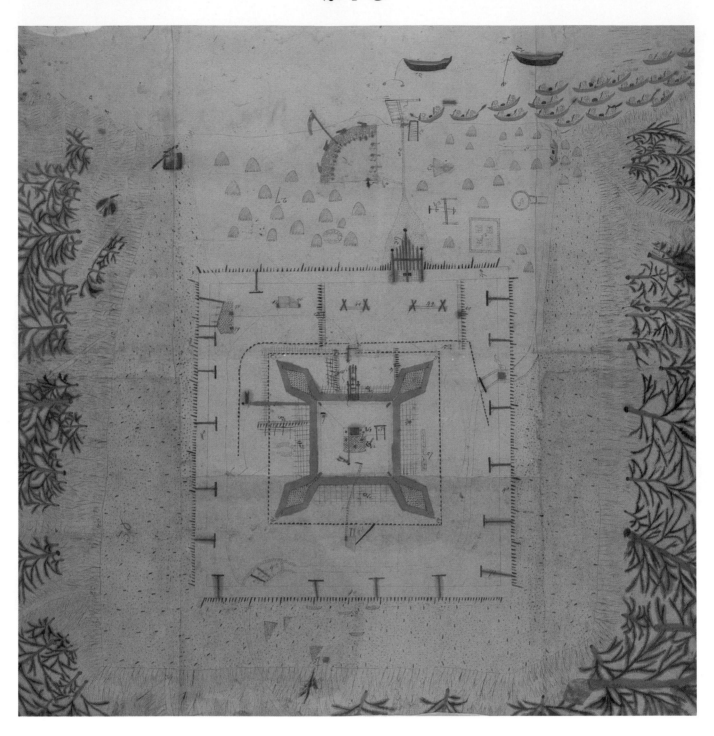

[Plan of Fort York. James Isham. Circa 1743]. Map, col. ms.; 92.7 × 95.3 cm.

This Hudson's Bay Company trading post was the starting-point for two expeditions into the West: William Stuart's in 1715–1716 and Anthony Henday's in 1754–1755.

Archives of the Hudson's Bay Company, Provincial Archives of Manitoba, Winnipeg: G. 2/5.

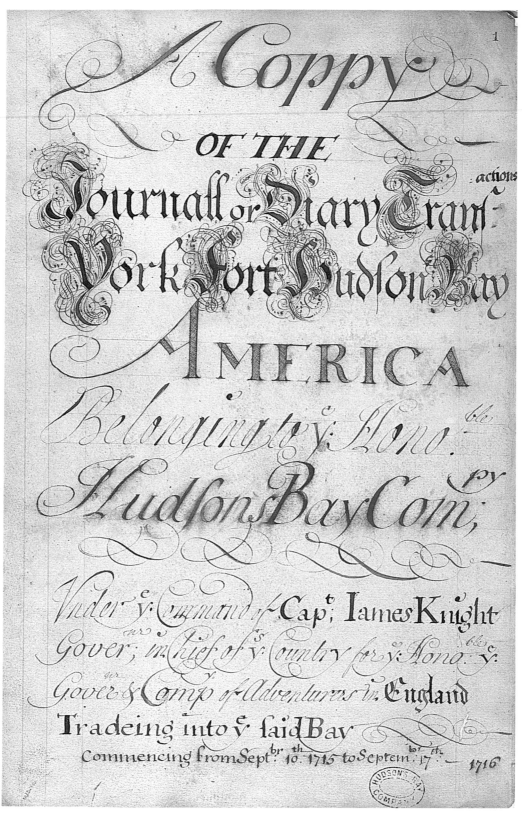

Journal kept at Fort York by James Knight, governor of the Hudson's Bay Company, September 1715 to September 1716.

In 1719, sailing northwards, James Knight explored part of the west coast of Hudson Bay. He was hoping to discover gold and copper mines and find a passage to Asia.

Archives of the Hudson's Bay Company, Provincial Archives of Manitoba, Winnipeg: B.239/a/2.

The French and the Western Sea

The king's abolition of trading licences in 1696 and the subsequent abandonment of most of the Western posts had brought French expansion northwest from Michilli-makinac temporarily to an end.

The loss of Hudson Bay at the time of the Treaty of Utrecht and the restoration of trading licences revived in New France the search for the Western Sea, which was imagined to be a gulf or an immense bay forming part of the Southern Sea (the Pacific Ocean) somewhere in northern California.

The first person to set off was Zacharie Robutel de La Noue: he was to establish three posts, or relay stations, on the route to the West, the most distant one being at Lake of the Woods. But he did not get beyond the first station, Kaministiquia, northwest of Lake Superior, where he seems to have remained until 1721.

In the meantime Father François-Xavier de Charlevoix was charged by the Conseil de Marine with making inquiries about the Western Sea. The Jesuit left from Montréal and at the end of June 1721 was at Michillimakinac; from there he went to Louisiana, questioning French and Indians on the way. It was a long trip and in the end brought little in the way of results.

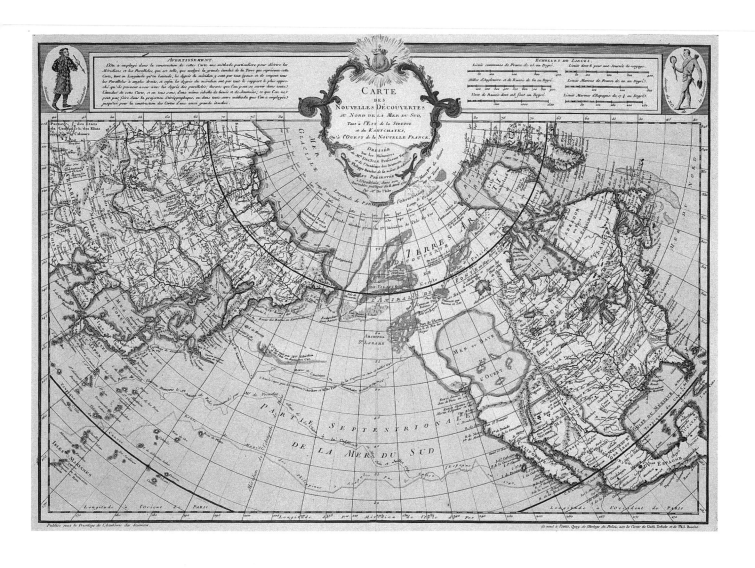

Map of the new discoveries to the north of the Mer du Sud . . . , Joseph-Nicolas De l'Isle and Philippe Buache. Paris: Quay de l'Horloge du Palais, [1752]. Map, hand-coloured, 36.8 × 62.6 cm.

It was believed that somewhere in the West there was a sea or bay that joined the Mer du Sud (the Pacific Ocean), which was the way to Asia. The statements by the Indians and explorers furthered the belief that this Western Sea was not too far away from the territories already known. This matter interested the politicians as much as it did the scientists.

Public Archives of Canada, Ottawa: National Map Collection (NMC 21056).

Canada

Conseil de Marine 7 Xbre 1717

121
376

M.rs de Vaudreüil et Begon ayant écrit l'année derniere que la decouverte de la Mer de l'Oüest seroit avantageuse à la Colonie, Il fut aprouvé, que pour y parvenir M. de Vaudreüil establit trois postes qu'il avoit proposé, et il fut marqué en mesme temps de faire faire cet etablissement sans qu'il encourast rien au Roy attendu que le commerce devoit indemniser ceux qui les feroient et d'envoyer un projet en detail de ce qu'il en cousteroit pour continuer cette decouverte.

Il a marqué en reponse que M. de Vaudreüil a fait partir au mois de Juillet dernier le S.r de la Noüe Lieutenant avec 8 Canots pour suivre le projet de cette

[Left margin:]
L'on ne doit porté a Monseigneur le Duc d'Orleans

14 Decembre 1717

S. A. R. ordonne que l'on suive cette [...], que l'on establisse [...] postes, et qu'elle fera des fonds deposés [...] cette Depense, mais [...] la condition le [...] qu'ils [...]

L. 20. 7.bre 1717

Deliberation of the Conseil de Marine upon a letter from Vaudreuil and Bégon, 7 December 1717.

". . . last July M. de Vaudreuil sent off Sieur de La Noue, lieutenant, with 8 canoes to pursue the project to discover [the Western sea]." Complying with the decision of His Royal Highness (noted in the margin), he ordered him to build three posts, one on the Kaministiquia River, one at Rainy Lake, and one at Lake of the Woods.

Archives nationales, Paris: Fonds des Colonies, série C11A, vol. 37, fol. 376.

Photo Studio Littré.

Letter from the Jesuit Pierre-François-Xavier de Charlevoix to the Comte de Morville, 1 April 1723.

The Duc d'Orléans, regent of France, was interested in the question of the Western sea, which arose from his curiosity about the sciences and which would perhaps increase the possibilities of trade with Asia. He "resolved to send someone to the principal posts in Canada and Louisiana who would find out . . . how one should go about making the discovery that was anticipated and whether there was any likelihood of succeeding in it." Father Charlevoix was "honoured with this commission."

Archives nationales, Paris: Fonds des Colonies, série C¹¹ᴱ, vol. 16, fol. 106.

Photo Studio Littré.

Pierre Gaultier de La Vérendrye

Trois-Rivières was the smallest town in New France. It nonetheless furnished coureurs de bois in large numbers and famous explorers, such as Jacques de Noyon and Pierre Gaultier de Varennes et de La Vérendrye.

La Vérendrye, who had first been a soldier, was over forty when, around 1728, on becoming commandant of a trading company at Kaministiquia, he began to be interested in the Western Sea and to dream of discovering it, a task with which he was officially entrusted in 1731 by Governor Charles de Beauharnois de La Boische.

The explorer, who was at the same time a merchant, was going to set up seven posts along the route to the Northwest. His partners, several of whom were close relatives, travelled all over the territory, while he himself remained more fixed and attended mostly to commercial and diplomatic relations with the Indians.

By order of his father, Louis-Joseph Gaultier de La Vérendrye went as far as Wyoming in 1742–43; in 1741–43 another son, Pierre, was charged by the explorer from Trois-Rivières with establishing the company on the Manitoba lakes. And it was precisely by the elder La Vérendrye's merit — even if he was strongly influenced by economic ambitions — that the northwest frontier of New France was extended as far as that present-day Canadian province.

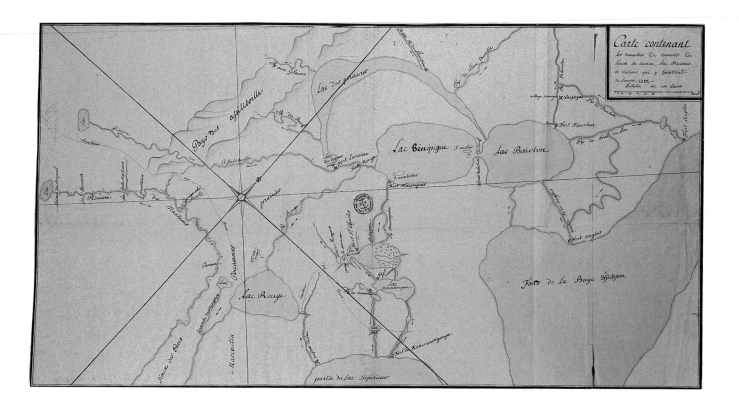

"Map with the recent discoveries made in the West of Canada . . . ." [Anonymous]. 1740. Map: col. ms., 45.0 × 84.0 cm.

This map shows the forts established by La Vérendrye and his men: Fort Maurepas, at the mouth of the Winnipeg River; Fort La Reine (Portage la Prairie); Fort Bourbon, to the northwest of Lake Winnipeg; Fort Paskoya, on the Saskatchewan River, and others. These trading posts, which saved the prairie Indians long voyages to the Hudson's Bay Company posts, hurt the English trade.

Service historique de la Marine, Vincennes, France; Service hydrographique, recueil 67, n° 23.

Photo Studio Littré.

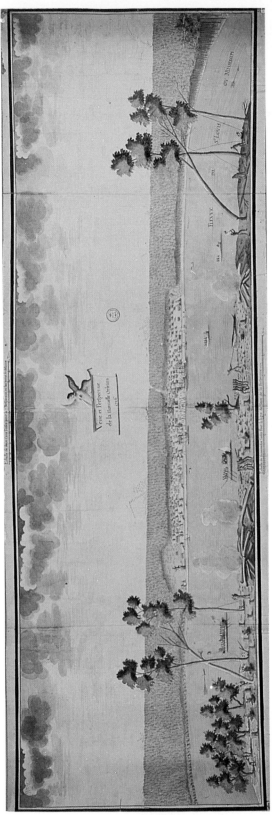

"View and perspective of New Orleans, 1726." Lassus. 1726. View: col. ms., 48.0 × 150.5 cm.

The travels of the explorers, missionaries, and coureurs de bois led to the founding of several settlements from northwest of the Great Lakes to the Gulf of Mexico.

Archives nationales, Paris: Section Outre-Mer, Dépôt des fortifications des colonies, Louisiane, portefeuille V1A, nº 71.

Photo Studio Littré.

The limits of French expansion

On 27 May 1750, soon after La Vérendrye's death at the end of 1749, Governor Jacques-Pierre de Taffanel de La Jonquière ordered Jacques Le Gardeur de Saint-Pierre to go and take possession of the explorer's posts, establish new ones, and continue the search for the Western Sea.

Le Gardeur installed himself at Fort La Reine, in Manitoba, from whence he sent off Joseph-Claude Boucher de Niverville, whose men built a fort named La Jonquière in what is today Saskatchewan, in 1751. In 1754 Louis de La Corne, who had succeeded Le Gardeur, built Fort Saint-Louis, which was still farther to the west than the preceding fort. Never had the French pushed so far towards the Western Sea, and never, under the French regime, would they get beyond that point.

New France had reached her utmost limits beyond the Great Lakes: to the northwest, the region of Fort-à-la-Corne, near the forks of the Saskatchewan in the province of the same name, and to the southwest, on the Mississippi, Louisiana, which under the government of Jean-Baptiste Le Moyne de Bienville and his successors had made progress after a fashion as a separate entity of the Canadian colony.

But at the beginning of the 1750s these new lands were threatened by the growing rivalries for possession of the Ohio country, to which Le Gardeur de Saint-Pierre was sent in 1753.

Order from Governor General de La Jonquière to Jacques Legardeur de Saint-Pierre "to go and look for the Western sea with nine canoes, each with a crew of seven men," Montréal, 27 May 1750.

Société du Musée du Séminaire de Québec: Fonds Verreau, carton 5, n° 37.

Photo Pierre Soulard.

L'ordre que j'avois donné à Mr le Chevalier de Niverville d'aller Etablir un fort à trois Cens lieües plus haut que celuy de Paskoya fut Executé le 29. May 1751 — il fit partir dix hommes en deux canots

Lesquels et monterens la Riviere du Paskoya jusques aux Montagnes des Roches, ou ils firent un bon fort que je Nommé le fort dajonquiere.

"Report or brief journal of Jacques Legardeur de Saint-Pierre's voyage . . . ," August 1752.

On 29 May 1751 the Chevalier de Niverville "despatched ten men in two canoes, who went up the Pasquia River as far as the Montagnes des Roches, where they built a good fort that I named Fort La Jonquière." This post was located in the heart of present-day Saskatchewan.

British Library, London: Haldimand Papers, Add. Mss. no. 21686, fol. 7v-8.

Portrait of Jean-Baptiste Le Moyne de Bienville (circa 1680–1767), governor of Louisiana. Artist unknown. Oil on canvas.

In 1699 Bienville began his career in Louisiana by exploring the Lower Mississippi with his brother Iberville. Up until 1743 he would contribute largely to settling the French in that colony by encouraging exploration, by favouring the establishment of several posts, and above all by demonstrating great diplomacy in dealing with the Indians.

Collection Le Moyne de Martigny, Rubelles, France.

Photo Graphic.

I

The Northwest Passage

After the failure of James Knight's exploration voyage by sea in 1719 and that of John Scroggs, who had sailed in 1722 to look for him, and with the exception of a half-hearted expedition mounted by the Hudson's Bay Company in 1737, England did not take an active interest in the Northwest Passage until 1740. Christopher Middleton, a former Hudson's Bay Company captain who had been dispatched by the Admiralty with George II's approval, sailed from England in 1741 and the following year ventured farther north than had anyone before him. Pushing on beyond Whale Point, which Scroggs had visited, he explored and named Wager Bay and continued on his route through Roes Welcome Sound, which, to his great disappointment, turned out to be a dead-end bay with a strait to the northeast that was completely blocked by ice floes. He named the bottom of the bay Repulse Bay and the inaccessible strait Frozen Strait.

In 1747 William Moor, a cousin of Middleton's who had accompanied him on his 1742 expedition and who was also a former Hudson's Bay Company employee, explored the west shore of Hudson Bay for private interests. He made observations to a distance of 150 miles inside Wager Bay, which ended in two non-navigable rivers; he did, however, discover and partially explore Chesterfield Inlet, which Middleton had not sighted.

In the end, despite the £20,000 reward promised by the British government in 1745 to whomever discovered it, the search for a Northwest passage was fruitless: the bay and the surrounding area apparently presented only openings with no outlets and impassable rivers, as the passages that were sighted one day would turn out the next day to be exasperating inlets without issue.

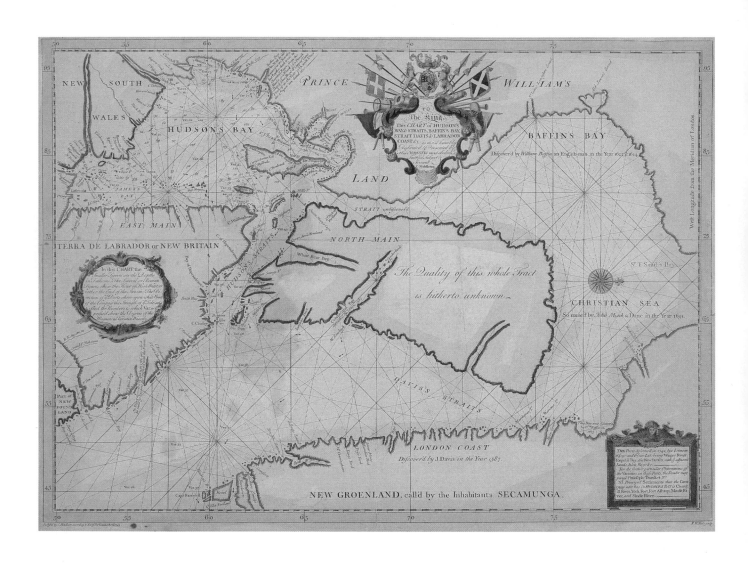

. . . This Chart of Hudson's Bay & Straits, Baffin's Bay, Strait Davis & Labrador Coast . . . . C. Middleton; [n.p.]: Publish'd by C. Middleton according to Act of Parliament, April 1743. Map: hand coloured, 45.2 × 64.1 cm.

Middleton was the first person to produce a fairly accurate outline of the west coast of Hudson Bay, which he had explored as far as its northern end.

Public Archives of Canada, Ottawa: National Map Collection (NMC 27782).

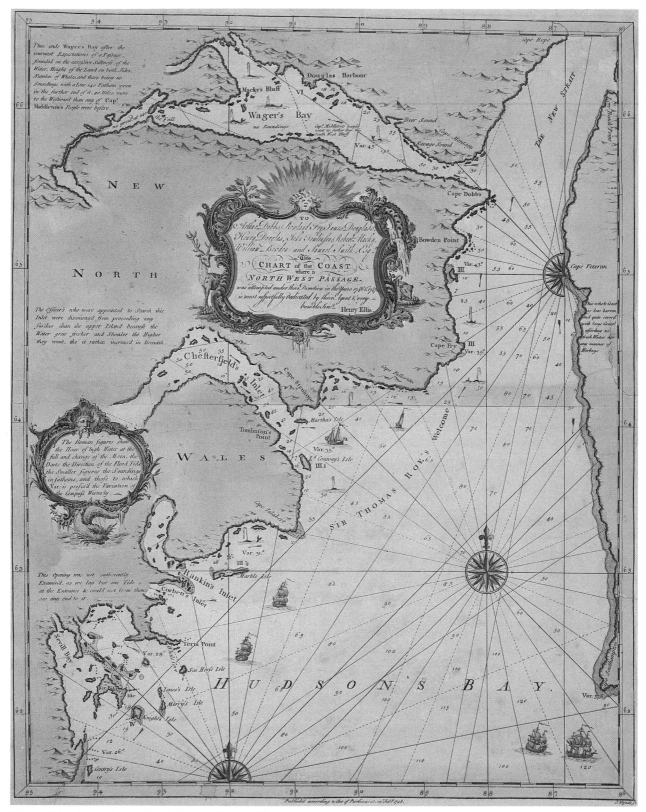

This Chart of the Coast where a North West Passage was attempted . . . . Henry Ellis. [N.d.: Anonymous], 12 February 1748. Map: hand coloured, 56.5 × 44.8 cm.

Henry Ellis, who took part in William Moor's expedition in 1747, drew this map of the west coast of Hudson's Bay, on which it can be seen that Wager Bay comes to a dead end.

Public Archives of Canada, Ottawa: National Map Collection (NMC 21058).

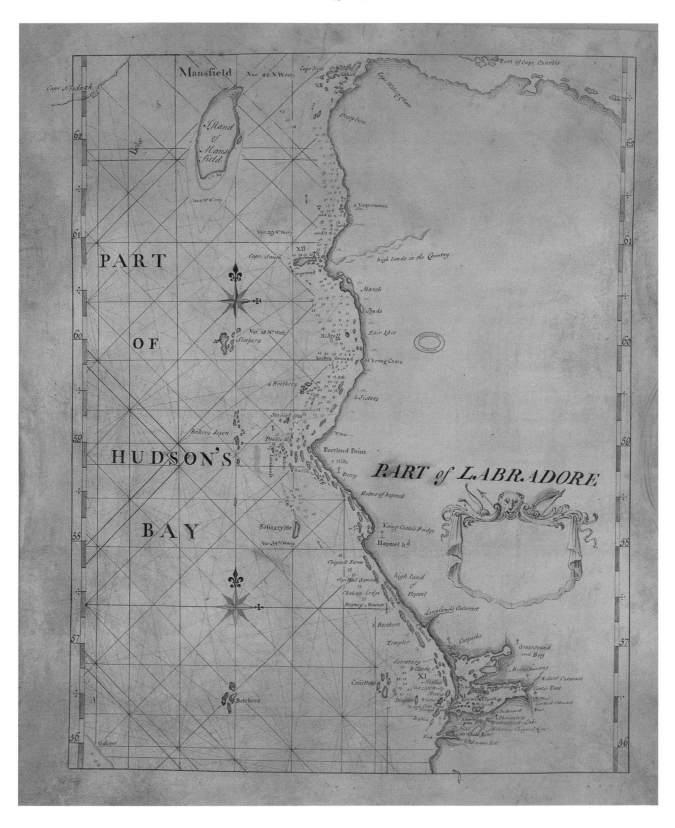

[Map of the east coast of Hudson Bay. William Coats, 1749]. Map: col. ms., 55.2 × 42.6 cm.

Coats, a captain in the service of the Hudson's Bay Company, was the first person to draw a fairly detailed map of the east coast of Hudson Bay, which he had explored over a distance of nearly 800 kilometres.

Archives of the Hudson's Bay Company, Provincial Archives of Manitoba, Winnipeg: G. 1/14.

Buffalo. Mark Catesby. Watercolour, circa 1724.

Buffalo abounded on the Canadian prairies in this period, and the Indians obtained from them their food, clothing and even a piece essential for making their tents. Anthony Henday, a Hudson's Bay Company employee who traversed these vast plains, noted on 15 September 1754: "The buffalo were so numerous that we were obliged to chase them out of our way."

Royal Library, Windsor Castle, England.

II

Population and Settlement

The territorial dimensions of New France had become so great that at the beginning of the eighteenth century the authorities no longer knew how to remedy the chronic shortage of manpower in the St. Lawrence valley. In 1706 the census enumerated 16,417 persons in the colony, of whom 7,751, that is to say 47.2 per cent, were under 15 years of age. And if the old people, the invalids, the coureurs de bois (numbering a few hundred) and the townspeople (who made up nearly a quarter of the population) are subtracted from the 8,876 men and women 15 and over, it is easy to understand why the governors and intendants were constantly looking for means to remedy the tragic situation in the rural areas, where no one was to be found to work the land. In 1700, for example, a year's pay was still being given to soldiers who became "habitants"; in the autumn of 1701, instead of training the soldiers who had just arrived, Governor Louis-Hector de Callière found himself under the necessity of "supplying them to the habitants to lighten their burden with their harvest." Once farm work was done, the soldiers were sometimes put to work building fortifications or "the roads most necessary for the convenience of the public."

Despite the "fertility" of Canadian women, which Roland-Michel Barrin de La Galissonière later praised, according to Intendant Jacques Raudot the inhabitants of Canada in 1705 had not "multiplied as much as one might hope, whether because of the wars or widespread maladies." Epidemics made terrible ravages, more than did the wars: one might say that in the eighteenth century, smallpox cost Canada the lives of almost as many people as the country took in as immigrants. Whatever the truth of that estimate, around the period 1713–20 the shortage of workers was felt more cruelly than ever in the Canadian colony; on the other hand, off in Acadia a new chapter was beginning in the history of French colonization during the same period.

If people talked unceasingly in Canada of the need to increase the population, the authorities in the mother country, maintaining the policy adopted by Louis XIV in 1673, gave no thought whatsoever to organizing large-scale departures of settlers. Throughout the period of French rule in the eighteenth century, a niggardly policy was followed in that respect: naturalization of foreigners who wanted to settle in the colony; obliging captains of merchant vessels to bring from three to six indentured servants, according to the ships' tonnage, to New France at each crossing; sending recruits to replace the soldiers who settled on the land; shipping off to Québec salt smugglers and poachers, but also young men from good families who had been banished from the kingdom for some wrongdoing. Except for criminals, few in number, who arrived in the 1720s, and to a certain extent the young men from good families, people were quite happy with these new arrivals, although, considering the needs, their number was insufficient.

And, to top it all, at the beginning of the eighteenth century the seigneurial system, the progress of which had been greatly hindered by the Iroquois wars, was suffering from various abuses, according to Intendant Raudot. In particular, not all the seigneurs and *censitaires* (settlers) were in a hurry to populate their fiefs or work their lands. This situation reached such a point that on 6 July 1711 the king published two edicts obliging those in both categories to carry out their respective engagements, on pain of forfeiting their properties. At first the colonial authorities were not very diligent in carrying out those edicts, being content to deal severely with a few recalcitrant settlers each year. Then between 1729 and 1732 Intendant Gilles Hocquart finally "pronounce[d] the reunion of 400 concessions to the seigneurs' domains because of failure by the settlers to take up residence." But it was not until 1741 that a score or so of abandoned seigneuries were incorporated into the royal domain. In the meantime, however, the Nouvelle-Beauce region on the Chaudière had been opened up with the granting of 7 seigneuries between 1736 and 1738, and between 1733 and 1739, 19 others had been granted on the Richelieu and in the Lake Champlain region. If Nouvelle-Beauce counted "about 120 families" in 1747, the Richelieu valley beyond Chambly and the Lake Champlain region made only a very small contribution to the total population of Canada, which in 1760 was estimated at 65,000.

On the east coast, after Acadia and Newfoundland had been ceded to England, the French authorities decided to occupy Cape Breton Island (Île Royale), where Philippe Pastour de Costebelle brought the garrison and entire colony of Plaisance (Placentia). At the same moment the "former" Acadians in Nova Scotia, who by virtue of the Treaty of Utrecht had "the freedom to withdraw elsewhere within the space of a year with all their personal possessions," were urged to settle on Île Royale. Very few of them, however, emigrated: on the one hand the Acadians were very much "undecided" and hesitated to leave their fertile lands for the rocky soil of Île Royale, and on the other, the English did everything they could to keep them from leaving, as much because they needed them for getting supplies as because they were afraid of reinforcing the new colony. Finally, France for her part was convinced that in the event of war the Acadians would rise en masse and would be more useful in Nova Scotia than on Île Royale. Île Saint-Jean (Prince Edward Island), which the

French also wanted to settle, would be a dependency of Île Royale, and more precisely of the fortified town of Louisbourg, which was the capital. At first granted in 1719 to Louis-Hyacinthe Castel de Saint-Pierre, who was required to render fealty and homage at the "Château de Louisbourg," the island was placed under the direct authority of Louisbourg in 1730. In 1752 it counted 2,751 settlers, and Île Royale 5,845, of whom 4,174 were living at Louisbourg. In Nova Scotia at that time the Acadians numbered about 13,000 – considerably more than the English on the peninsula, of whom more than half, that is to say about 4,000, were concentrated at Halifax, which had been founded on Chebucto Bay in 1749. Moreover, 1749 marked the beginning of an important immigration movement in Nova Scotia, thus far populated almost entirely by Acadians: in a short time, English from the colonies to the south, Irish, Germans and Swiss settled there in large numbers — the first influx of British and foreigners to present-day Canada.

Thousands of kilometres away from Acadia, the population of Louisiana in 1746 reached about 4,000, in addition to whom there were 4,730 slaves, Indians and blacks (the latter were in the majority); Nouvelle-Orléans counted 800 inhabitants (women and children excluded) and 300 slaves. Incidentally the St. Lawrence colony also had slaves: blacks, of course, but also Indians (Panis, Foxes, Comanches), in much smaller numbers however than those in Louisiana. On the other hand, owing in part to the work of the missionaries, it had its "settled" Indians: Hurons at Lorette, near Québec; Abenakis at Bécancour and Saint-François, near Trois-Rivières; Iroquois at Saint-Louis, and Algonkins, Nipissings and Iroquois at Lac des Deux-Montagnes, near Montréal. These natives of the country, all of them Catholics, were considered an integral part of the population of Canada.

A colony to be populated

Between 1700, when it counted perhaps 15,000 inhabitants, and 1747, when it counted nearly 50,000, Canada progressed enormously from the demographic point of view. If the other colonies produced greater riches, wrote Roland-Michel Barrin de la Galissonière, this one produced men, thanks to the fecundity of the Canadian women.

But by itself the birthrate, as remarkable as it was, had not been and still was not sufficient for the manpower needs. The settling of the waterfront lands along the St. Lawrence was consequently not going to be more or less completed until the 1730s and 1740s. It is true that at the beginning of the century certain seigneuries were beginning to extend inland, but in reality the situation was less brilliant than it appeared. In 1713, for example, the governor and the intendant had to ask the minister to send newly-enlisted soldiers to make up for "the scarcity of workers." The situation was so bad, according to statements of the authorities, that for lack of manpower it was "hardly possible any more to work the land or to harvest the crop."

How could one prevent "most of the land from becoming useless"? That was the question that Governor Philippe de Rigaud de Vaudreuil and Intendant Michel Bégon were asking themselves in 1714.

2⁶5

au contraire doit diminuer au bout d'un tems.

6° Que ce pays contient deja un assés
grand peuple propre a la fatigue; a la
guerre, et a la navigation, peuple qu'on perdroit
pour la plus grande partie avec le pays, et
qui avec le tems fortifieroit nos Ennemis,
Comme j'ai a craindre qu'il n'arrive dans
peu a l'Acadie.

7° Que si les autres Colonies produisent
plus de richesses, Celle ci produit des hommes,
Richesse bien plus estimable pour un grand
Roy que le Sucre et l'indigo, ou si l'on
veut tout l'or des Indes.

8° Que la fecondité est telle qu'elle
peut remplacer en partie la perte immense
de monde que nous coutent tous les ans
la martinique et S.t Domingue; on m'a
fait remarquer depuis long tems que les
Canadiens etoient les moins sujets de tous
aux maladies qui desolent quelquefois
cette derniere jsle, et j'ai lieu de croire que
la meilleure et peutêtre la seule façon

Letter from La Galissonière, acting governor of Canada, to the minister, Québec, 24 October 1747.

La Galissonière was less inclined than were the authorities in the mother country to judge the value of a colony solely by its economic profitability: if "the other colonies produce greater wealth, this one produces men, a treasure far more worthy of esteem for a great king than sugar and indigo, or, if you wish, all the gold of the Indies."

Archives nationales, Paris: Fonds des Colonies, série C[11A], vol. 87, fol. 265.

Photo Studio Littré.

Portrait of Roland-Michel Barrin, Marquis de La Galissonière (1693–1756), acting governor of New France from 1747 to 1749. Artist unknown. Oil on canvas.

Since, around 1750, New France was seriously threatened by the political expansion of the English, La Galissonière recommended, among other things, sending settlers and troops there "solidly establishing [increasing the population in] the vicinity of Fort Saint-Frédéric and the posts of Niagara, Detroit and Illinois," and erecting posts in the Ohio region.

Musée de l'île Sainte-Hélène, Montréal.

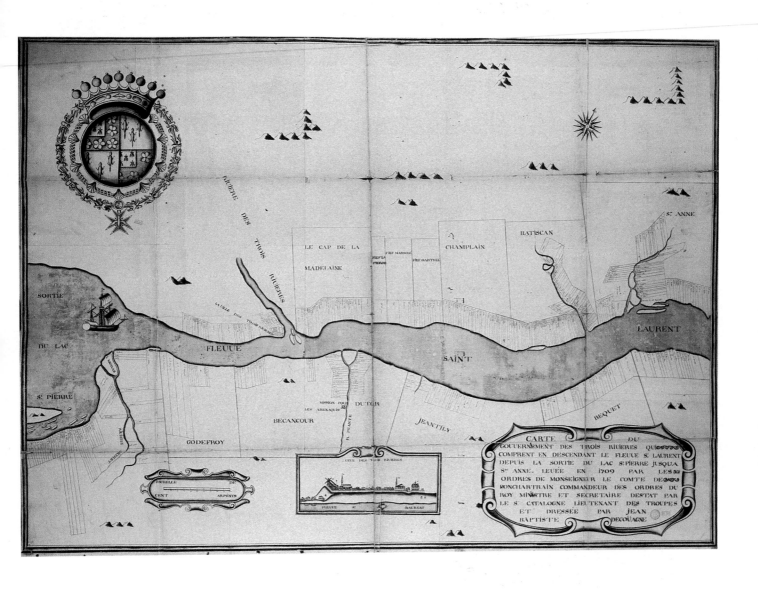

"Map of the Government of Trois-Rivières." Gédéon de Catalogne and Jean-Baptiste de Couagne, 1709. Map: col. ms.

Land grants in Canada were generally much longer than they were wide, which brought the settlers closer to one another, thus combatting isolation and increasing the number who had access to the waterways, which provided communications within the colony.

Bibliothèque nationale, Paris: Département des cartes et plans, Service hydrographique de la Marine, portefeuille 127, 2.

Population influxes from outside Canada

Since organized immigration had just about ceased after 1673, the authorities, both in the colony and in the mother country, had recourse to various means to populate the colony.

Many foreigners, most of them from New England and former prisoners of war, were naturalized; in addition, it became the practice to send salt smugglers to Canada, many of whom turned out to be excellent subjects.

Then, since the governors and intendants had noticed that the best soldiers willingly became settlers, the king regularly destined newly-enlisted soldiers for Canada to replace those who were taking up land.

Also, captains of merchant vessels were obliged on each voyage to transport to New France a certain number of indentured servants or soldiers. Considering the number of ships that cast anchor off Québec every year, the population of the colony must have been increased considerably through this measure, although the king's orders on the matter were not always respected.

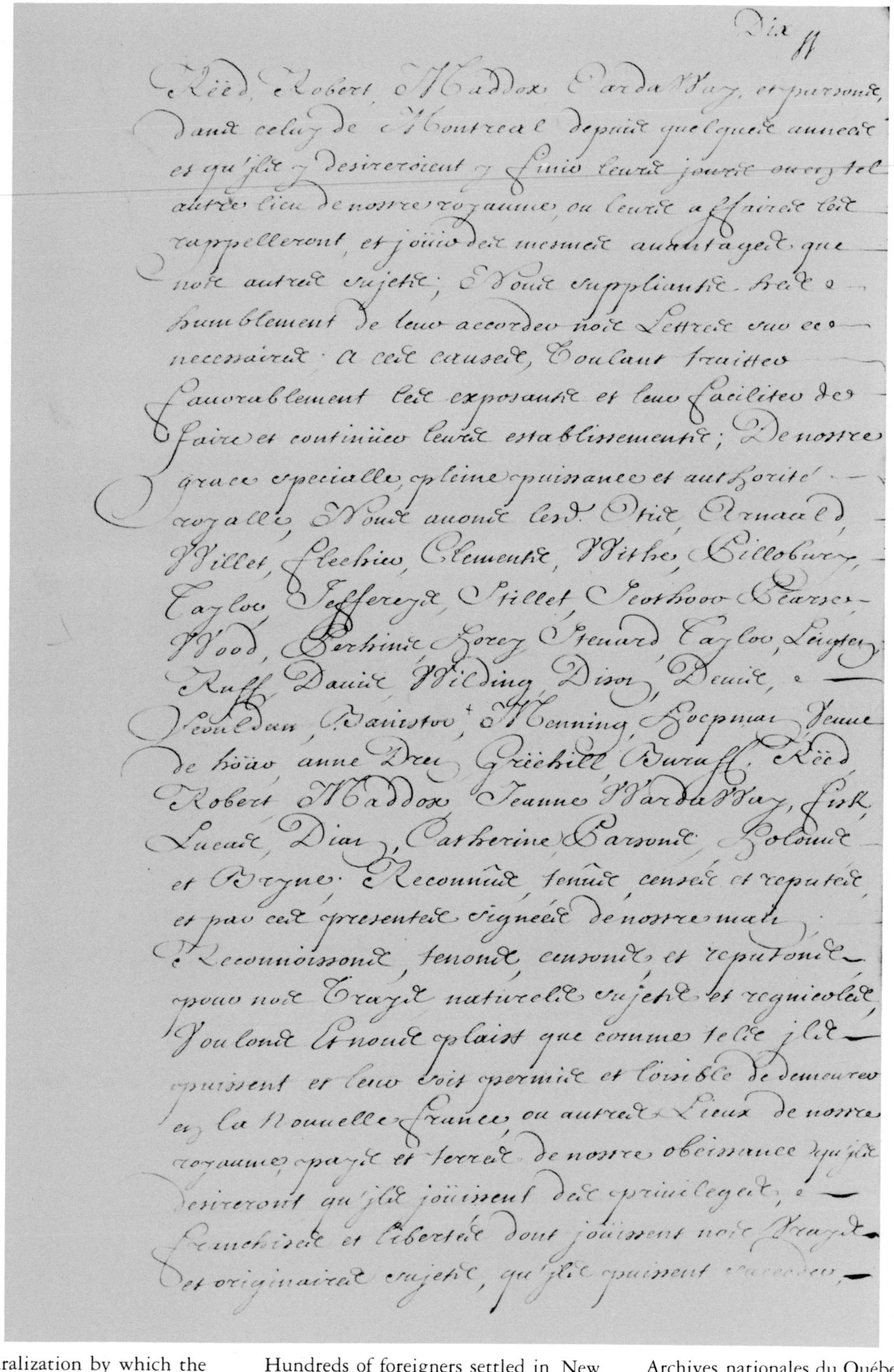

Dix 11

Rééd, Robert, Maddox, Cardaway, et parsons,
dans celuy de Montreal depuis quelques années
et qu'ils y desireroient y finir leurs jours ou en tel
autre lieu de nostre royaume, ou leurs affaires les
rappelleront, et jouir des mesmes avantages que
nos autres sujets; Nous suppliants tres
humblement de leur accorder nos Lettres sur ce
necessaires. A ces causes, voulant traitter
favorablement les exposants et leur faciliter de
faire et continuer leurs establissements; De nostre
grace specialle, pleine puissance et authorité
royalle, Nous avons lesd. Otis, Arnaud,
Willet, Fletcher, Clements, Withe, Billobury,
Taylor, Jeffereys, Stillet, Scothoor, Pearse,
Wood, Perkins Horey, Steward Taylor, Langley,
Ruff, Davids, Wilding, Dixon, Denis,
Seoldan, Banistor, Henning, Hopman Jeanne
de Hoar, anne Dren, Griehill, Buraff, Rééd,
Robert Maddox Jeanne Wardaway, Fink,
Lucas, Dian, Catherine Parsons, Holones
et Bryne. Reconnus, tenus, censés et reputés,
et par ces presentes signées de nostre main
Reconnoissons, tenons, censons et reputons
pour nos vrays naturels sujets et regnicoles;
Voulons et nous plaist que comme tels ils
puissent et leur soit permis et loisible de demeurer
en la Nouvelle France, ou autres Lieux de nostre
royaume, pays et terres de nostre obeissance qu'ils
desireront qu'ils jouissent des privileges,
franchises et libertés dont jouissent nos vrays
et originaires sujets, qu'ils puissent succeder,

Letters of naturalization by which the King of France recognized foreigners as his "true and natural subjects," expressing his will that "it will be permissible and open to them to live in New France," Rambouillet, June 1713.

Hundreds of foreigners settled in New France under the French regime.

Archives nationales du Québec, Centre d'archives de Québec: Insinuations du Conseil supérieur, vol. 4, fol. 10.

Photo Belvédère.

Elle a ordonné et ordonne (tout ce entend) qu'à commencer de ce jourd'huy il sera inseré dans les passeports qui seront expediés pour les bâtimens allans en la nouvelle France la Condition d'y porter 3. Engagés pour ceux de soixante Tonneaux et au dessous 4 pour ceux depuis soixante jusques à 100. Tonneaux et 6 pour ceux au dessus de 100. Tonneaux. qui auront au moins 18. et ne ne pourront être plus agés de 40. et seront de la grandeur au moins de 4 p.ds

permet Sa Maj.té mod.t Capitaines qui voudront se dispenser de porter lesd. engagés de porter à la place de Chaque Engagé Soldats de recrue pour les Compagnies que Sa Maj.té entretient en garnison aud.t pays de la nouvelle France lesquels Soldats leur seront remis par les intendants Commissaires de la Marine ou des Classes des Ports ou les bâtiments seront Expediés et dont mention sera faite dans les Rolles des Equipages.

"Ordinance requiring merchant ships going in the future to New France to carry there" indentured servants or soldiers, Versailles, 20 March 1714.

Merchant ships sailing to New France will have "to carry there 3 indentured servants for those of sixty tons burden or less, 4 for those of from sixty to 100 tons, and 6 for those of over 100 tons . . . . His Majesty permits [them] to carry army recruits in place of each indentured servant."

Archives nationales, Paris: Fonds des Colonies, série B, vol. 36, fol. 337-337v.

Photo Studio Littré.

View of the port of La Rochelle. Claude-Joseph Vernet (1714–1789). Oil on canvas, 1762.

It was at La Rochelle that a good part of the persons who contracted to go to work in Canada, on Île Royale or on Île Saint-Jean, boarded ship. Many became settlers once their contracts ended.

Musée de la Marine, Paris.

Photo Musées nationaux.

Canada. à 8.bre 1731

83.

M.re le M.s de Beauharnois
à Hocquart

Monseigneur

M. Le Comte des *[illegible]* nous
a remis les 60 faux sauniers
et les quatre contrebandiers qui
avoient esté embarquez par
vos ordres Sur le vaisseau du Roy.
jls se sont tous trouvez gens

de bon service. Nous les avons
distribuez Sur le champ aux
particuliers qui nous en ont
demandés et qui en avoient
besoin, a l'éxception de quatre
Seulement que M.r De Beauharnois
a incorporés dans les troupes
et qui se sont engagés de bonne
Volonté

Nous vous suplions Monseigneur
de continuer de nous en faire
envoyer toutes les années. y
en eust il quatre cents nous
n'en serions pas embarrassez

Letter from Governor de Beauharnois
and Intendant Hocquart to the minister,
Québec, 5 October 1731.

" . . . the 60 salt smugglers and four
smugglers who by your order had been
put on board the king's ship . . . have
all turned out to be serviceable people."
Several hundred salt smugglers settled in
Canada between 1730 and 1749.

Archives nationales, Paris: Fonds des
Colonies, série C¹¹ᴬ, vol. 54, fol. 83-
83v.

Photo Studio Littré.

Letter from Governor General de Beauharnois and Intendant Hocquart to the minister, Québec, 14 October 1733.

"In accordance with the king's intentions it has always been the custom upon the arrival of the new recruits to discharge the soldiers who have gotten married. As a rule it is the best ones who take up residence . . . ." Of the 10,000 people who settled in Canada under the French regime, about 3,500 were soldiers.

Archives nationales, Paris: Fonds des Colonies, série C11A, vol. 59, fol. 184-184v.

Photo Studio Littré.

The towns

The people who landed at Québec in the eighteenth century were not always coming to settle on the land; merchants and craftsmen, senior judicial officers and minor officials, young men from good families and salt smugglers, many came to swell the ranks of the city dwellers.

By Jean Talon's time about a quarter of the population of Canada lived in the towns — an enormous proportion for the period. Throughout the French rule in the eighteenth century that proportion remained approximately the same, and even then it took Intendant François Bigot's intervention in the 1750s to curb the flight from the land.

In the period from 1700 to 1760, thanks above all to commerce and officialdom, Québec and Montréal became comparatively large towns. Trois-Rivières, which was less favoured in all respects, remained a small urban centre.

In the English colonies to the east, the three main towns — Halifax, founded in 1749, Lunenburg, founded in 1753, and St. John's, which was much older — were populated mostly by English, Irish or Germans.

A General View of Quebec, from Point-Lévy. Vue Generale de Quebec, prise de la Pointe-Lévy.
To the Hon.ble S.r CHARLES SAUNDERS Vice Admiral of the Blue, and Knight of the most Honourable Order of the BATH.
These Twelve Views of the Principal Buildings in QUEBEC, are most Humbly Inscribed by his most Obedient Humble Servant Richard Short.

View of Québec from Pointe-Lévy.
Richard Short (known 1759–1761).
Etching by P. Canot, printed by
Thomas Jefferys, 1761.

Québec called to mind Old France with
its buildings in the classical style, its
port where European ideas and fashions
circulated, and the lifestyle of its
government officials, merchants and
military officers, who were always
inclined to imitate what was being done
in the mother country.

Public Archives of Canada, Ottawa:
Picture Division (Negative no. C-355).

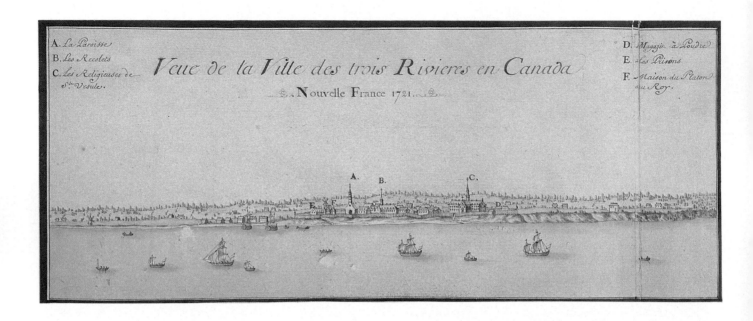

A. La Paroisse
B. Les Recolets
C. Les Religieuses de S.te Ursule.

Veue de la Ville des trois Rivieres en Canada

Nouvelle France 1721.

D. Magazin à Poudre
E. Les Prisons
F. Maison du Platon du Roy.

"View of the town of Trois-Rivières in Canada . . . . " [Anonymous], 1721. View: col. ms., 15.3 × 38.8 cm. Page, also containing views of Chambly, Montréal, Québec and Niagara Falls.

According to Nicolas-Gaspard Boucault, Trois-Rivières had "a local governor, a king's lieutenant, and a town major and adjutant of the troops garrisoned there." The royal jurisdiction (court) of the town was "composed of a lieutenant-general for civil and criminal affairs, a king's attorney and a court clerk." The parish church was served by the Récollets, and the town had a hospital that was run by the Ursulines, who also concerned themselves with education for the girls.

The Newberry Library, Chicago: Edward E. Ayer Collection.

View of Montréal from Île Sainte-Hélène. Thomas Davies (circa 1737–1812). Watercolour, 1762.

Since it was in contact with the West and the world of the Indians, Montréal seemed more open to the currents of influence circulating on the new continent than was Québec. Its townspeople were said to be more adventuresome, more warlike and less "civilized" than those of Québec.

National Gallery of Canada, Ottawa.

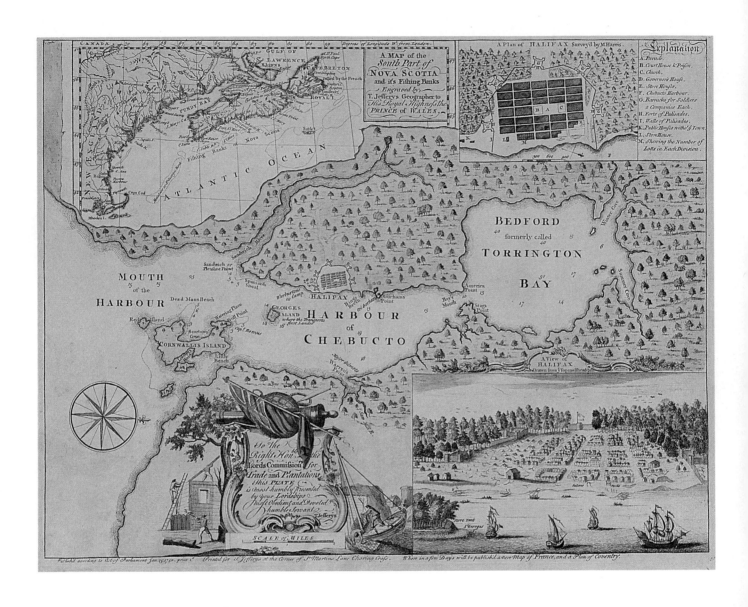

[Halifax and environs]. T. Jefferys. [London]: Printed for T. Jefferys at the corner of St. Martins Lane, Charing Cross, 25 January 1750. Map: hand coloured, 31.7 × 41.2 cm.

Thirty-five years after it had been conquered by Great Britain, Nova Scotia was still populated almost entirely by Acadians. Since she could not trust this French population too much, Great Britain decided to bring in a large number of English, German, Swiss and other settlers. These immigrants founded settlements such as Halifax in 1749 and Lunenburg in 1753.

Public Archives of Canada, Ottawa: National Map Collection (NMC 1012).

The country

Many Canadians, both seigneurs and settlers, perhaps preferring the life in the woods or town life to agricultural labour, let their lands lie fallow. On 6 July 1711, with an aim to developing the land in New France, the king obliged them all, under pain of confiscation of their properties, to keep to the terms of their land-grant obligations.

If not all Canadians displayed a strong liking for farm work, hardworking *censitaires* nevertheless represented the greatest number, and certain seigneuries, such as Batiscan, east of Trois-Rivières, were being settled at a very satisfactory rate.

Moreover, in the 1730s lands for settlement were opened up on one of the tributaries of the St. Lawrence, the Chaudière, and in the Lake Champlain region. It is true that beyond Chambly in the Richelieu valley and on the shores of Lake Champlain, settlement was scarcely pushed before 1760; but on the Chaudière, Nouvelle-Beauce would experience rapid growth.

Even at Detroit settlement had made great progress: despite being so far from Canada, the post counted some 600 inhabitants in 1751.

75.

*trouuent moins de terres a occupées dans les lieux
qui peuuent mieux conuenir au Commerce; A quoy
Voulant Pourvoir. Sa Majesté estant en
Son Conseil, a ordonné et ordonne que dans vn
an du jour de la publication du present arrest pour
toutes prefixions et delayst, les Habitants de la
Nouuelle france ausquels Sa Majesté a accordé
des terres en Seigneurie, qui n'ont point de domaine
deffriché, Et qui n'y ont point d'habitants Seront
tenus de les mettre en culture, et d'y placer des
Habitants dessus, faute dequoy, Et les temps passé,
Veut Sa Majesté qu'elles Soient réünies a Son
Domaine a la dilligence du Procureur general du Con.
Superieur de Quebec, Et Sur les ordonnances qui en
Seront rendües par le Gouverneur et Lieutenant gnal
de Sa Majesté Et l'Intendant aud. pays;
Ordonne aussy Sa Majesté que tous les Seigneurs
audit pays de la Nouuelle france, ayent a conceder
aux Habitants les terres qu'ils leur demanderont
dans leurs Seigneuries, a titre de redevances, et Sans
Exiger d'eux aucune Somme d'argent pour raison des
Concessions, Sinon et a faute de ce faire, Permet aux d.
Habitants de leur demander lesd. terres par Sommation,
Et en cas de refus de Se pourvoir par deuant les
Gouuerneur et Lieutenant general, Et l'Intendant
aud. pays ausquels Sa Majesté ordonne de les
Conceder aud. Habitants les terres par eux demand.
dans lesd. Seigneuries au x mesmes droicts imposez
Sur les autres terres concedées dans lesd. Seigneuries
lesquels droicts Seront payez par les nouueaux
Habitants entre les mains du receueur du domaine
de Sa Majesté En la Ville de Quebec, Sans que les
Seigneurs en puissent pretendre aucun Sur eux, de
quelque nature qu'ils Soient, Et Sera le present*

Decree by the Conseil d'État concerning the seigneuries in Canada, Marly, 6 July 1711.

"[Within one year, those who own] seigneuries, who have no cleared land on their domains and who have no settlers on them, will be required to bring them under cultivation and to put settlers on them, failing which, and the said period having elapsed, His Majesty wills that they be re-attached to his domain."

Archives nationales du Québec, Centre d'archives de Québec: Insinuations du Conseil supérieur, vol. 3, fol. 75.

Photo Belvédère.

76.

[Manuscript text in 18th-century French handwriting — a decree by the Conseil d'État, 6 July 1711]

Decree by the Conseil d'État concerning lands granted in the seigneuries, Marly, 6 July 1711.

"The settlers in New France who are not living on the lands that have been granted them will be required to take up residence on them and to work them, failing which [they will] have forfeited the property, and the said lands will be re-attached to the domain of the seigneuries."

Archives nationales du Québec, Centre d'archives de Québec: Insinuations du Conseil supérieur, vol. 3, fol. 76.

Photo Belvédère.

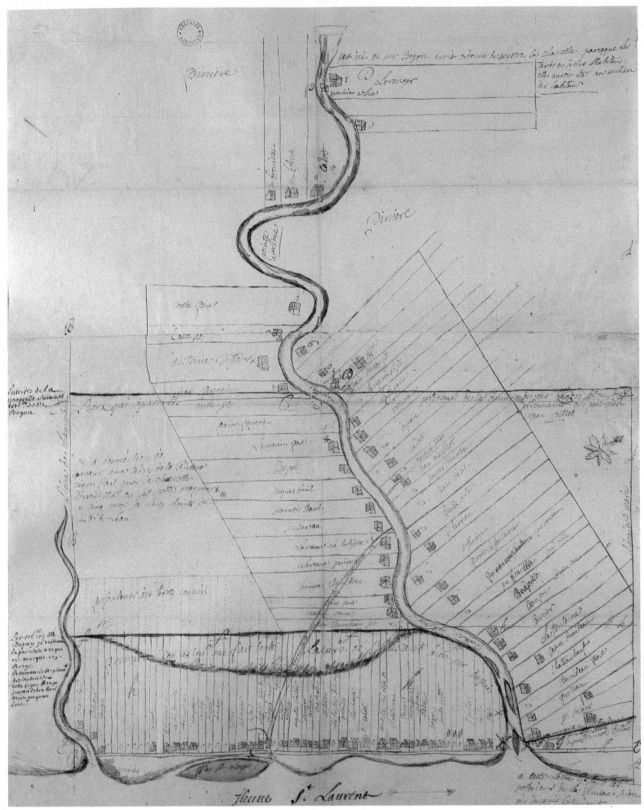

[Cadastral survey of Batiscan, a seigneury belonging to the Jesuits. Anonymous, 1725]. Map: col. ms., page 47.3 × 62.6 cm.

In the middle of the eighteenth century a third of the Canadian population lived on seigneuries that belonged to religious institutions and that were generally among the most progressive in the colony.

Archives nationales, Paris: Section Outre-Mer, Colonies, G¹, vol. 461. Recensements (ancienne cote).

Photo Studio Littré.

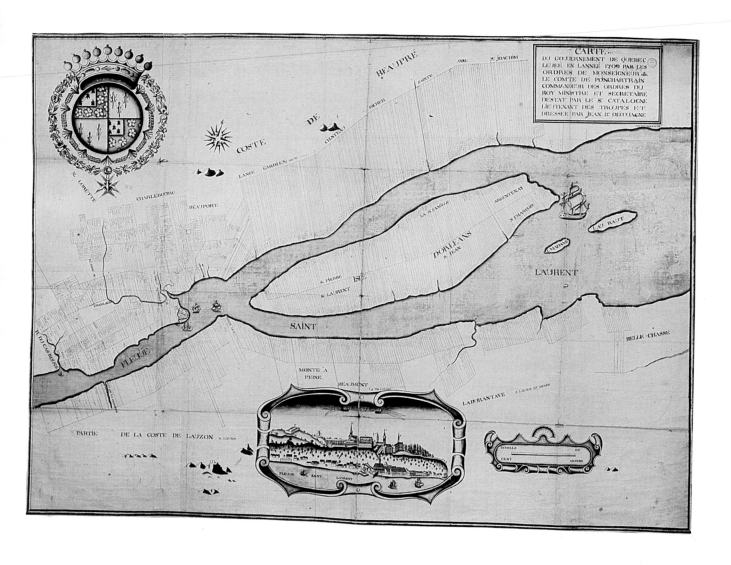

"Map of the Government of Québec . . . ." Gédéon de Catalogne and Jean-Baptiste de Couagne. 1709. Map: col. ms.

At the beginning of the eighteenth century the Government of Québec counted a population of about 9,000, that is to say, more than half of that of Canada. Its most heavily populated seigneuries were located a short distance from the town of Québec. Throughout the colony the tendency was to settle near the towns, where various services and conveniences were to be found.

Bibliothèque nationale, Paris: Département des cartes et plans, Service hydrographique de la Marine, portefeuille 127,2.

Les jeunes gens ont continué de se-
jetter et deprendre des (Établissemen ( )
sur la rivière du Saut de la chaudière),
Ils s'y croyent livrés deportée d'estre
attaquez par L'Enemy ; Les
propriétaires des differentes Seigneuries)

ne negligent rien pour les peuples et le
pays nourrit ceux qui l'habitent au
Nombre, d'environ 120: familles qui y
tiennent feu et lieu et de 100: jeunes gens
qui ont commencé des défrichemens .

Letter from the acting governor, La Galissonière, and Intendant Hocquart to the minister, Québec, 24 September 1747.

In ten years the Nouvelle-Beauce region has experienced rapid growth, thanks above all to the dynamism of a few seigneurs, who have even had a road built there. Now this region "feeds those who live there, to the number of about 120 families who reside there, and about 100 young men who have begun to clear land."

Archives nationales, Paris: Fonds des Colonies, série C¹¹E, vol. 10, fol. 69v-70.

Photo Studio Littré.

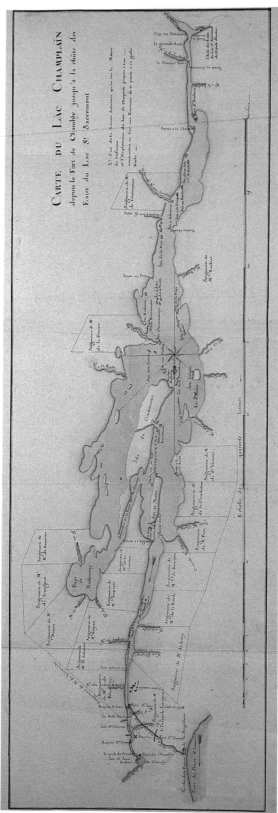

[Map of the Richelieu valley and the Lake Champlain region. Louis Franquet. Circa 1752]. Map, col. ms., 31.0 × 97.0 cm.

In Louis Franquet's "Report drawn from the observations made on the principal places that I travelled through in my tour from Montréal to Lake Champlain and other places in the period from 24 July to 23 August 1752."

The seigneuries in the Richelieu valley and the Lake Champlain region were lightly populated, partly because of the war, and partly because of the seigneurs' negligence. Beyond Chambly the most important population centre was at Fort Saint-Frédéric, near Lake Champlain.

Bibliothèque de l'Inspection du Génie, Paris: Ms f°210°, n° 6.

Photo Studio Littré.

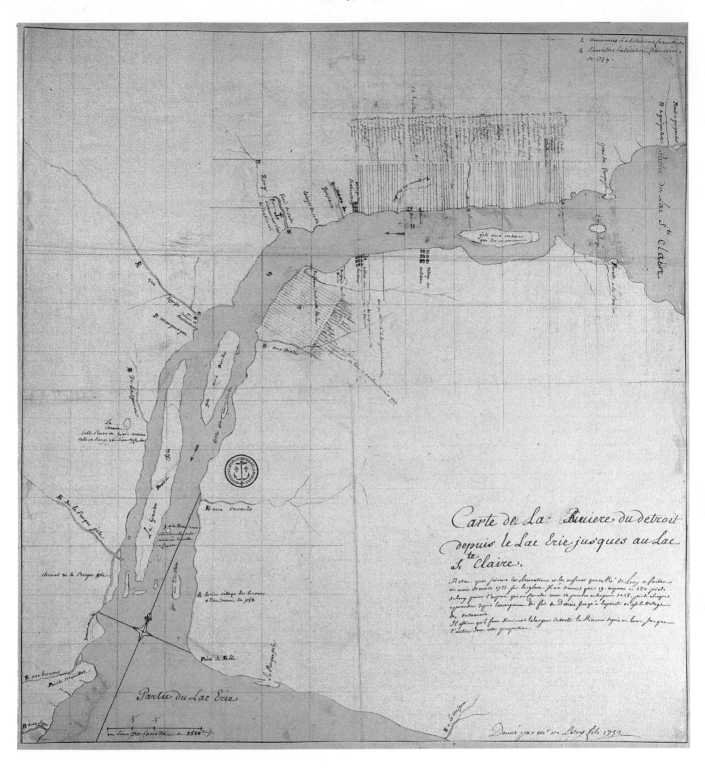

"Map of the Detroit River from Lake Erie to Lake St. Clair." Gaspard-Joseph Chaussegros de Léry (the younger). 1752. Map: col. ms., 50.0 × 47.0 cm.

The land grants that appear on this map belonged above all to Canadians, who constituted the population of the post of Detroit. According to a report of the period (1758), "the settlers at Detroit harvest in a normal year 25,000 *minots* of wheat, a good deal of oats and corn . . . . In a normal year between 800 and 1,000 bales (of pelts) go out from here."

Service historique de la Marine, Vincennes, France: Service hydrographique, recueil 67, n° 71.

Photo Studio Littré.

From one census to another

A certain number of censuses furnish fairly accurate figures on the population of Canada in the period of French rule in the eighteenth century.

In 1716, for example, the curé of Notre-Dame de Québec parish, which took in the town of Québec and its suburbs, recorded the names of some 2,300 people living there.

In 1737, 6,872 families and 39,970 persons — 20,708 males and 19,262 females — were counted in the colony. This population was very young: 17,486 boys and girls — 43.7 per cent of the total — were under 15 years of age.

A document from 1754 reveals that in that year, of the 55,000 people living in Canada, 42,200 lived in the country and 12,800 (22.2 per cent) in the towns. Interestingly, despite its strategic importance for the fur trade, Montréal, which counted 4,000 people, came after Québec, the capital of the colony and a seaport, whose population (8,000) had increased almost fourfold in 40 years.

Quantdessus est pierre heu dit Cournoyer fils
dud heu qui possede quatre arpens de front sur lad
profondeur le quel na qune grange et sept arpens de
terre labourable et un arpent de prairie,

quantdessus en pierre La Callée gendre dud heu qui
possede quatre arpens de front sur lad profondeur le
quel a maison grange et Etable quatre arpents de
terre labourable et un arpent de prairie,

quantdessus est une terre de quatre arpents de
front sur lad profondeur qui estoit concede par led
paul heu a feu joseph heu son fils sur laquelle il
y a une grange quatre arpens de terre labourable
et un arpent de prairie,

quantdessus en pierre salvaye gendre dud paul
heu qui possede quatre arpens de front sur laditte
profondeur lequel a maison grange et Etable les
quatre arpens de terre labourable,

Quantdessus en estienne heu fils dud paul heu
qui possede quatre arpens de front sur lad profondeur
lequel a maison grange et Etable et quatre arpens
de terre labourable,

quantdessus en paul heu dit despins fils dud paul
heu qui possede quatre arpens de front sur laditte
profondeur lequel a maison grange et Etable et
huit arpens de terre labourable,

Quantdevant de lad Concession et suite fleuve
st laurens en une isle vulgairement nommée L'isle

Extract from the *aveu et dénombrement* for
the fief Yamaska, 3 June 1723.

The censuses, *aveux et dénombrements*,
parish registers, notarial minutes and
judicial registries give us information
about the colonists and their way of life
(family life, social life and financial
status).

Public Archives of Canada, Ottawa:
Manuscript Division, MG 8, F 97,
p. 16.

Extrait du Recensement general
De la Colonie de la nouvelle france pour l'année 37.

Sçauoir.

Maisons Royalles	
Eglises	102.
Cures ou missionnaires	80.
Presbitaires	72.
Chanoines et Prestres du seminaire	33.
Jesuites	22.
Recolets	42.
Religieuses de l'hôtel Dieu	83.
Religieuses Vrsulines	89.
Religieuses de l'hôpital general	55.
Soeurs de la Congregation	67.
Moulins à bled	107.
Moulins à Scie	66.
familles	6872.
hommes au dessur de 50. ans	1791.

hommes au dessous	5347.
hommes absents	240.
femmes et veuues	6804.
Garçons au dessus de 15. ans	4263.
Garçons au dessour	9067.
filles au dessus de 15. ans	4039.
filles au dessour	8419.
Terres en valeur	158805. arpens
Prairies	19763. arpens
bled françois	333388. minots
bled d'Inde	4185. minots
Pois	52197. minots
avoine	130152. minots
Orge	2669. minots
Tabac	93867. livres
Lin	104120. Jd.
Chanvre	3375. Jd.

Extract from the general census of
Canada for the year 1737.

From 1737 to 1760 the population of
Canada rose from 40,000 to 65,000.

Archives nationales, Paris: Section
Outre-Mer, série G¹, vol. 460.

Photo Studio Littré.

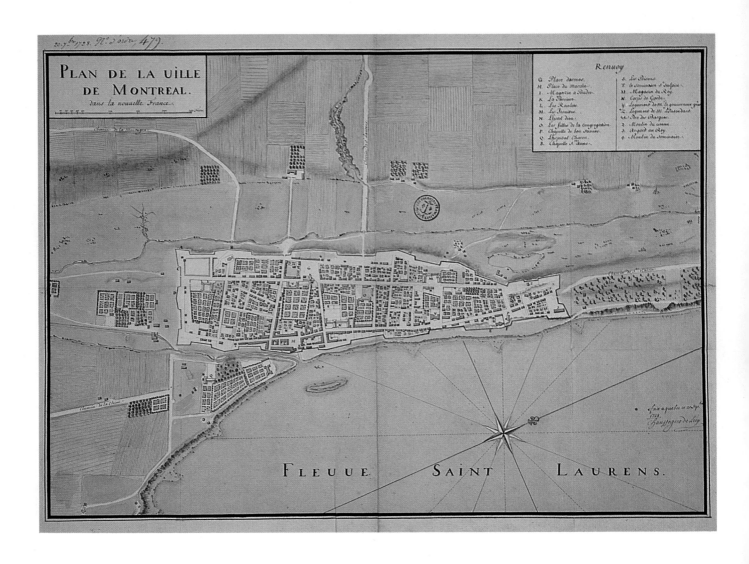

"Plan of the town of Montréal, in New France," Gaspard-Joseph Chaussegros de Léry. 20 September 1728. Map: col. ms., 44.7×63.8 cm.

On this plan are shown the church (K), the Sulpician seminary (T), the Hôpital Général (Q), the Hôtel-Dieu (N), the houses of the Récollets, the Jesuits, and the sisters of the Congrégation de Notre-Dame (O), the marketplace (H) and the prisons (S).

Archives nationales, Paris: Section Outre-Mer, Dépôt des fortifications des colonies, Amérique septentrionale, 479 B.

Photo Studio Littré.

D. l'autrepain . . . . 152325.#

12291. ames
29909. . . . Ame chesse de famille, leur femmes, qui les faut
       Domestiques, passée p.r 18000. attendû
       les Enfants au dessous de 7 ans a 2o.sol . . . 18000.
                                                    _____
42200. ames   170325.#

Récapitulation

Quebec . . . . 8000. ames . . . . 32650.#

Montreal . . . . 4000 . . . . 19870.

3. R.es du f. ger . . 800 . . . . 2997.

Campagne . 42200. . . . . 170325.
                                        _____
                    55000. ames . . 225842.#

Plan for a poll-tax, 1754.

Three quarters of the Canadians lived in the country, where farming, livestock-raising, woodcutting, hunting, fishing and now and then a little trading afforded them a certain degree of comfort. On the whole, being squeezed less by taxes, seigneurial dues and tithes, they enjoyed better living conditions than did the peasants in France.

Archives nationales, Paris: Fonds des colonies, série C11A, vol. 99, fol. 533v.

Photo Studio Littré.

The colonies in the East and Southwest

After the loss of Acadia, about all that remained to the French on the Atlantic coast were Île Royale and Île Saint-Jean, which were from then on called French Acadia, as opposed to the former Acadia, which came under British jurisdiction in 1713 along with its 1,800 or so inhabitants.

Because of Île Royale's geographical situation, no time was lost in occupying it after the Treaty of Utrecht, with the Acadians being invited to settle there — an invitation that was not met with an overwhelming response. In 1734 a census recorded 3,407 inhabitants, most of them engaged in fishing and in coastal and ocean-going trade.

As for Île Saint-Jean, granted in August 1719 to Louis-Hyacinthe Castel, Comte de Saint-Pierre, who was to settle it along with Île Miscou (granted to him at the same time) and establish inshore cod-fishing on it, in 1739 it counted a population of only 422.

If, on the other hand, the English population of Newfoundland barely exceeded a thousand around 1700, it grew gradually, reaching some 7,300 in the 1750s, while the English colony of Nova Scotia experienced a great surge in population due to immigration.

And at the other end of the continent the French colony of Louisiana counted 3,987 persons, 44 per cent of whom were slaves, in 1726.

LETTRES PATENTES DE CONCESSION

DE L'ISLE DE SAINT JEAN, ET DE CELLES
DE MISCOU, situées dans le Golfe de S. Laurent,
pour M. le Comte de S. Pierre.

Du mois d'Aoust 1719.

LOUIS par la Grace de Dieu Roy de France &
de Navarre, à tous presens & à venir, SALUT.
Nous avons favorablement écouté la demande
que le Sieur Comte de Saint-Pierre, Premier
Ecuyer de nostre très-cher & très-amée Tante la Duchesse
d'Orleans, Nous a faite d'une Concession d'Isles dans le
Golfe de Saint Laurent, pour y établir des Habitans &
une Pêche sédentaire de Moruës. Un pareil établissement
estant avantageux à nôtre Royaume & au Commerce de
nos Sujets ; A CES CAUSES & autres, à ce Nous
mouvans, de l'avis de nostre très-cher & très-amé Oncle
le Duc d'Orleans Petit-Fils de France, Regent de nostre
Royaume, de nostre très cher & très amé Oncle le Duc
de Chartres Premier Prince de nostre Sang, de nostre
très-cher & très-amé Cousin le Duc de Bourbon, Prince
de nostre Sang, de nostre très-cher & très-amé Oncle le
Comte de Toulouse, Prince Legitimé, & autres Pairs de
France, Grands & Notables Personnages de nostre
Royaume, & de nostre grace speciale pleine puis-

sance, & autorité Royale, Nous avons concedé,
donné, & octroyé audit Sieur Comte de Saint-Pierre
les Isles de Saint Jean & de Miscou, avec les Isles,
Islots & Battures adjacentes situées dans le Golfe Saint
Laurent, pour en joüir par ledit Sieur Comte de Saint
Pierre, ses heritiers ou ayans cause, à perpetuité, comme
de leur propre, à titre de Franc-Aleu Noble, cependant
sans justice, que Nous Nous sommes reservée. Donnons
faculté audit Sieur Comte de Saint Pierre de conceder les
terres qui sont contenuës dans lesdites Isles à rente, sans
que pour raison de la presente Concession il soit tenu de
Nous payer, ni à nos successeurs Rois, aucune finance,
ni indemnité ; desquelles, à quelques sommes qu'elles
puissent monter, Nous lui avons fait don & remise, à la
charge de porter foi & hommage au Château de Loüis-
bourg dont il relevera sans aucune redevance, de conserver & faire conserver par ses tenanciers les bois de chênes
propres à la construction de nos Vaisseaux, de Nous donner avis, ou au Gouverneur & Commissaire Ordonnateur
de l'Isle Royale, des Mines, Minieres, & Mineraux, si
aucunes s'y trouvent sur l'étenduë des terres concedées
par les Presentes, lesquelles Nous Nous sommes reservé
de conserver ou indemniser les Habitans qui peuvent y
estre établis, de faire passer sur icelles pendant le courant
de l'année prochaine cent personnes pour s'y habituer,
& pendant les années suivantes cinquante autres personnes chacune année, jusqu'à ce que lesdits Isles soient
entierement habitée avec les bestiaux necessaires ; d'y
tenir feu & lieu, & le faire tenir par ceux qu'il établira,
d'essarter & faire essarter incessamment lesdites terres,
laisser les chemins necessaires pour l'utilité publique. Et
en cas que dans la suite, Nous eussions besoin d'aucune

Letters patent from the king granting
"the Comte de Saint-Pierre the islands
of Saint-Jean and Miscou," with the
obligation of bringing there "in the
course of the next year 100 people to
settle there, and 50 more each year
during the following years," Paris,
August 1719.

The Comte de Saint-Pierre's company
established the first population nucleus
on Île Saint-Jean (Prince Edward Island).
The population of the island would
grow appreciably only in the years
1749–1758, when some thousands of
Acadians came to seek refuge there.

Archives nationales, Paris: Archives
imprimées, série AD, VII, 2a, n° 36.

Recensement de l'Isle Royale

1734.

Habitans . . . . 318.

Femmes . . . . 256.

Garçons au dessus de 15. ans . . . . . 107.

Garçons au dessous de 15. ans . . . . 357.

Filles . . . . 404.

Servantes et autres domestiques . . . . . 321.

Matelots et pecheurs au Service des
habitans . . . . 1644.

      Total des ames . . . . 3405.

Chaloupes des habitans po. la pêche . . . . 259.

Batteaux et Goelettes Jd. . . . . 28.

Navires et autres Batimens des
habitans po. le comerce et le cabotage . . . . . 48.

      Total des Batimens de Mer . . . . 335.

Census of Île Royale, 1734.

Île Royale (Cape Breton Island) was above all populated by fishermen, workmen and tradespeople who came from Newfoundland (Plaisance), Nova Scotia (Acadia), and the maritime regions of the kingdom such as Brittany, Gascoyne, Normandy, Aunis, Saintonge, Poitou and Labourd.

Archives nationales, Paris: Section Outre-Mer, série G[1], vol. 466.

Photo Studio Littré.

Medal with head of Louis XV to commemorate the founding of Louisbourg, 1720.

The fortress of Louisbourg, which was built in the years 1719–1744, would be taken twice by the British, who landed troops west of the town, on the land side, and attacked it from the rear.

Parks Canada, Fortress of Louisbourg.

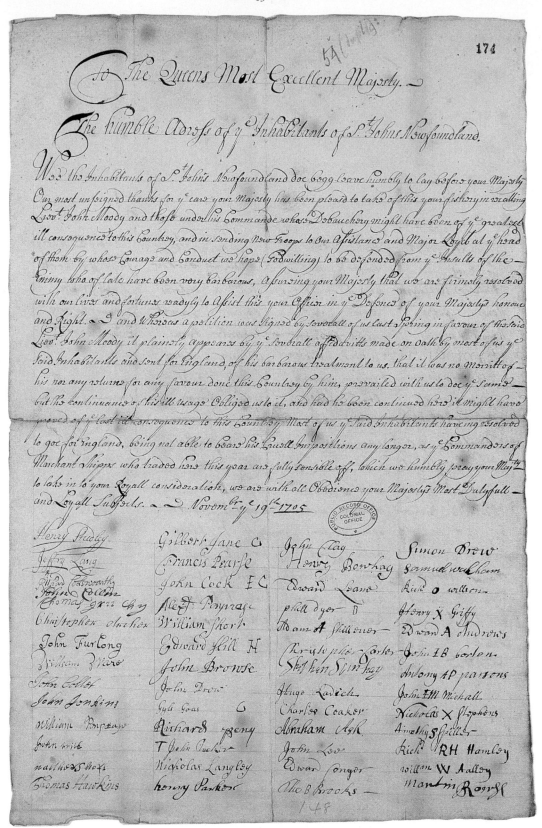

Address from 118 inhabitants of
St. John's to the queen of England,
19 November 1705.

Up until about 1730, the population of
Newfoundland was largely English. In
the following decades, however, a great
many Irish settled on the island.

Public Record Office, London: Series
C.O. 194, vol. 22, p. 174.

View of the Town & fort of Annapolis Royal Nova Scotia taken on the Spot by Cap.t Hamilton of His Majest.s 40th Reg.t foot

View of Annapolis Royal. John Hamilton (known 1753–1777). Watercolour.

From 1710 to 1748, the English in Nova Scotia were few. They settled mostly at Annapolis Royal and at Canso. From 1749 on, the thousands of immigrants sent over from England could establish themselves only in places that were well fortified (Halifax, Lunenburg, Lawrencetown), raids by the Indians (and later by the Acadians)

totally preventing the dispersal of the population.

Public Archives of Canada: Picture Division (Negative no. C-2706).

76 VOYAGE

Presque dans toutes les familles on voit cinq & six Enfans, & souvent beaucoup plus ; il faut voir comme la marmaille y fourmille ; & si l'on ne va point là comme ailleurs en Pellerinage pour en avoir, ils se suivent de prés, & l'on diroit qu'ils sont presque tous d'un même âge.

> Dans un Pays qu'on va rarement secourir,
>
> Et qui souffre souvent la derniere misere,
>
> On s'étonne de voir que le Pere & la Mere
>
> De leur petit travail en puissent tant nourrir.

Mais c'est la richesse du Pays, quand ils sont en état de travailler, ce qu'ils font de bonne heure ; ils épargnent à leurs Peres des journées d'hommes qui coûtent là vingt-cinq & trente sols, & cela va à une dépense qu'ils ne sçauroient faire. Il en coûte beaucoup pour accommoder les terres qu'on veut cultiver, celles qu'ils apellent Hautes, & qu'il faut défricher dans les Bois ne sont pas bonnes, le grain n'y leve pas bien, & quelque peine que l'on prenne pour le faire venir par des Engrais dont on a trés-peu, on n'y recüeille presque rien, & on est quelquefois contraint de les abandonner. Il faut pour avoir des Bleds dessecher les

DE L'ACADIE. 77

Marais que la Mer en pleine marée inonde de ses eaux, & qu'ils apellent les Terres Basses ; celles-là sont assez bonnes, mais quel travail ne faut-il pas faire pour les mettre en état d'être cultivées ? On n'arrête pas le cours de la Mer aisément ; cependant les Acadiens en viennent à bout par de puissantes Digues qu'ils apellent des Aboteaux, & voicy comment ils font ; ils plantent cinq ou six rangs de gros arbres tous entiers aux endroits par où la Mer entre dans les Marais, & entre chaque rang ils couchent d'autres arbres de long les uns sur les autres, & garnissent tous les vuides si bien avec de la terre glaise bien battuë, que l'eau n'y sçauroit plus passer. Ils ajustent au milieu de ces Ouvrages un Esseau de maniere qu'il permet à la marée basse, à l'eau des Marais de s'écouler par son impulsion, & défend à celle de la Mer d'y entrer. Un travail de cette nature qu'on ne fait qu'en certains temps que la Mer ne monte pas si haut, coûte beaucoup à faire, & demande bien des journées ; mais la moisson abondante qu'on en retire dés la seconde année, aprés que l'eau du Ciel a lavé ces terres, dédommage des frais qu'on a faits. Comme elles apartiennent à plusieurs, ils y

G j

Dièreville. *Relation du voyage du Port Royal de l'Acadie, ou de la Nouvelle France*. Rouen: Chez Jean-Baptiste Besongne, 1708. pp. 76–77.

From 1700 to 1748, the French population of Acadia (Nova Scotia) went from about 1,500 to 12,000. According to Dièreville, "in nearly all the families, one saw five or six children, and often many more." Agriculture and stock-farming were the main activities of the Acadians, fishing not often being a good source of livelihood. Rather than clear the forest, they preferred to "drain the marshlands, which the sea at floodtide inundated with its waters," to provide pastureland. To turn back the sea, they built "powerful dikes that they called *aboteaux* [aboiteaux]."

Public Archives of Canada, Ottawa: Library (Negative no. C-125667).

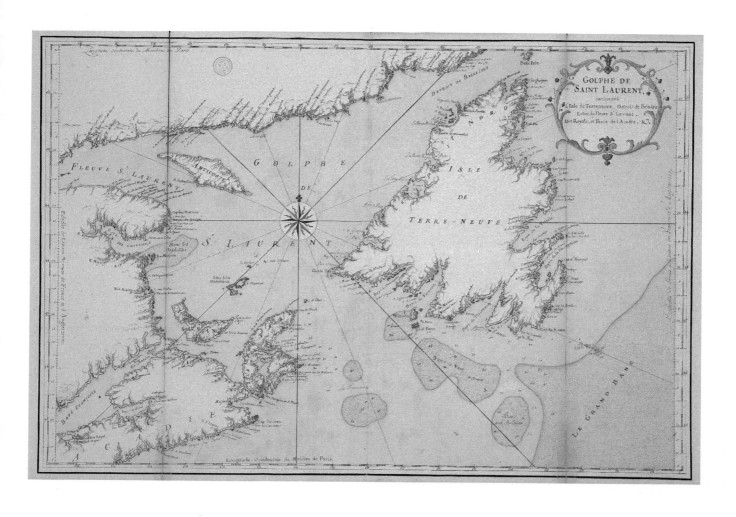

"Gulf of St. Lawrence . . . ." Jacques-Nicolas Bellin. [1752]. Map: col. ms., 51.9 × 78.2 cm.

In Jacques-Nicolas Bellin "Cartes de la Nouvelle-France ou Canada." 1752. (Manuscript atlas).

In the 1750s the population of the British colonies was a cosmopolitan one: English and Irish in Newfoundland; and Acadians, immigrants from New England, Irish, German and Swiss in Nova Scotia.

Public Archives of Canada, Ottawa: National Map Collection (NMC 15012).

Suitte de la Concession de Mr Renault aux Illinois

Noms des habitans	Enfans legitimes	apprentis esclaves	Terre de Cu Vallue	Negres hom & fem	Neg.ion 12	Negrilon 12 & au des	Esclaves Indiens	Esclaves Indiens	Boeufs	Vaches	Chevaux	Cochons	Maisons	Moulin	Granges	Ecuries
Montant de l'autre part																
Bosset	2		26						2	7	6	20	1		1	1
Blondin			20						2	2	1					
Guessenon et femme	1		24						2	2	2	5	1			
Germain	2		20						2	6	1	20				
Boutain			8						6	6						
La Ramée	1									2		15				
	17	250	471	14	3		5	4	1	28	42	25	160	9	2	7	5

Nota qu'il y a toujours nombre de voyageurs allant et venant aux Illinois de 50 hommes

Recapitulation generalle de tout le pays des Illinois

hommes			femmes	Enfans legitimes	orphelins et esclaves	arpents en surface	Terre de Cu Vallue	Negres hom & fem	Neg. 12	Negrillon 12 & au des	Esclaves Indiens	Esclaves Indiens	Boeufs	Vaches	Chevaux	Cochons	Maisons	Moulins	Granges	Ecuries
42	La Prairie du fort de chartres	27	66	6	160	827	13	6	18	19	20	116	122	59	376	41	5		19	
48	Cascassias	36	87	14	126	2054	38	23	41	30	38	256	237	108	896	52	11		28	
5	Cahoquias					39	3		1		7	3	7	30	10	30	2			1	
12	Concession de Renault	3	17			471	14	3	5	1	1	28	42	25	160	9	2		7	5
3	officiers																			
41	soldats																			
4	Jesuites																			
3	seminaire																			
159		39	170	20	266	3391	68	33	64	57	62	407	431	202	1462	104	18		55	5

"General recapitulation of the entire Illinois country," 1732.

Many Canadians settled in this region of the Upper Mississippi, which in 1752 counted nearly 800 settlers. They lived on farming, hunting and trading with the Indians. They provided Lower Louisiana with flour, salted meats and animal skins.

Archives nationales, Paris: Section Outre-Mer, série G[1], vol. 464.

Photo Studio Littré.

Census of Louisiana for the year 1726.

In Louisiana the population of Canadian and French origin lived above all in the north (the Illinois country) and the south (the Mobile and Nouvelle-Orléans regions as far as the country of the Natchez). Between the agglomerations in the north and south, which were separated by hundreds of kilometres, one encountered only small trading posts surrounded by Indian tribes that were not always favourable to the presence of the French.

Archives nationales, Paris: Section Outre-Mer, série G¹, vol. 464, p. 38–39.

Photo Studio Littré.

II

The Indians

In the eighteenth century, more than in the preceding one, the Indians were in evidence in the daily life of the French. In Montréal, groups belonging to various tribes were seen wandering about the streets, and at Québec the Hurons, who lived near the town, mingled readily with the whites, from whom they could often be distinguished only by the rather garish colours of their European-style clothes.

Trade with the West led to close relations with several new tribes, and the requirements of diplomacy led the authorities to maintain virtually constant contact with the Iroquois. Moreover, the often hostile relations that, as a result of expansion over the continent by the Europeans, were established among tribes that up till then had been strangers to one another, obliged the French to negotiate with many distant tribes such as the Illinois, Foxes, Chactas, Sioux and Crees.

Moreover, whether they were considered French subjects or enemies, the Indians had a way of life of their own, an original civilization, from which the French population in particular benefited as it established itself permanently in Canada.

Portrait of the Iroquois chief Sa Ga Yeath Qua Pieth Tow (baptized Brant). John Verelst (circa 1648–1734). Oil on canvas, 1710.

The Iroquois and other Christian Indians living in the vicinity of the towns retained habits different from those of the Canadians, and they refused to obey French laws. Few of them consented to speak French.

Public Archives of Canada, Ottawa: Picture Division (Negative no. C-92419).

Indians from several tribes. Alexandre de Batz. Watercolour, 1735.

The various regions of North America were peopled with Indian tribes that were often different in language, form of government, and family and social structures. Batz's drawing depicts Indians from the Great Lakes region (Foxes), the Upper Mississippi valley (Illinois) and Lower Louisiana (Attacapas).

Peabody Museum, Harvard University, Cambridge, Massachusetts.

Photo Hillel Burger.

Sauvages Tchaktas matachez en Guerriers qui portent des chevelures.

Choctaw Indians tattooed as warriors and carrying scalps. Alexandre de Batz. Watercolour, circa 1732.

The French were absolutely dependent upon their Choctaw and Alibamu allies, among others, for holding their ground in Louisiana. But these allies were not at all trustworthy, particularly since the English in Carolina and Georgia worked continually at winning them over to their cause.

Peabody Museum, Harvard University, Cambridge, Massachusetts.

III

Government

From the beginning of the eighteenth century, the colony of Canada had an administrative structure that had been tested in the previous century and that met its requirements. This structure would not undergo any notable changes until 1760; only certain adjustments, which were accompanied by an increase in the number of officials, would be made to alter it slightly as a result of the increase in the population, rapid expansion (particularly into the West) and growing economic activity.

In 1719, it is true, an Admiralty Court began sitting at Québec; if the court was newly instituted, it merely relieved the Provost Court of Québec (which since the 1680s had also been called the Provost and Admiralty Court of Québec) of the jurisdiction that it exercised over maritime affairs. It was, besides, the only new administrative institution set up during the century in the St. Lawrence valley — with the exception of a "Royal Jurisdiction of the South Shore" that was set up at the end of the French regime — and little is known of it.

Otherwise, the duties of the governor general and the intendant did not change, although the number of their assistants (local governors and king's lieutenants for the governor, subdelegates and commissaries of the Marine for the intendant) increased along with the number of posts and "habitations" in New France. As for the Conseil supérieur, which had at first assumed important administrative responsibilities, it hardly ever intervened any more in extra-judicial matters — administrative regulations, for example — and then only with the help or consent of the governor and the intendant, or at the very least of the latter, who generally preferred to act alone. As the Conseil had again become above all the court of final appeal in Canada, justice continued to be exercised as previously, appeals from seigneurial courts being heard by the royal jurisdictions, and those from the latter by the Conseil supérieur, which also heard appeals from the Admiralty Court.

III

In the eighteenth century, however, something new could be noted: the pursuit within the administration, in particular the administration of justice, of greater stringency, and consequently of greater efficiency. Perhaps as a result of the strong concern voiced by Intendant Jacques Raudot around 1707, and despite the extreme difficulty in finding competent persons for judgeships, there was an attempt to bring order into the lawcourts, confirm land-titles, authenticate surveyors' and notaries' incomplete deeds, regulate the notarial profession, and so on. Inquiries were conducted on the state of notarial registries, where the archives of the courts and notaries were deposited, and appropriate measures for ensuring their preservation were prescribed. Negligence, together with ignorance and a certain casualness, had given rise to numerous abuses. To correct them there seemed to be only two means: teach those Canadians who displayed an aptitude for posts in the judicial system, and persuade the judges — even those of the Conseil supérieur — to "sacrifice" their personal interests to the service of the king and the welfare of the general public.

Within as well as outside the St. Lawrence valley, in the newly created colonies of French Acadia and Louisiana, new administrative institutions, copied pretty much from those in Canada, were seeing the light of day. Officially these colonies were put under the jurisdiction of Québec, the governor general and the intendant having authority, by virtue of their commissions, over "Canada, Île Royale, Île Saint-Jean and others dependent on it, Louisiana, and other countries in New France"; in practice they corresponded directly with the mother country, took their orders from it, and attended to their own internal administration, although there was at times indispensable consultation on questions of common interest between Québec and Louisbourg, or Québec and Nouvelle-Orléans.

Île du Cap-Breton, which in September 1713 was inhabited by a single Frenchman and 25 or 30 Indian families, had scarcely been renamed Île Royale and the population and garrisons of Newfoundland moved to it after the Treaty of Utrecht, than the king set up on the island at Port-Dauphin, Port-Toulouse and Louisbourg three royal *bailliages*, courts of first instance that would sit in judgment "in civil, personal, real and mixed actions, and criminal matters." Appeals from these courts would come before the Conseil supérieur of Louisbourg, which was set up by the same edict of June 1717 and which would deliver judgments "in both civil and criminal affairs." The following year — a year before Québec had one — an Admiralty Court was sitting in Louisbourg. Needless to say, Île Royale had its local governor and its financial commissary, both members of the Conseil supérieur, the latter acting as first councillor on it.

This judicial system, it is true, never materialized entirely. The *bailliages* of Port-Toulouse and Port-Dauphin never saw the light of day — subdelegates dispensed justice in both places — and the *bailliage* of Louisbourg was not set up until 1734. In the meantime the Conseil supérieur had been hearing cases of the first instance there.

Not far from Île Royale, the Acadians living on the peninsula, although under British rule, remained virtually without any form of government until their expulsion. In that regard all of Nova Scotia was for a long time in the same situation, because scarcely any English were encountered outside the garrisons. In 1720, it is true, Governor Richard Philipps, mitigating somewhat the military regime, established a kind of civil administration by creating a council of twelve members (including himself) made up of officers and civilians. Nothing changed for the Acadians: they had representatives — at first appointed by the governor, then elected by their compatriots — who played the role of intermediaries between them and the authorities and who sometimes even rose to the rank of negotiators, but they had absolutely no power. It took the founding of Halifax, which replaced Annapolis Royal as the capital in 1749, and a sudden influx of English-speaking settlers, to accelerate the evolution of the province. In 1758 Nova Scotia had its House of Assembly, its executive and legislative councils, and its judicial system, which was presided over by a chief justice, the first British institutions in the territory that is now Canada. At that time, and although it had acquired an embryonic judicial system, Newfoundland was still under the rule of the "commodores" and "fishing admirals" — and the Acadians had been chased out.

Finally, far away from the valley of the St. Lawrence, Louisiana followed the model of the other French colonies as far as administration was concerned: a local governor, a financial commissary and a Conseil supérieur. Independent of Québec, pursuing an economic policy that annoyed the Canadian authorities, Louisiana had scarcely any relations with them unless it was obliged to, or unless concerted action seemed imperative because its security was threatened. Among the sovereign countries, there was no collaboration in the face of a common enemy.

Authority, gentleness and humaneness

Throughout the period of French rule in the eighteenth century, the governor general and the intendant continued to hold supreme authority in the colony. On every occasion the king reminded them of the need to "live on good terms" and how to do so, which was "for each to confine himself to his specific functions" and to collaborate in those "that were shared."

The king and the minister insisted still more frequently that they should govern "the settlers with gentleness and humaneness . . . preventing any oppressive measure from being imposed upon them by the officers" of the armed forces and generally "by looking into the needs of the settlers," so that "the little man is not hurt by the powerful one, and officers of the law do not use their authority abusively."

If the governor general and the intendant might have seemed somewhat inaccessible to the simple settlers in the rural areas, they were nonetheless represented in each parish or seigneury by the militia captain, a local inhabitant who received their orders and saw to it that they were carried out.

Portrait of Louis XV (1710–1774), king of France from 1715 to 1774. Studio of Louis-Michel Van Loo (1707–1771). Oil on canvas, after 1761.

As the holder of the supreme power, the king decided upon the most important matters concerning the colonies. His will was carried out above all through the agency of the minister of Marine, to whom he had entrusted administration of the colonies. It was generally the minister who defined policy, adopted the important measures and ordered them to be applied.

Public Archives of Canada, Ottawa: Picture Division (Negative no. C-604).

Royal arms of France. Attributed to
Noël Levasseur. Wood carving, circa
1727.

Public Archives of Canada, Ottawa:
Picture Division.

Portrait of Jean-Frédéric Phélypeaux, Comte de Maurepas (1701–1781), secretary of State (minister) for the Marine from 1723 to 1749. Artist unknown. Engraving.

Maurepas was probably the best minister for New France in the eighteenth century. He provided large sums of money from his ministry to strengthen the defences of the North American colonies and assure their economic development. He took a particular interest in Canada, seeking through various means to increase its trade and diversify its economy.

Bibliothèque nationale, Paris: Cabinet des estampes.

"Memoir from the king to serve as a guide" for Governor General de La Jonquière and Intendant Bigot, Versailles, 30 April 1749.

Being anxious to govern "as a good head of a family," the king regularly recommended treating "the settlers with gentleness and humanity," and the governor general and the intendant regularly treated them thus: their personal convictions were reinforced by the desire not to antagonize a people whose "spirit of independence" they feared.

Archives nationales, Paris: Fonds des Colonies, série B, vol. 89, fol. 55.

Photo Studio Littré.

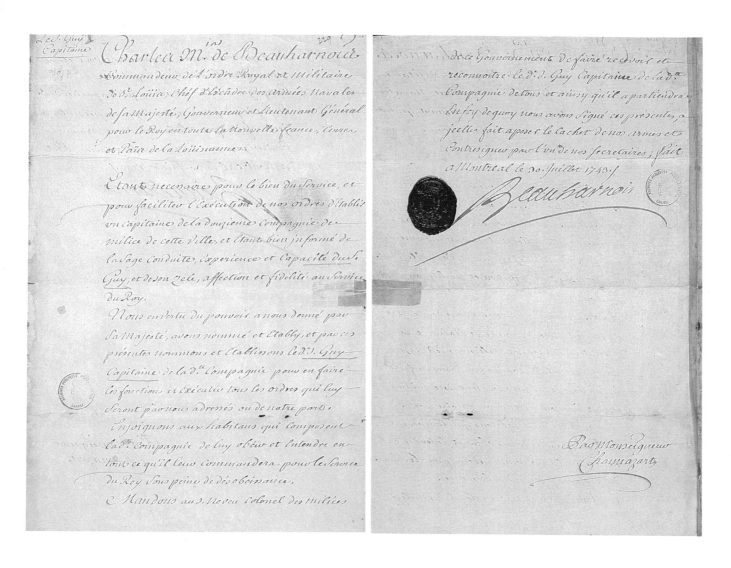

Militia captain's commission granted to Pierre Guy by Governor General de Beauharnois, Montréal, 30 July 1743.

Within his parish, the militia captain was responsible for transmitting orders from the governor and the intendant and seeing that they were carried out. He was in charge of the corvées for public works, and called the men up for military exercises.

Public Archives of Canada, Ottawa: Manuscript Division, MG 23, G III, 28.

Portrait of Charles de Beauharnois (1671–1749), governor general of New France from 1726 to 1747. Oil on canvas.

The concentration of political and military power in the hands of the governor general as a rule permitted him to react quickly and efficiently in the face of difficulties incurred with the English or the Indians. This centralization guaranteed the colony a certain superiority over the British colonies, where the division of power often hindered action.

Musée de l'île Sainte-Hélène, Montréal.

On the judicial system

The Conseil supérieur sat as usual, but the number of judges, which had been increased to seven in 1675, was "too small" for it, and was often "smaller than what had been set by the [royal] ordinances"; on 16 June 1703 Louis XIV therefore increased by five the number of councillors, among whom there would always be an ecclesiastic. The composition of the Conseil would be changed twice more, in 1733 and 1744.

In the three governments the royal courts remained as they were at the end of the seventeenth century, except for the Provost Court of Québec, which in 1719, after an Admiralty Court had been created, officially lost the jurisdiction that it had exercised for some forty years over maritime affairs.

Administration of justice was under the intendant's jurisdiction. Now, on 10 November 1707 Jacques Raudot had asked the minister to "afford the settlers in this country a great measure of relief in their lawsuits by reducing the number of levels of jurisdiction." As it was, they had to appeal decisions of the seigneurial courts (where they existed) to the royal court in their government, and from there to the Conseil supérieur at Québec. According to the intendant, that entailed a great deal of lost time.

[Handwritten text in French, 17th–18th century script:]

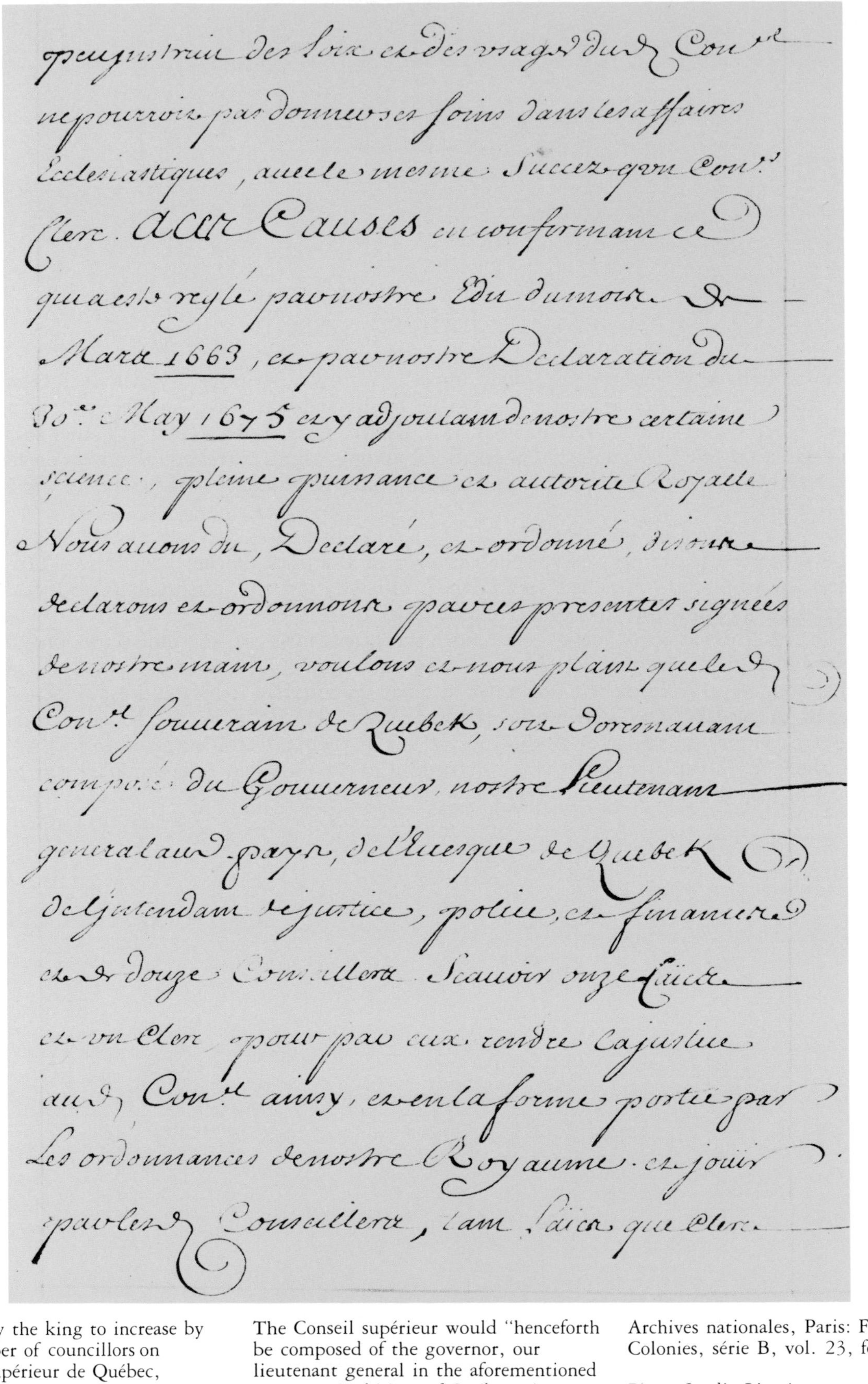

...que justice des loix et des usages dud. Con.
ne pourroit pas donner ses soins dans les affaires
Ecclesiastiques, avec le mesme Succez qu'un Con.r
Clerc. A Ces Causes en conformant ce
qu'a esté reglé par nostre Edit du mois de
Mars 1663, et par nostre Declaration du
30.me May 1675 et y adjoutant de nostre certaine
science, pleine puissance et autorité Royalle
Nous avons dit, Declaré, et ordonné, disons
declarons et ordonnons par ces presentes signées
de nostre main, voulons et nous plaist que led.
Con.l souverain de Quebek, soit dorenavant
composé du Gouverneur, nostre Lieutenant
general aud. pays, de l'Evesque de Quebek
de l'Intendant de justice, police, et finances
et de douze Conseillers Scavoir onze Laïcs
et un Clerc, pour par eux rendre la justice
aud. Con.l ainsy, et en la forme portée par
Les ordonnances de nostre Royaume. et jouïr
par lesd. Conseillers, tant Laïcs, que Clerc.

Declaration by the king to increase by five the number of councillors on the Conseil supérieur de Québec, Versailles, 16 June 1703.

The Conseil supérieur would "henceforth be composed of the governor, our lieutenant general in the aforementioned country; the bishop of Québec; the intendant for justice, public order and finances; and twelve councillors, that is to say eleven laymen and one member of the clergy."

Archives nationales, Paris: Fonds des Colonies, série B, vol. 23, fol. 228v.

Photo Studio Littré.

A View of the Intendants Palace.   Vue du Palais de l'Intendant.

Drawn on the Spot by Rich.ᵈ Short,   Engraved by William Elliott.

Published according to Act of Parliament Sept.ʳ 1ˢᵗ 1761. by Rich.ᵈ Short,   and Sold by Tho.ˢ Jefferys the Corner of S.ᵗ Martins Lane.

View of the intendant's palace at Québec. Richard Short (known 1759–1761). Etching by William Elliott, printed by Thomas Jefferys, 1761.

The palace housed a good part of the colony's administrative services: offices of the intendant, the Conseil supérieur, and the Provost and Admiralty Courts of Québec.

Public Archives of Canada, Ottawa: Picture Division (Negative no. C-360).

4

trées que par des Ordonnances particulieres, Et par des Jurisdictions Establies exprés pour les faire observer; SA MAJESTÉ, de l'avis du Duc d'Orleans son Oncle Regent, a resolu le present Reglement.

TITRE PREMIER.

Des Juges d'Amirauté & de leur Competence.

ARTICLE PREMIER.

IL y aura à l'avenir dans tous les Ports des Isles & Colonie Françoises, en quelque partie du monde quelles soient situées, des Juges pour connoistre des causes Maritimes, sous le nom d'Officiers d'Amirauté privativement à tous autres Juges, Et pour estre par eux lesdites causes jugées suivant l'Ordonnance de 1681. & autres Ordonnances & Reglemens touchant la Marine.

II.

LA nomination desdits Juges appartiendra à l'Amiral comme en France, sans toute-fois qu'ils puissent exercer qu'aprés avoir sur ladite nomination obtenu une Commission de Sa Majesté au grand Sceau, laquelle Commission sera revocable *ad Nutum.*

III.

ILs pourront estre choisi parmi les Juges des Jurisdictions ordinaires, sans estre obligez de prendre des Lettres de compatibilité; Ils rendront la Justice au nom de l'Amiral, conformément à l'Ordonnance de 1681. & au Reglement de 1669. Et les appels de leurs Sentences seront relevez en la maniere prescrite par ladite Ordonnance & ainsi qu'il sera expliqué cy aprés; Ils ne pourront en mesme temps estre Juges de l'Amirauté & Officiers des Conseils Superieurs.

IV.

LEUR Competence sera la mesme qui est expliquée par l'Ordonnance de 1681. Livre premier Titre II. Et par l'Edit de 1717.

V.

IL y aura dans chaque Siege d'Amirauté, un Lieutenant, un Procureur du Roy, un Greffier & un ou deux Huissiers suivant le besoin, avec les mesmes fonctions qui leur sont attribuées dans l'Ordonnance de 1681.

VI.

LES Lieutenans & les Procureurs du Roy seront reçeûs au Tribunal où se porteront les appels de leurs Sentences; Les Greffiers & les Huissiers seront reçeûs par les Officiers de leur Siege.

VII.

LES Lieutenans & les Procureurs du Roy ne pourront estre reçeûs qu'ils ne soient âgez de vingt-cinq ans; Seront dispensez d'estre graduez pourveû toutesfois qu'ils ayent une connoissance suffisante des Ordonnances & des affaires Maritimes, sur lesquelles ils seront interrogez avant que d'estre reçeûs.

VIII.

LES Lieutenans rendront la Justice & tiendront les Audiances dans le lieu où se rend la Justice ordinaire, Et on conviendra des jours & des heures afin que cela ne fasse point de confusion.

IX.

EN cas d'absence, mort, maladie, ou recusation d'aucun desdits Officiers, ses fonctions seront faites par le Juge ordinaire le plus prochain, jusqu'à ce qu'il y ait esté pourveû, lequel Juge sera tenu de faire mention expresse dans ses Sentences & procedures de sa Commission.

X.

LE Greffier sera tenu de se conformer exactement à l'Ordonnance de 1681. pour ce qui regarde ses fonctions, Et en cas d'absence, mort ou maladie il y sera commis par le Lieutenant jusqu'à ce qu'il y ait esté pourveû.

XI.

LES Huissiers seront reçeûs & exploiteront conformément

A iij

"Statute concerning the admiralty courts that the king desires to be set up in all the ports of the French islands and colonies . . . ," Paris, 12 January 1717.

The Admiralty Court that was set up at Québec was a court of first instance to judge suits concerning the sea service and sailing. It issued sailing permits to captains and shipowners. Its officers maintained law and order in the port by inspecting ships and cargoes.

Archives nationales, Paris: Archives imprimées, série AD, VII, 1, n° 150.

Photo Studio Littré.

Jl me Simble aussy, Monseigneur, que
Jvous pourriez donner auxhabitans deceprïes
vngrand Soulagement dansleurs proces, en
leurs diminuant les degrées de juridiction
quîls ont a essuier, jls Sont obligez d'abord
deproceder devant les juges des Seigneurs
dans les endroitts oujls yen a d'Establis
ensuitte par appel aux prevostez d'ou jls
resortissent, et enfin en Dernier resort
au Conseil, cela poura estre bon quelque jour
mais dans lestems que cet ordre de juridiction
a esté Establi rien n'a esté plus pernicieux.
pour Ces pauvres habitans lesquels en Souff
encore apresent beaucoup puisque le tems
quîls devroient donner au travail ou leurs c.
fair consommer laplus grande partie à
plaider,

Letter from Intendant Jacques Raudot to the minister, 10 November 1707.

Raudot asks for a reduction of the "levels of jurisdiction" that the settlers "had to undergo. First, they had to go before the seigneurial court in the places where these were established, then appeal to the appropriate provost court [or royal jurisdiction] and finally as a last resort to the Conseil" supérieur.

Archives nationales, Paris: Fonds des Colonies, série C¹¹A, vol. 26, fol. 159-159B.

Photo Studio Littré.

III

Seigneurial justice

In asking for a reduction in the number of "levels of jurisdiction," the intendant was proposing abolition of the royal jurisdictions, so that a settler would appeal a decision of the seigneurial court directly to the Conseil supérieur. It is difficult to see how the situation would have been improved by this. However that may be, if there was any change, it was to the detriment of the seigneurs: since the final years of the seventeenth century, in fact, the administration had no longer been willing to grant seigneuries with the right of high justice; quite to the contrary, in 1707 the exercise of high justice in two fiefs was transferred elsewhere, to the Provost Court of Québec in one case, and to the Royal Jurisdiction of Trois-Rivières in the other.

Since competent candidates for judgeships were very scarce, we can understand the authorities' concern for limiting the right to exercise justice in the seigneuries, and their distrust of the judges and other officers who did so.

Consequently, on 23 February 1750, following a complaint by one of its members, according to whom administration of justice in the jurisdiction of Château-Richer "was not being carried out with all the attention that one would wish to see brought to it," the Conseil supérieur charged one of the councillors with conducting an inquiry; and on the following 16 March it ordered that a whole series of measures to correct the abuses be put into effect.

Decree of the Conseil supérieur concerning the administration of justice in Château-Richer, Québec, 16 March 1750.

The first councillor went to Château-Richer "to examine the manner in which" justice "is exercised there . . . whether there is a location assigned for hearings, and whether in the aforementioned location there is a convenient place where the clerk can secure the acts of jurisdiction and the records of deceased notaries."

Archives nationales du Québec, Centre d'archives de Québec: Jugements et délibérations du Conseil supérieur, vol. 64, fol. 115.

Photo Belvédère.

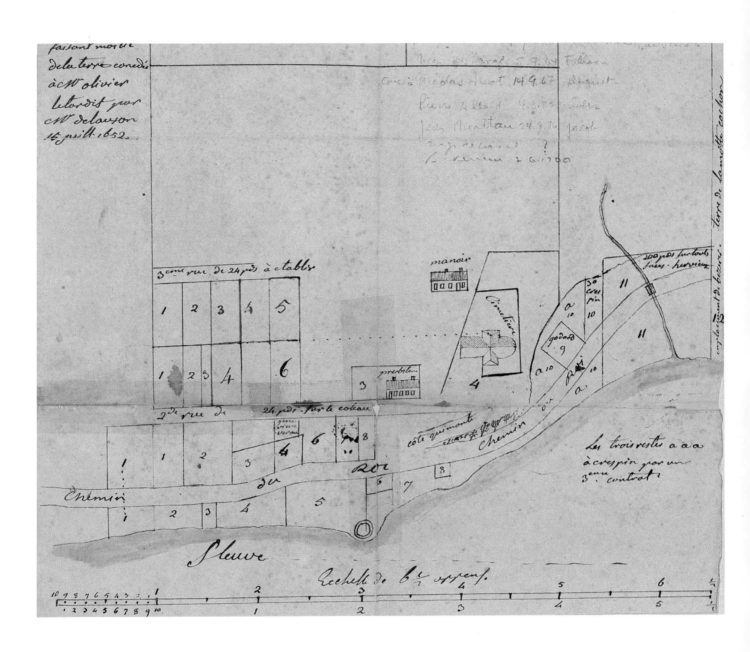

[Plan of the village of Château-Richer. Circa 1760.] Plan: col. ms.

Canada had few villages. Château-Richer had a church, a presbytery, a girls' school that was run by the sisters of the Congrégation de Notre-Dame, and a seigneurial manor-house "where justice was dispensed for the whole of the Côte de Beaupré."

Société du Musée du Séminaire de Québec: Procure, folio 26.

Photo Pierre Soulard.

The representatives of the law

Besides the law officers themselves (judges, attorneys, court clerks), there were a certain number of representatives of the law in the colony: notaries, surveyors and, at the bottom of the scale, process-servers, including the personnel of the constabulary — the Maréchaussée.

The notaries, who were relatively numerous in the eighteenth century, could nonetheless not cover all the territory being settled because of distances and the climate. In 1722, therefore, the missionaries in the colony, whether they belonged to the secular or the regular clergy, were authorized to receive wills — a privilege that French law accorded only to curés of fixed parishes. Similarly, in 1733 parish priests, captains and other officers of the militia were authorized to draw up marriage contracts in localities remote from the towns and in the absence of a notary.

Surveyors for their part did not have any deputies. All were appointed by the intendant, and some of them who worked "in the côtes" — the concessions along the St. Lawrence — covered great distances by canoe or on snowshoes to practise their profession. They were less numerous than the notaries, nevertheless they left a great number of plans that are often very useful for shedding light on notarial deeds.

The duty of the Maréchaussée was to serve criminal justice. Consisting of a provost marshal, police officers and soldiers of the watch, it constituted the police force of the time and was attached to the royal jurisdictions.

Quarante cinq

villes privé souvent les mourans de la consolation quils désireroient avoir de faire quelque disposition testamentaire, a quoy etant necessaire de pourvoir en attendant que touttes les cures de cette colonie ayent eté renduës fixes suivant l'intention du Roy NOUS AVONS *authorisé et authorisons par provision les prestres seculiers ou reguliers faisant les fonctions curiales en qualité de missionnaires dans les paroisses de cette colonie pour recevoir les testaments des habitans de leurs paroisses en y apelant trois témoins masles agéz de vingt ans acomplis qui ne pourront etre legataires non plus que le missionnaire, et faisant mention dans le testament quil a eté dicté, nommé par le testateur et a luy relu en presence tant dudit missionnaire que des témoins, et le faisant signer par le testateur et lesd. témoins ou faisant mention de la cause pour la quelle ils n'ont point signé conformement audit article 289 de la coutume de paris* MANDONS *aux officiers de la prevosté de cette ville, et des juridictions*

Ordinance by Intendant Bégon authorizing "by confirming letters secular or regular priests who are carrying out the duties of parish priests as missionaries in the parishes of this colony to receive wills by the settlers in their parishes," Québec, 30 April 1722.

Archives nationales du Québec, Centre d'archives de Québec: Ordonnances des intendants, cahier 8, fol. 45.

Photo Belvédère.

François Bigot &c.

Janvier 12.

*Commission d'arpenteur
à Montréal pour
Jean Bte. Perrault*

Estant necessaire de commettre une personne capable d'exercer l'office d'arpenteur dans l'étenduë du Gouvernement de Montreal et estant Informé de la capacité et experience de Jean Baptiste Perrot résidant au dit Montreal au fait de l'arpentage et mesurage des terres. Vû le Certificat du S. Bonnecamps Jesuitte et professeur de mathematiques daté a Quebec le 22. 7bre dernier comme ledit Perrot est capable d'exercer le dit office d'arpenteur. Nous en vertû du pouvoir a nous donné que sa Majesté a nous donné et octroyé, Donnons et octroyons par ces presentes au dit Jean Baptiste Perrot l'office de Juré arpenteur pour l'exercer par luy dans toute l'étenduë du Gouvernement de Montreal aux droits et emoluments y attribués. Mandons

Commission from Intendant Bigot granting "Jean-Baptiste Perrot the office of sworn surveyor, to be exercised by him throughout the Government of Montréal," Québec, 12 January 1753.

Canadians held mainly junior posts in the civil administration: judges and attorneys in the lower jurisdictions, bailiffs, clerks of court, clerks, notaries and surveyors.

Archives nationales du Québec, Centre d'archives de Québec: Ordonnances des intendants, cahier 40, fol. 51v.

Photo Belvédère.

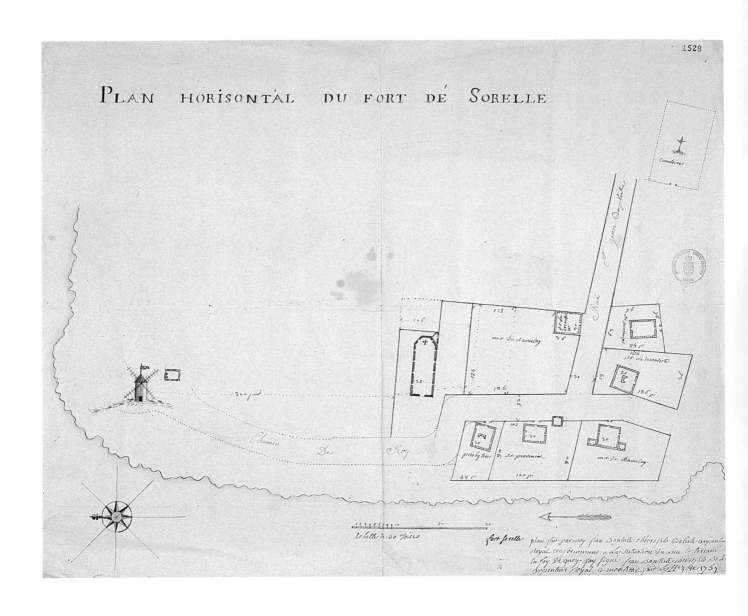

"Horizontal plan of the fort at Sorel."
Jean-Baptiste Chevrefils Belisle.
22 December 1757. Map: col. ms.,
40.9 × 52.0 cm.

In New France many representatives of
the ruling class sought to become rich
through trade or industry. The
Ramezays are a good example of this,
because of the diversity of their
enterprises: developing seigneuries
(including Sorel), the wood business,
milling and the tanning trade, among
others.

Public Archives of Canada, Ottawa:
National Map Collection (NMC 16634).

est d'usage.

La colonie s'estendant tous
les jours, les crimes se
multiplient: il seroit bien
nécessaire, Monseigneur, qu'il
vous plust augmenter la
marechaussée d'un exempt et
de trois ou quatre archers a
Montréal, la depense en
seroit peu considerable et
serviroit beaucoup à maintenir
le bon ordre, le Prevost et leur archers
ne pouvant suffire.
Nous sommes avec un très
profond respect

Monseigneur

a Quebecq,
15 — Octobre 1730.

Vos très humbles et
très obeissants Serviteurs.

Beauharnois Hocquart

Letter from Governor General de Beauharnois and the financial commissary, Hocquart, to the minister, Québec, 15 October 1730.

The *Maréchaussée* – the constabulary – was responsible for hunting down and arresting criminals; now, "as the population of the colony is growing every day, crimes are multiplying. It would be quite necessary . . . to augment the Maréchaussée by an officer of the watch and three or four soldiers of the watch in Montréal; the cost would not be very great and would be of great service in maintaining order."

Archives nationales, Paris: Fonds des Colonies, séric C[11A], vol. 52, fol. 84v.

Photo Studio Littré.

Portrait of Gilles Hocquart (1694–1783), intendant of New France from 1731 to 1748. Artist unknown. Oil on canvas.

If in the 1730s Canada made unprecedented strides, it was partly thanks to Hocquart who, in addition to convincing the mother country to increase the funds it invested in the colony, multiplied initiatives in many areas: land development, creation of industries, road construction, extension of trade outside the country and expansion of the fur trade, among other things.

Musée régional de Vaudreuil-Soulanges.

Local administrative personnel

According to a plan for a poll tax, in 1754 Québec's administration counted, in addition to the governor, the intendant, and their assistants, 19 law officers, a *grand-voyer* or chief road officer, a provost marshal, a comptroller of the Marine and a port captain. The comptroller of the Marine had under his orders a treasurer, a storekeeper and 21 clerks. The port captain was assisted by a lieutenant and a port master, and he collaborated with the master shipbuilder. In all there were 49 employees. For its part Montréal had 4 law officers and 8 *officiers de plume* or recording officers, whereas Trois-Rivières had in all only 3 law officers and a storekeeper.

The administration of the Domaine d'Occident, which oversaw the King's Domain, consisted of a director, a receiving agent, and a comptroller, 3 *visiteurs* (inspectors), 6 clerks and a captain of the guards (the number of the latter is not known).

Many other inhabitants of Canada worked from time to time for the State, either conducting hydrographic surveys (many people who were not port captains made such surveys), or being requisitioned for tasks that were sometimes more irksome than they were remunerative.

De l'autrepart . . . . 6415.#

Ursulines

18. filles . . . . a 15.# . . . . 675.

Hôtel Dieu

40. filles . . . . a 15.# . . . . 600.

Hôpital général

30. filles . . . . a 15.# . . . . 450.

Soeurs de la Congrégation

5. filles . . . . a 15.# . . . . 75.

Officiers Militaires

Un Gouverneur en chef . . . . 200.

12. Capitaines . . . . a 90.# . . . . . 1080.# ⎫
12. Lieutenants . . . . a 60.# . . . . . . 720. ⎬ 2436.
12. Enseignes en pied . a 30.# . . . . . . 360. ⎪
12. Enseignes en Second . a 23.# . . . . . 276. ⎭

Officiers de Justice

Le premier Conseiller . . . . 90. ⎫
9. Conseillers . . . . . . a 40.# . . . . 360. ⎪
Le procureur général . . . . 108. ⎬ 666.
Le greffier en chef . . . . 100. ⎪
Le premier huissier . . . . 8. ⎭

11515.

Plan for a poll-tax, 1754.

Et Cetra 1151# 530

Prevosté

Le Lieutenant general .... 58#
Le Lieutenant particulier .... 50. } 233.
Le Procureur du Roi .... 25.
Le greffier .... 100.

Le grand Prevost .... 50. } 100.
Le grand Hostie .... 50.

Amirauté

Le Juge .... 50.# } 100.
Le greffier .... 50.

Officiers de plume

Le Controlleur de la Marine .... 150.#
2. Ecrivains principaux a 75.# .... 150.
4. Ecrivains ordinaires a 50.# .... 200. } 950.
15. Ecrivains non Brevetés a 30.# .... 450.

Le Tresorier .... 125.# } 250.
Le garde des Magasins .... 125.

Officiers de port

Le Capitaine .... 100.# _____

1.3150.#

This plan mentions several of the colony's administrators and civil servants such as members of the Conseil supérieur and the Provost and Admiralty Courts, the comptroller of the Marine, the head of shipbuilding, the director of the Domaine d'Occident, the port captain and the chief road officer.

De l'autre part . . . . 13150.#

Suitte des officiers de port

De l'autre part . . . . . . 100.#

Le lieutenant . . . . 70. } 220.

Le Maître . . . . 50.

Le Chef de construction . . . . 200.

Domaine du Roy

En lieutenant general ⟨ Le Directeur

Sont Conseillers { Le Receveur

Le Controleur

3. Visiteurs . . . . . . a 125.# . . . . . 375.t }

6. Commis . . . . . . a 30.# . . . 180. } 605.

Le Capitaine des gardes . . . . 50.

Compagnie des Indes

Un agent . . . . 150.#

Un Controleur . . . . 125. }

Un Receveur . . . . 100. } 425.

Un Commis . . . . 50.

Un Medecin . . . . 100.# }

Un Chirurgien Major . . . . . 100. } 250.

Un Chirurgien en second . . . . . 50.

274.

. . . . 14850.#

Archives nationales, Paris: Fonds des
Colonies, série C11A, vol. 99, fol. 529v–
530v.

Photo Studio Littré.

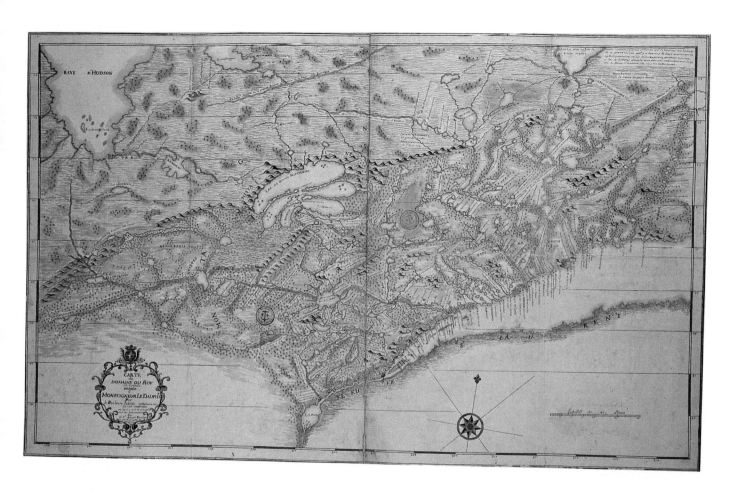

"Map of the Domaine du roy in Canada . . . ." Pierre-Michel Laure and Guyot, 1733. Map: col. ms., 56.5 × 91.0 cm.

According to Hocquart, the Domaine du Roi extended "from Île aux Coudres to two leagues below Sept-Îles, in which area were the posts of Tadoussac, Chicoutimi, Lac Saint-Jean . . . Sept-Îles and the Moisie River," among other places. The revenue drawn from the exploitation of this Domaine (the fur trade, hunting, fishing and agriculture)

served to defray part of the colony's expenses.

Service historique de la Marine, Vincennes, France: Service hydrographique, recueil 67, n° 10.

Photo Studio Littré.

Petition from Richard Testu de La Richardière, port captain of Québec, 1 April 1737.

This port captain "has applied himself carefully to making known the navigation of the St. Lawrence River," to making it less dangerous, and to "training pilots . . . . Besides, it is he who has the responsibility of piloting the king's ships on this same river . . . ." He was also in charge of getting the port of Québec into shape to receive ships.

Archives nationales, Paris: Fonds de la Marine, série C[7], dossier 319.

Photo Studio Littré.

III

Louisiana and Île Royale

On 27 September 1717 the King's Council of State incorporated the Illinois country into the government of Louisiana, a colony that had come under the jurisdiction of the Compagnie d'Occident the month before.

Louisiana was joined anew to the royal domain in 1731. Nouvelle-Orléans, which had been the capital of the colony since 1722, was the place of residence of the governor and the financial commissary as well as the seat of the Conseil supérieur.

To the east, in June 1717 the king endowed Île Royale with three royal *bailliages* (each consisting of a judge, an attorney and a court clerk) and a Conseil supérieur — a court of final instance that would sit at Louisbourg and would be composed, in addition to the governor general and the intendant of New France, of the local governor for Île Royale, a first councillor (the financial commissary), the king's lieutenant, two other councillors, an attorney general and a court clerk.

But this fine system was premature: only the Conseil supérieur, and in 1718 an Admiralty Court, were set up, institutions that would do until 1734.

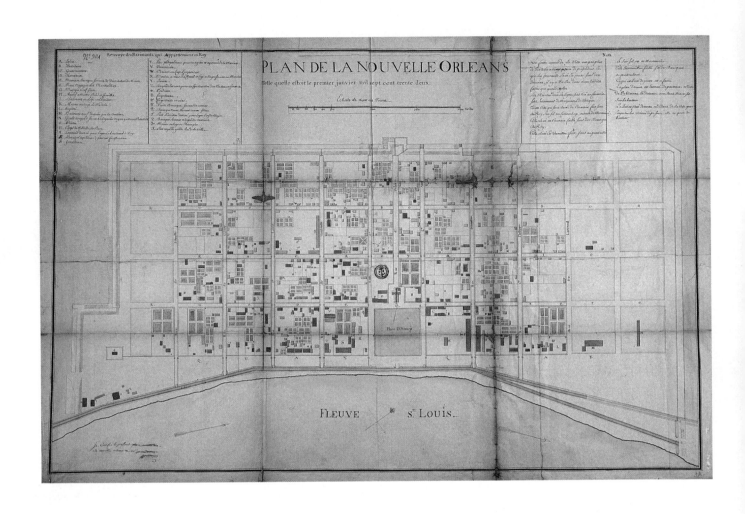

"Plan of Nouvelle-Orléans . . . ." I.F. Broutin. 20 January 1732. Map: col. ms., 77.0 × 119.0 cm.

Around 1750 Nouvelle-Orléans had a parish church, a hospital, an Ursuline house, a Jesuit house and a Capuchin convent. The governor's mansion, the financial commissary's house and that of the Conseil supérieur attested to the fact that this city was the capital of Louisiana.

Archives nationales, Paris: Section Outre-Mer, Dépôt des fortifications des colonies, Louisiane, Portefeuille V1A n° 90.

Photo Studio Littré.

Arrest qui unit et incorpore au Gouvernem.t de la Louisianne le pays des sauuages Ilinois.

27. 7bre 1717.

Le Roy estant en son cons.l s'estant fait representer en son cons.l les lettres patentes en forme d'Edit du mois d'Aoust dernier portant etablissem.t d'une comp.e de commerce sous le nom de Comp.e d'occident ensemble celles du 14 7bre 1712. accordées au S.r Crozat et estimant qu'il conuient pour le bien de son service et pour l'auantage et l'vtilité de la Comp.e d'occident d'augmenter le gouuernement de la Prouince de la Louisianne et d'y joindre le pays des sauuages Ilinois Ouy le rapport et tout consideré.

Sa Ma.té estant en son conseil de l'auis de M. le Duc d'orleans regent son oncle a uni et incorporé le pays des sauuages Ilinois au Gouuernement de la Prouince de la Louisianne, veut et entend que la d. comp.e d'occid.t jouisse des terres comprises sous le nom du d. pays de la mesme maniere qu'elle doit jouir de celles acquises par les d. lettres patentes du mois d'aoust d.er et que les Commandants Officiers soldats habitans et autres qui sont ou pourront estre au d. pays reconnoissent le commandant gn.al de la louisianne et luy obeissent et entende. sans y contreuenir en quelque sorte et maniere que ce soit a peine de desobeiss.ce fait au Con.l d'estat du Roy. Sa Ma.té y estant tenu a. &c.

Decree from the king's Conseil d'État incorporating the Illinois country into the Government of Louisiana, 27 September 1717.

This decision was taken "to be profitable and of service to the Compagnie d'Occident," which owned Louisiana and which wanted to exploit the mineral resources of the Illinois country. The territory would remain incorporated in Louisiana.

Archives nationales, Paris: Fonds des Colonies, série A, vol. 21, fol. 95v.

Photo Studio Littré.

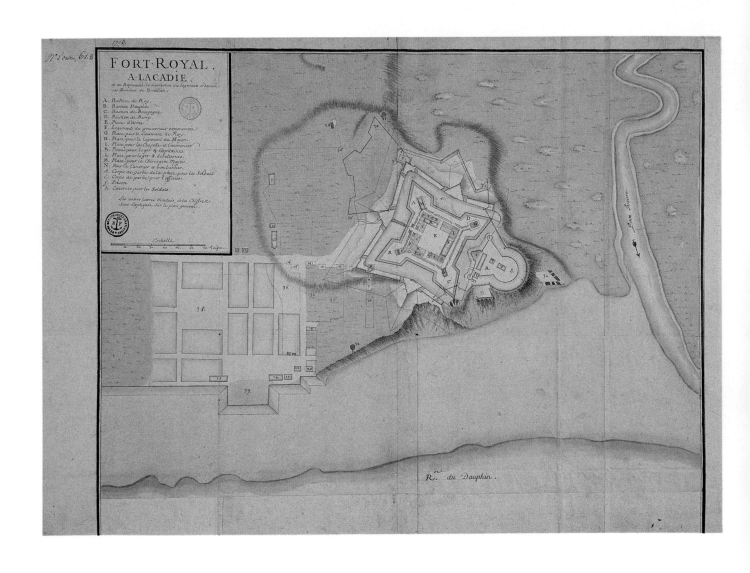

"Fort Royal in Acadia." [de Labat. 29 November 1703]. Plan: col. ms., 50.0 × 62.5 cm.

Under French rule, Port-Royal, the seat of the government of Acadia, scarcely looked like a capital. In 1699–1700 the traveller Dièreville found there only "some very badly built thatched cottages" and a church that he "took for a barn rather than for a temple of the true God."

Archives nationales, Paris: Section Outre-Mer, Dépôt des fortifications des colonies, Amérique septentrionale, 61 B.

Photo Studio Littré.

Edict by the king creating a Conseil supérieur at Louisbourg and three "*bailliages* for the whole of Île Royale, namely a court seat and *bailliage royal* at the port of Louisbourg, another at Port Dauphin, and a third at Port Toulouse," Paris, June 1717.

Archives nationales, Paris: Fonds des Colonies, série B, vol. 39, fol. 300v–301.

Photo Studio Littré.

"View of the town of Louisbourg from inside the port." Claude-Étienne Verrier. 1731. View: col. ms., 36.3 × 103.1 cm.

Around 1740 Louisbourg gave the impression of a large town with its gigantic fortifications and the large number of ships in its harbour. The capital of Île Royale had a hospital, a convent of the sisters of the Congrégation de Notre-Dame, a Recollet house and . . . several taverns. The most imposing building, the Bastion du Roi, supplied lodgings for the governor, the military officers, and part of the troops.

Bibliothèque nationale, Paris: Département des cartes et plans, Rés. Ge. C. 5019.

Wars

When Governor General Louis-Hector de Callière learned in 1702 that war had just been declared in Europe, he refused to take any military action that would compromise the results of the Great Peace of Montréal, which had been signed the previous year, and above all that would prompt the Iroquois to abandon the neutrality they had promised to observe at that time. He persuaded the French minister that the Five Nations and their former allies in the colony of New York had to be dealt with tactfully, so as to avoid a new Iroquois war. At the same time attacks would be carried out against the New England colonies, in particular through the intermediary of the Abenakis, who it was feared might otherwise go over completely to the English side in the East. That policy was pursued by his successor, Philippe de Rigaud de Vaudreuil, who through raids into the enemy's territories, and particularly into Massachusetts, succeeded in retaining the Indians' loyalty to France by keeping them occupied.

It was in Newfoundland that hostilities in the War of the Spanish Succession were opened in America. Beginning in 1702 English and French in turn ravaged one another's fishing installations and engaged in privateering operations around the island. Plaisance remained until the end in the hands of the French, who seized Bonavista in 1705 and razed St. John's to the ground in 1709. During that time expeditions launched from Acadia and Canada made brutal surprise attacks on several New England settlements. In retaliation the English acted in the same manner in Acadia, where they destroyed Abenaki villages in 1703 and part of Pentagouet in 1704; that same year they laid waste Les Mines (Grand Pré) and Beaubassin (Chignecto); finally, after failing twice before Port-Royal (Annapolis Royal) in 1707, they forced the fortress to surrender on 13 October 1710. The great offensive against New France was already under way. In 1711 a powerful fleet under the command of Admiral Hovenden Walker was sailing towards Québec, while an army corps under the command of General Francis Nicholson was on its way to invade the colony along the Richelieu route. Eight of his ships having been wrecked on the reefs of Île-aux-Oeufs, Walker turned back, and on hearing this Nicholson did the same.

The Treaty of Utrecht, which put an end to the war in 1713, proved extremely costly for New France. Newfoundland, Acadia, Hudson Bay and its entire hydro-graphic basin were handed over to England. In addition the Iroquois became British subjects, while the Indians in general received the right to trade with either the French or the English as they wished. From then on a serious threat hung over the French fishing industry in the East and the fur trade in the West. Furthermore France no longer had the assurance that her ships could sail freely in the gulf, and the security of Lake Ontario, to which the colony of New York would have access through the Iroquois territories, appeared seriously compromised.

What remained of New France had to be fortified with the utmost urgency. On the Atlantic side the project for occupying Cap-Breton, renamed Île Royale, was followed up, and in 1719 the construction of the fortress of Louisbourg was begun. In 1716 a start was made on building a surrounding wall in stone around Montréal, although the king refused until 1745 to improve Québec's fortifications. Then attention turned to blocking the principal invasion routes at the frontiers: in the Ohio region, where the English were already trying to establish themselves, Fort des Ouiatanons was built in 1719, Fort des Miamis in 1722, and Fort Vincennes in 1731–32; in the Illinois country Fort de Chartres was built in 1720; Fort Niagara was built on the south shore of Lake Ontario in 1726 and Fort Saint-Frédéric on Lake Champlain in 1731.

A certain number of dangers threatened New France, not the least of them being the expansion of the English from Pennsylvania, Virginia and Carolina towards the Ohio region and the Illinois country. If they were to get established there, then New France would be cut into two sections: if Louisiana were isolated, she would not long resist the enemy's covetousness; if deprived of the furs from the West, Canada would not have survived economically. Now, the forts that were built in those regions could not by themselves assure that France would remain in possession of them; it was absolutely essential to ensure the loyalty and constant support of the allied Indians, whom the English were courting assiduously. Strengthening the alliances, maintaining peace among some thirty tribes, several of which were hereditary enemies, controlling the Foxes in particular, who several times were on the point of setting the West ablaze — all this required great firmness, and even greater diplomacy, on the part of the authorities in Canada and the post commandants.

After the War of the Austrian Succession, which was marked by the loss of Louisbourg in 1745 and two attempts by the French to regain Nova Scotia, and after the Treaty of Aix-la-Chapelle, which handed Louisbourg and Île Royale back to France in 1748, the authorities again lost no time in fortifying Lake Ontario and the Ohio region. In the latter region the construction of Fort Duquesne caused the renewal of hostilities with the English in 1754, right in the middle of a period of peace. The war of the conquest was beginning. If Coulon de Villiers had seized Fort Necessity, in the Ohio country, in 1754, Dieskau suffered a setback the following

IV

year at Lac Saint-Sacrement (Lake George), in the Lake Champlain region. Again in 1755 the French were victorious on the Monongahela, in the Ohio country, but in Acadia Fort Beauséjour and Fort Gaspereau fell, and in Nova Scotia the deportation of the Acadians was beginning.

During the Seven Years' War the French at first won some great victories in America: the capture of Oswego in 1756 and of Fort William Henry in 1757, followed by the brilliant victory at Carillon in 1758; in that year, however, they surrendered at Louisbourg and Fort Frontenac. In 1759 the end of French power in North America could be foreseen by the month of July: the French had to surrender at Niagara, on Lake Ontario, and in the Lake Champlain region they abandoned Fort Carillon and Fort Saint-Frédéric, which they blew up, to fall back upon the Richelieu. At that moment James Wolfe was besieging Québec. On 13 September, after an unremitting bombardment of the town that lasted two months, he won the battle of the Plains of Abraham; on 18 September Québec surrendered. Montréal followed suit on 8 September 1760. The last French feat of arms, the victory of Sainte-Foy in the spring of 1760, had not been able to ward off fate.

New France was no more.

The War of the Spanish Succession

In Newfoundland the War of the Spanish Succession was the occasion for the renewal of hostilities between the French at Plaisance and the English on the island. In 1705 Jacques Testard de Montigny took the field by the command of Daniel d'Auger de Subercase. The settlers along the coasts were disarmed and their properties burned; Bonavista surrendered. But the French victory did not have any lasting effect, and St. John's remained in English hands until 1709.

The English in New England mounted several expeditions against Acadia and the Abenakis, who were allied with the French: in 1703, 1704 and 1707 they destroyed villages and sowed terror. Finally, on 13 October 1710, Port-Royal surrendered and passed into British hands for good.

Exasperated by the raids into their territory by the French and their Indian allies, the New England authorities planned nothing less than the conquest of Canada. But in 1711, after the shipwreck of several of his ships on the reefs off Île-aux-Oeufs in the St. Lawrence, Admiral Hovenden Walker, who had the mission of besieging Québec, turned about with his entire fleet. The rejoicing there was as great as the fear had been.

The Treaty of Utrecht, which was disastrous for New France, put an end to this war in 1713.

315

Extrait du journal du Sr de Montigny Il commandoit un party de Canadiens et de Sauvages composé de 72. hommes qui a accompagné M. de Subercaze dans son entreprise le long de la coste angloise jusqu'au port du fourillon a son retour de St Jean il le quitta le 13.e mars 1705. après avoir receu ses ordres Le 15.e il se mit en marche pour aller brusler et détruire les bayes ports et habitation de la Conception, la Trinité la Carbonniere et Bonneviste; Le 16.e il a apperceu le Sonde de la Baye de la conception, Le 17.e il trouva un petit haure dans lequel il n'y avoit que deux maisons habitées de

Extract from the journal of Jacques Testard de Montigny's expedition against the English settlements in Newfoundland, 1705.

On 15 March Montigny "set out to burn and destroy the bays, ports and settlements of Conception, Trinity, Carbonear and Bonavista." His campaign was crowned with success.

Archives nationales, Paris: Fonds des Colonies, série C¹¹C, vol. 4, fol. 315.

Photo Studio Littré.

Nous eûmes l'honneur, Monseigneur l'année

derniere de vous rendre compte des raisons qui

nous avoient obligés de brouiller l'angloise avec

l'abenaxise, et du coup considerable que nous

avions fait faire pour ce sujet par le S.r De

Beaubassin, peu de temps apres qu'il se fut

Abenakis contre
les anglois

retiré, les angloise ayant ─ tués quelqu'uns

de ses sauvagex, ila nous en donnerent auix

et nous demanderent en mesme temps du ─

secours, ce qui nous obligea Monseigneur

d'y envoyer le S.r de Rouville officier dans

les troupes avec pres de deux cent hommes

ila ont attaqué un fort, où au raport de tous

les prisonniers il y avoit plus de cent hommes

portans les armes, ont fait plus de cent cinq.te

le exploit

prisonniers, tant hommes que femmes

et se sont retirés n'ayant perdus que trois

hommes et une vingtaine de blessés,

Letter from Governor General de Vaudreuil and Intendant de Beauharnois to the minister, Québec, 17 November 1704.

It was necessary to "set the English and Abenakis at odds." This was achieved by having the Indians take part in Leneuf de Beaubassin's expedition, which ravaged several settlements in Maine in 1703, and Hertel de Rouville's, which took the market town of Deerfield in Massachusetts by surprise the following year, taking "more than one hundred and fifty prisoners, men and women."

Archives nationales, Paris: Fonds des Colonies, série C¹¹A, vol. 22, fol. 12–12v.

Photo Studio Littré.

1708
July the 27th

Plantations General

111

Canada Surveyed, or the
French Dominions on
the Continent of America
briefly Considered. with
Proposals for subduing them

Canada Survey'd;

Or the French Dominions upon the Continent
of America briefly Considerd in their Situation
Strength, Trade & Number, more particularly
how vastly prejudicial they are to the
British Interest, And a Method Proposed
of Easily removing them.

Vide. Repᵗ fˢ 269.

It Cannot but be wondered att, by all thinking
Men, who know the Valuableneſs of the British
Monarchy in America, both with regard to their
Power and Trade, That a Nation so Powerful in
Shiping, so Numerous in Subjects, and other ways
so Jealous of their Trade, should so tamely allow
Such a troublesome Neighbour as the French, not
only to sit Down Peaceably beside them, but with
a handful of People vastly Dispersed, to Poſseſs a
Country of above four thousand Miles Extent, quite
Encompaſsing and hemming in betwixt them and
the Sea, All the British Empire upon the said
Continent of America; By which they have
already so Mightily Obstructed the British Trade
all America Over, and must in time totally Ruin
the Same, unleſs seasonably Prevented, as will
Appear by the following Considerations (and what
renders Us Entirely inexcusable, is, that the half
of one Years Loſt We Sustain in Trade by them
besides the Vast Expence both the Crown & Country
is at, in Maintaining of Troops and Garrisons
upon their Frontiers, Bribing of the Natives for
their Friendships, or indeed more properly speaking
being

Memoir of Samuel Vetch, 1708.

Vetch explains that the French colonies must be conquered because they are slowing down the development of the British colonies: through the empire that they have carved for themselves out of an immense part of the North-American territory, the French are "quite encompassing and hemming in betwixt them and the sea, all the British Empire upon the said continent of America, by which they have already so mightily obstructed the British trade, all America over, and must in time totally ruin the same . . . ."

Public Record Office, London: Series C.O. 324, vol. 9, p. 221.

13 octob. 1710.

95

France et
angleterre

Acadie

Articles de Capitulation accordée pour la
Reddition du fort du Port Royal entre François
Nicolson Escuyer general et commandant en chef
touttes les forces de sa sacrée majesté anne par la
grace de dieu Reine de la grande Bretagne france
et Irlande Deffenderesse pour la foy Et Monsieur
de Subercasse chevalier de lordre militaire de
St Louis et gouverneur pour le Roy du fort du
Port Royal Province de lacadie.

Sçavoir

1.
Que la garnison sortira avec armes et Bagages tambour
Battant et drapeau deploye.

2.
Quon nous fournira un nombre suffisant de bons bastimens
munis de vivres pour nous transporter à la Rochelle ou à
Rochefort par le plus court chemin ou on leur fournira
des passeports pour leur Retour.

3.
Que je pourray sortir six canons et deux mortiers à mon
choix

4.
Que les officiers emporteront leurs effets de quelque
nature qls soient sinon en vaymens les vendre lequel
payement leur sera fait de bonne foy

5.
Que les habitans de la Banlieüe resteront sur leurs
biens avec leurs bleds Bestiaux et autres meubles pendant
deux ans sinon en vaymens en sortir auant ce
temps apres les deux annees escoulies, Ils seront

Capitulation de la
reddition du fort et
du Port Royal en
acadie entre François
Nicolson et celle de
Subercasse

Terms of the surrender of Port-Royal, Acadia, 13 October 1710.

In the face of British troops whose numerical superiority was too great, Governor Subercase was forced to surrender. " . . . the [French] garrison will march out with all its equipment and with drums beating and flags flying."

Archives nationales, Paris: Fonds des Colonies, série C[11D], vol. 7, fol. 95.

Photo Studio Littré.

482 HISTOIRE DE L'HÔTEL-DIEU

à petites journées, afin qu'on eut ici le tems de se préparer à les recevoir; les Anglois s'appercevant qu'il retardoit leur route, le menacerent de le punir s'il ne se pressoit de les faire arriver, ainsi quand ils furent au Nord de l'Isle aux œufs, le Capitaine Paradis eut beau leur dire que l'endroit étoit très-dangereux, qu'il ne falloit point le passer la nuit, surtout avec un vent du Sud, qui les poufferoit sur la terre, ils s'imaginerent, que ce Pilote François vouloit leur inspirer une terreur panique, ils l'obligerent donc à marcher. Le Navire où il étoit, passa assés heureusement le premier, tous les autres le voulurent suivre, mais le vent du Sud ayant fraîchit, & étant devenu orageux, il soufla avec tant d'impetuosité qu'en moins de demi heure, huit des plus gros Vaisseaux se briserent, avec une violence épouvantable sur les Rochers, & sur la bature, à grande peine les autres pûrent-ils se conserver, en jettant promptement leurs Ancres. Les éclairs & le tonnerre se mêlant au bruit des flots, & des vents, & aux cris perçans de tous ces naufrages, augmentoient l'éffroy : ceux qui en furent temoins, nous ont dit depuis, qu'ils s'étonnoient que nous n'en eussions rien

DE QUEBEC. 483

entendu à Quebec, & que c'étoit l'image de l'enfer, il semble que la justice de Dieu les poursuivit, & les châtiât de toute maniere, car le tonnerre tomba sur un de leurs Vaisseaux, & le fit sauter si loin que la quille qui avoit plus de 50. pieds de long, fut trouvée bien avant sur la grêve ; tous ces miserables tacherent de gagner terre, & environ 3000. moururent dès qu'ils y furent arrivés, sans compter ceux qui furent submergés. Ils se perdirent la nuit du 2. au 3. de Septembre, & le pêcheur qui leur avoit échappé, & qui nous assura qu'il avoit vû leur flotte dans la baye de Gaspé, ne les y rencontra qu'après le naufrage, comme il s'en retournoit, il crût qu'il faisoit la route de Quebec, en quoi il se trompa, car dès le lendemain de cet accident, quand ils eurent un peu repris leurs esprits, ils tinrent un conseil de guerre pour voir ce qu'ils avoient à faire ; celui qui devoit commander les troupes, étoit d'avis que l'on vint assiéger Quebec, quoiqu'ils eussent fait une si grande perte, ils se croyoient encore assés forts pour nous prendre, l'Amiral fut d'un avis contraire, ne jugeant pas à propos de perdre le reste de sa flotte, & son sentiment l'emporta.

Ss ij

Soeur Jeanne Françoise Juchereau de La Ferté, dite de Sainte-Ignace. *Histoire de l'Hôtel-Dieu de Québec*. Montauban: Chez Jerosme Legier, 1751, pp. 482–483.

"In less than half an hour, eight of the largest vessels [of Hovenden Walker's squadron] smashed with terrible violence on the rocks and reefs [of Île aux Oeufs]. Not thinking it advisable to risk the rest of his fleet," Walker gave up the idea of attacking Québec.

Public Archives of Canada, Ottawa: Library. (C-125030).

Medal with head of Louis XIV commemorating the Treaty of Utrecht. Struck in bronze, 1713.

By the Treaty of Utrecht France surrendered to Great Britain "the island of Newfoundland," "Hudson Bay and Hudson Strait" and "Nova Scotia, in other words Acadia in its entirety, in keeping with its former boundaries."

Public Archives of Canada, Ottawa: Picture Division (Negative nos. C-14900 obverse and C-14901 reverse).

de S.t Laurent demeureront a l'avenir a la France, avec
l'entiere faculté au Roy tres Chrestien d'y fortifier une, ou
plusieurs places.

14/

Il a esté expressement convenu que dans tous les lieux et
Colonies qui doivent estre cedez ou restituez en vertu de ce traité
par le Roy tres Chrestien, les Sujets dud. Roy auront la liberté
de se retirer ailleurs dans l'espace d'un an avec tous leurs effets
mobiliaires qu'ils pourront transporter ou il leur plaira; Ceux
neantmoins qui voudront y demeurer et rester Sous la domination
de la Grande Bretagne doivent jouir de l'exercice de la Religion
Catholique et Romaine en tant que la permettent les loix de
la Grande Bretagne.

15/

Les habitans du Canada et autres Sujets de la France, ne mole-
steront point a l'avenir les cinq nations ou Cantons des Indiens
Soumis a la Grande Bretagne, ni les autres nations de l'amerique
amies de cette Couronne; Pareillement les Sujets de la Grande
Bretagne se comporteront pacifiquement envers les Americains
Sujets ou amis de la France; Et les uns et les autres jouiront
d'une plaine liberté de se frequenter pour le bien du Commerce,
et avec la mesme liberté les habitans de ces Regions pourront
visiter les Colonies Françoises et Britanniques pour l'avantage
reciproque du Commerce Sans aucune molestation, ni empechement
de part ni d'autre, Au Surplus les Commissaires regleront
exactement et distinctement quels Seront ceux qui Seront, ou

Treaty of Utrecht, 11 April 1713.

Article 15 of this treaty opened the way to the West for the English: first, it allowed them to get a foothold on the Great Lakes region by stipulating that the Iroquois "cantons" (south of Lake Ontario) were "subject to Great Britain"; then it recognized the right of the English, as well as of the French, to trade with the Western tribes.

Archives du ministère des Affaires étrangères, Paris.

"Fortify Canada"

It was clear that the English were aiming to take over all the French possessions in North America. At the beginning of 1716, therefore, Governor Philippe de Rigaud de Vaudreuil issued the watchword: take advantage of the peace to "fortify Canada."

Québec, which had been attacked by William Phips in 1690 and threatened by Admiral Walker in 1711, and whose fall would be fatal to the colony as a whole, ought to have received large defence works. In the period 1716–45 plans for building fortifications kept following one another, but in actual fact very little was done to ensure the town's security.

Off in the direction of the Great Lakes, the Niagara River was taking on special importance strategically. In the seventeenth century a post had already been built there, at the point where the French colony and the Iroquois territories met; in 1720 a trading post was established there, then in 1726–27 a stone fort was put up on the right bank of the river.

Fortifying Canada also meant maintaining and tightening the alliances with the Indians, on whom gifts were lavished and who were further rewarded on occasion with medals for services rendered. This policy was all the more necessary because the Indians contributed greatly to "guarding the approaches" to the colony, and also because peace between rival tribes in the West or between one or another of them and the French, whether in Canada or in Louisiana, was never assured.

"Plan of the town of Québec, capital of New France." Gaspard-Joseph Chaussegros de Léry. 30 September 1730. Map: col. ms., 55.0 × 74.3 cm.

In the period from 1700 until about 1745, several plans were put forward for fortifying Québec, but little or no action was taken on them. In 1746 a beginning was made on building a surrounding wall, but the work advanced slowly and would never be completely finished.

Archives nationales, Paris: Section Outre-Mer, Dépôt des fortifications des colonies, 410.

Photo Studio Littré.

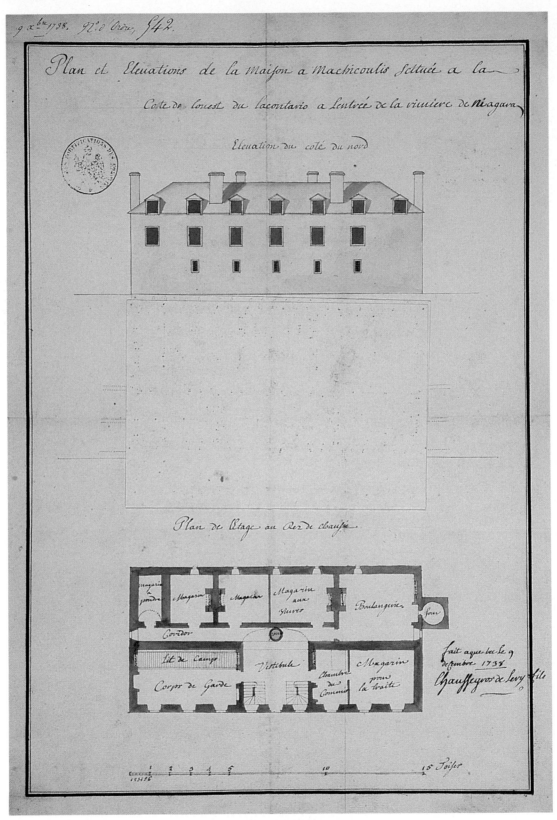

"Plan and elevations of the machicolated building situated . . . at the entrance of the Niagara River." Gaspard-Joseph Chaussegros de Léry (the younger). 9 December 1738. Plan: col. ms., 47.2 × 31.5 cm.

In the 1720s the French built a trading post and a fort at Niagara. They were hoping thus to curb New York State's growing trade in the Great Lakes region and divert towards the St. Lawrence the Indians who passed by on their way to trade at Albany.

Archives nationales, Paris: Section Outre-Mer, Dépôt des fortifications des colonies, 542 C.

Photo Studio Littré.

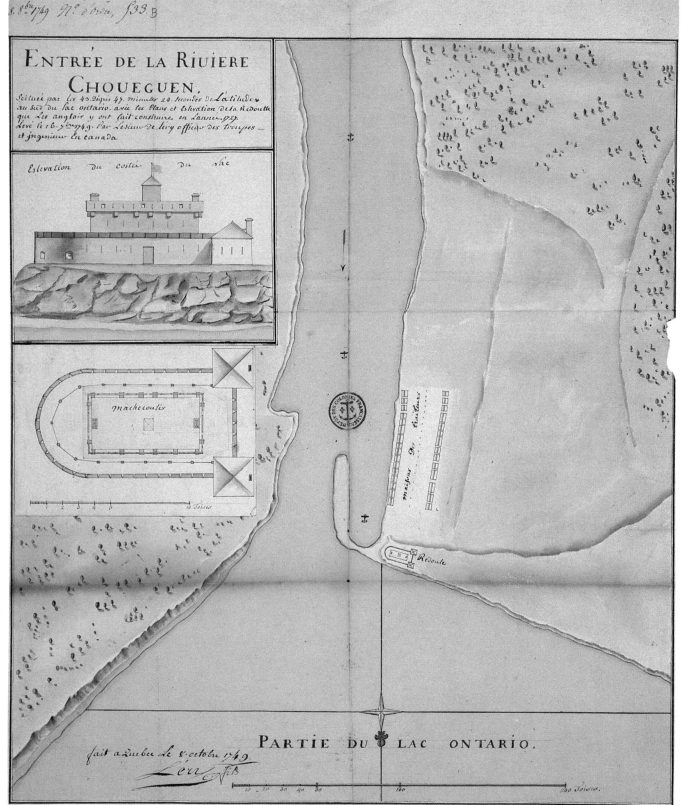

"Entrance to the Rivière Choueguen . . . ." Gaspard-Joseph Chaussegros de Léry (the younger). 8 October 1749. Map: col. ms., 50.3 × 44.0 cm.

According to La Galissonière, in the Great Lakes region, it was at Chouaguen (Oswego) "that the English attract all the Indian tribes [to trade there] and that they try through giving them presents not only to win them over but also to urge them to murder the French traders."

Archives nationales, Paris: Section Outre-Mer, Dépôt des fortifications des colonies, Amérique septentrionale, 532 C.

Photo Studio Littré.

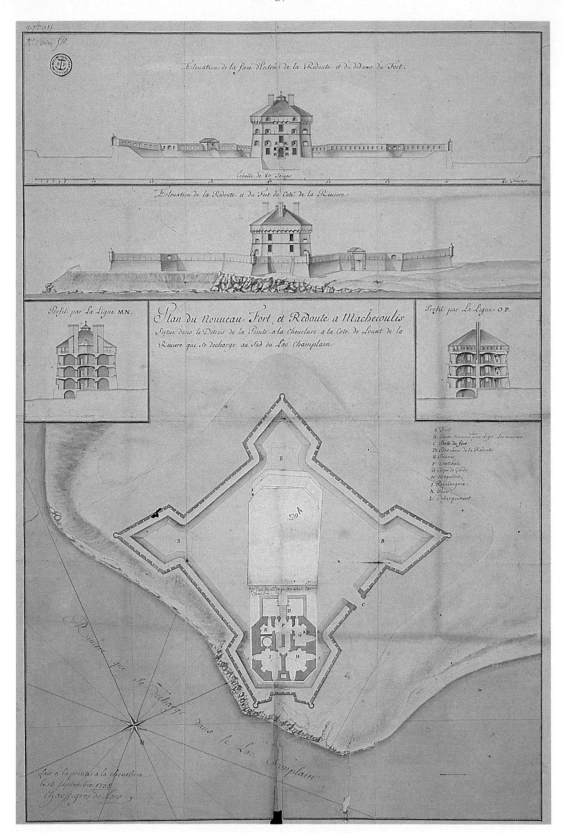

"Plan of the new machicolated fort and redoubt located in the strait of the Pointe-à-la-Chevelure . . . ." Gaspard-Joseph Chaussegros de Léry (the elder). 15 September 1735. Plan: col. ms., 88.6×58.0 cm.

The construction of Fort Saint-Frédéric (or Fort de la Pointe-à-la-Chevelure) was designed to prevent the British from establishing themselves in the Lake Champlain region and to close to them the invasion route leading from New York to Montréal.

Archives nationales, Paris: Section Outre-Mer, Dépôt des fortifications des colonies, Amérique septentrionale 510 A.

Photo Studio Littré.

[Handwritten French memoir, circa 1758]

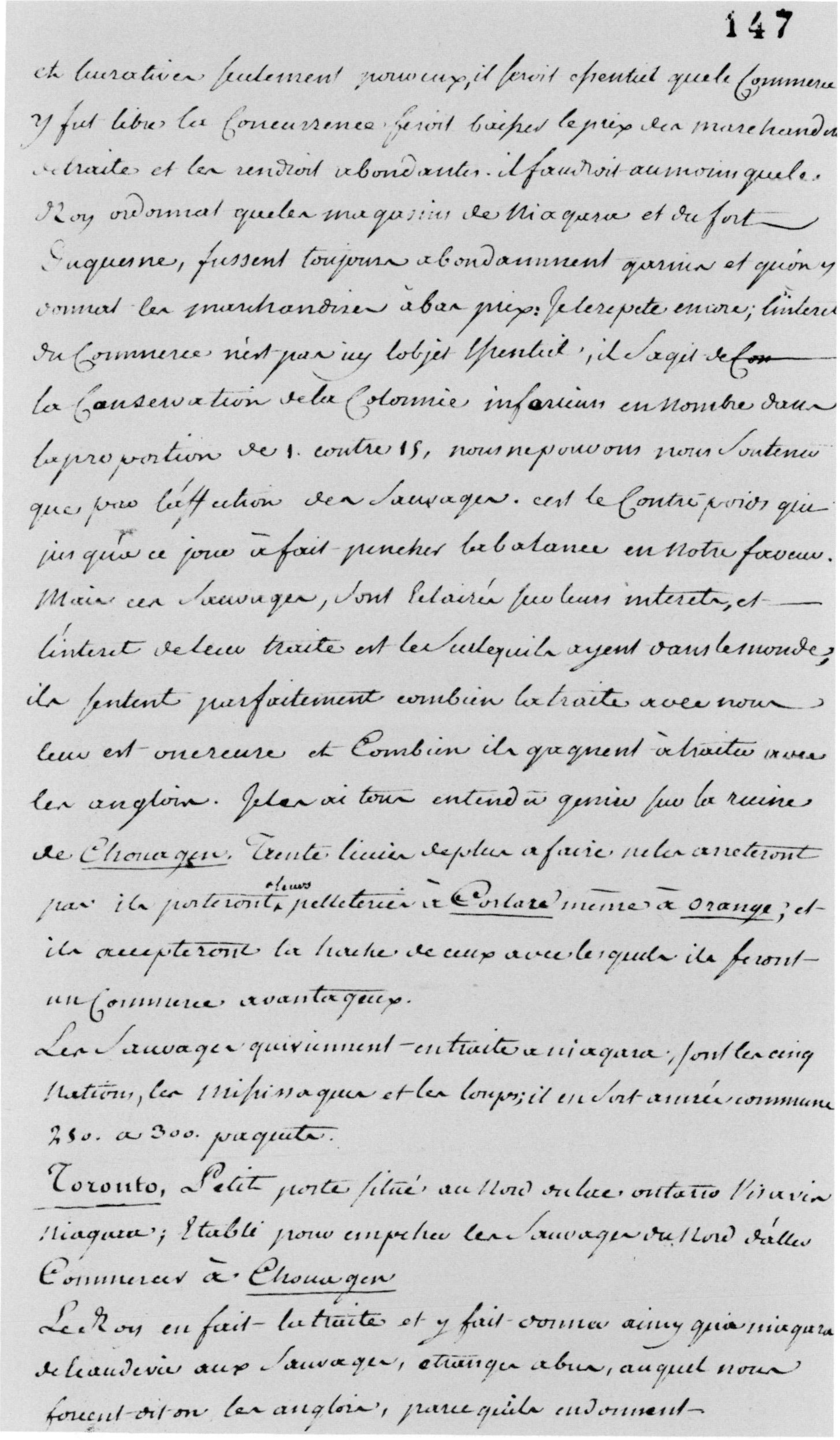

Memoir concerning French posts, circa 1758.

Because she is "very much inferior in numbers in the proportion of 1 to 15" to the British colonies, New France can "last only through the attachment of the Indians." But the Indians are conscious of the degree to which trade with the French "is onerous for them and how much they gain by trading with the English." There is a good chance that they will take up "the hatchet of those with whom they will be carrying on a profitable trade." Since the beginning of the century the inability of the French to offer deals as good as those of the English had imperilled, if not ruined, many of their alliances.

Archives nationales, Paris: Fonds des Colonies, série C¹¹E, vol. 13, fol. 147.

Photo Studio Littré.

Medal of Louis XV, distributed to the Indian chiefs for services rendered. Struck in silver, circa 1740.

Presents, medals and trading goods were used to win the Indians' support. Fairly often, however, the main reason that incited them to side with the French was the fear and respect that the latter inspired in them through their shows of force and feats of arms. "When they feel that we are the stronger, they will all be our friends," wrote La Galissonière.

Public Archives of Canada, Ottawa: Picture Division (Negative nos. C-62181 obverse and C-62182 reverse).

Letter from Governor General de Beauharnois and Intendant Dupuy to the minister, Québec, 25 October 1727.

During the thirty years of peace that followed the Treaty of Utrecht, the rivalries between the English and French settlers showed up in various ways: " . . . the English, who are jealous of the trade that the French carry on with the Indian tribes in the *pays d'en haut*, try all sorts of ways to take this trade away from the French . . . ." They sent "underground belts to all the tribes on whose territories the French have posts or establishments to incite them to get rid of them and to massacre the garrisons."

Archives nationales, Paris: Fonds des Colonies, série C[11A], vol. 49, fol. 48-48v.

Photo Studio Littré.

Canada   10. 0ctob 1730

Mr. Lems.* de Beauharnois

Monseigneur.

J'ay veu par la Lettre que vous m'avés
fait l'honneur de m'écrire le 11. avril dernier,
la satisfaction que sa majesté a eüe de
l'attention que j'apporte a maintenir les
abenakis dans les Interests des François
et a veiller aux tentatives des anglois qui
demandent une plus particuliere attention)
que celle que l'on a eüe jusqu'a present par
les Justances Sollicitations et les propofitions
avantageuses que les anglois leurs font

[surtout] aux abenakis de l'acadie, ainsy
que vous verrés, Monseigneur, par la copie
du rapport que le S.* de Hassin m'a fait, (qui
est venu cet été avec Six sauvages) que
j'ay l'honneur de joindre icy, qui prouve le
dessein que les anglois ont de s'emparer
de leur pays par les forts et les garnisons
qu'ils y établissent, et que les Sauvages
ne seront plus maîtres de repousser si
leurs projets ont leur Execution.
Quoy qu'ils me parroissent toujours dans les
Sentiment de ne point vendre ny ceder
leurs terres, il est a craindre que les
anglois ne les gagnent par des présens
ou des promesses qu'ils ne leur tiendront
pas s'ils en Sont une fois les maîtres
ce que je leur ay bien fait entendre dans

Letter from Governor General de
Beauharnois to the minister, Québec,
10 October 1730.

The English were making "attractive
propositions" to the Abenakis with a
view to "taking possession of their
country," where they had begun to
establish garrisons and settlers. This
expansion might well give them control
of the buffer zone (present-day Maine
and New Brunswick) that separated
Canada from New England.

Archives nationales, Paris: Fonds des
Colonies, série C[11A], vol. 52, fol. 196-
196v.

Photo Studio Littré.

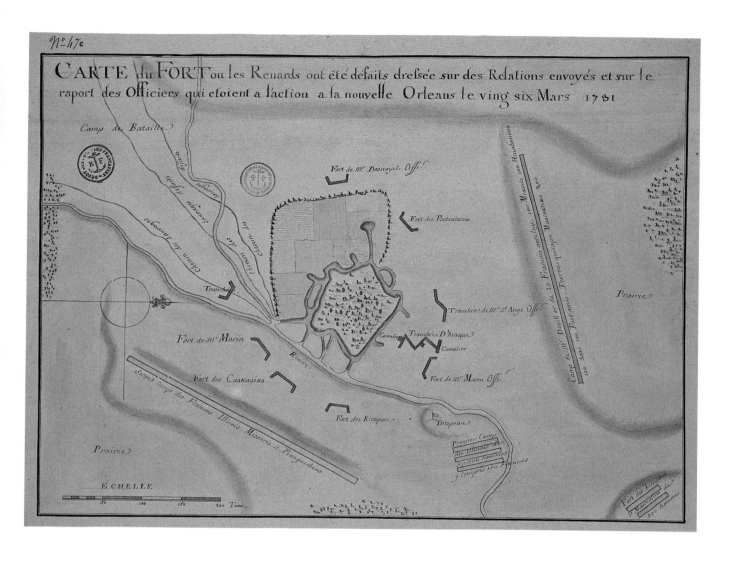

"Map of the fort where the Foxes were defeated . . . ." 26 March 1731. Map: col. ms., 29.5 × 44.6 cm.

Because they were hurting the fur trade by attacking French voyageurs and the allies of the French in the West, the Foxes were to be exterminated. In 1730 hundreds of them were killed at the Rivière Saint-Joseph des Illinois by French and Indian forces led by Groston de Saint-Ange, Noyelles de Fleurimont, and Coulon de Villiers.

Archives nationales, Paris: Section Outre-Mer, Dépôt des fortifications des colonies, Louisiane, portefeuille V1C, 47.

Photo Studio Littré.

IV

The War of the Austrian Succession

As soon as it was learned at Louisbourg in 1744 that war had broken out in Europe, François Du Pont Duvivier led an expedition against Annapolis Royal in the hope of recovering the former Acadia. But the bid failed.

The following year it was Louisbourg's turn to be besieged by troops from New England and a British fleet under command respectively of William Pepperrell and Peter Warren. After 47 days Louis Du Pont Duchambon surrendered: the "impregnable" fortress, the town and their dependencies passed into the hands of the English.

The loss of Louisbourg was a major disaster for France. In 1746 a fleet under command of Jean-Baptiste-Louis-Frédéric de La Rochefoucauld, Duc d'Anville, was dispatched with the task of recovering Louisbourg, Nova Scotia and Placentia. Bad weather and sickness wrecked the plan.

Louisbourg was nevertheless going to become a French possession again with the signing of the Treaty of Aix-la-Chapelle in 1748.

Letter from Commandant Louis Du Pont Duchambon to the minister, 13 August 1745.

". . . on 27 June last I was forced to hand Louisbourg with its outlying areas over to the English after sustaining a siege for 47 days . . . lacking powder and men to defend it . . . ."

Archives nationales, Paris: Fonds des Colonies, série C¹¹B, vol. 27, fol. 34.

Photo Studio Littré.

L'on ne doit pas se flatter que nôtre reconciliation avec les Anglois soit bien sincere, au moins de leur part, la paix concluë à Aix-la-Chapelle ne prouve que le besoin où l'on étoit en Angleterre et en France de terminer une guerre qui étoit egalement onereuse aux deux Puissances, et que l'on ne pouvoit continuer d'epart ni d'autre par la situation forcé des finances.

Tout enfin doit faire sentir et penser que l'Angleterre n'attend qu'une conjoncture favorable qui peut être même, elle fera naître sous le plus legeo pretexte pour nous faire la guerre en Amerique, sy emparer de toutes nos possessions, detruire entierement notre Commerce, et nous mettre par la hors d'Etat d'avoir jamais une marine telle qu'il convient à un aussi grand Etat

Memoir from the Maréchal de Noailles, 1749.

" . . . the peace concluded at Aix-la-Chapelle only proves the need in which England and France found themselves to end a war that was equally onerous for both powers . . . ." But this peace was only a truce: " . . . England is only waiting for a favourable situation . . . to make war on us in America, take all our possessions there, utterly destroy our trade . . . ."

Service historique de l'Armée, Vincennes, France: série A¹, vol. 2997, fol. 211v-212.

From one war to another

English competition was making itself strongly felt on Lake Ontario, particularly through the post of Oswego (Chouaguen). But the threat extended much farther, into the immense territory situated between Canada and Louisiana. If the English were successful in establishing themselves there, it would be all over for the Mississippi colony, and Canada's internal trade would collapse.

In addition to tightening the alliance with the Indians in the region, it was then necessary to fortify the West. In the space of a few years Fort La Présentation, west of Montréal, and Fort Rouillé on the north shore of Lake Ontario were built, as were Fort Presqu'île, Fort Le Boeuf, Fort Venango and Fort Duquesne, from Lake Erie to the Ohio.

The construction of Fort Duquesne, at the junction of the Ohio and the Monongahela, was going to set off hostilities in the region. On 3 July 1754 Fort Necessity, commanded by George Washington, surrendered to Louis Coulon de Villiers; a year later, on 9 July 1755, on the Monongahela, the French repulsed Major-General Edward Braddock, who had come at the head of an army of nearly 2,000 men to capture Fort Duquesne.

Even before war was declared in Europe, another battle was taking place on Lac Saint-Sacrement (Lake George), in the colony of New York, in which the French troops commanded by Jean-Armand, Baron de Dieskau, suffered a partial defeat.

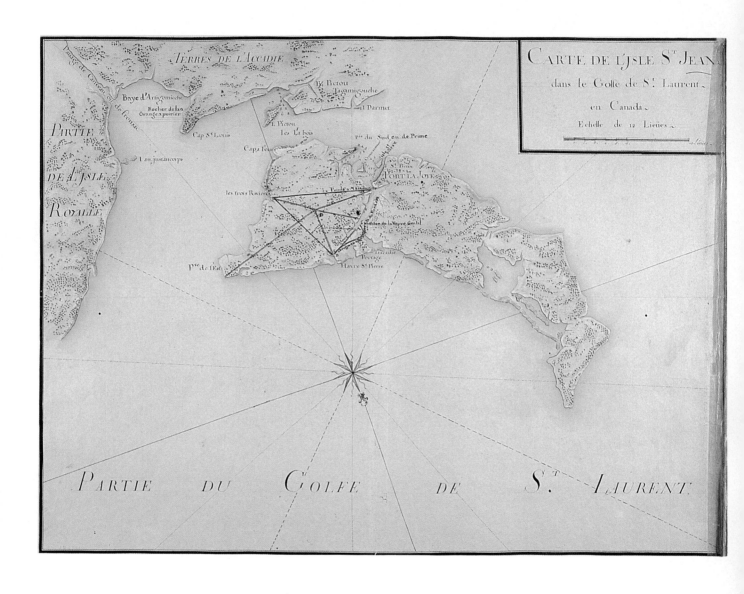

[Map of Île Saint-Jean (Prince Edward Island). Louis Franquet 1751]. Map: col. ms.

In the period 1749–1755 the Acadians left Nova Scotia by the thousands to settle in the French colonies of Île Royale and Île Saint-Jean. The arrival of foreign immigrants in their country, rumours of deportation and the oath of allegiance that was being forced upon them were just so many factors that prompted them to emigrate.

Public Archives of Canada, Ottawa: Manuscript Division, MG 18, K 5.

121

quelque chose de bon et de vrai dans

ce que j'ai marqué cy dessus, je l'ai

puisé dans ses lettres.

C'est aussi de là que je tire une

remarque essentielle au Sujet. Si la

Colonie illinoise forte de monde peut

vexer les Colonies Angloises, Elles n'on

gueres moins de facilité à S'emparer

des illinois qu'on laisseroit dans l'etat

languissant d'aujourd'huy, c'est de tout le

pays que nous occupons celuy ou ils

peuvent venir le plus aisément avec un

peu de forces, et Après avoient une fois

reussi à Se fourrer ainsi entre nos

deux Colonies la perte du Mississippi

et la ruine du commerce interieur du

Canada Seroient assurées, et les Colonies

Espagnoles même le Mexique en

tres grand danger.

Il resulte de tout cela qu'en reunissant

les illinois au Canada on gagnera peu

Letter from Acting Governor de La Galissonière to the minister, Québec, 1 September 1748.

If the English colonies seized the Illinois country, succeeding in "thus getting in between our two colonies [Canada and Louisiana], the loss of the Mississippi and the ruin of Canada's inland trade would be assured, and the Spanish colonies, even Mexico, would be in very great danger."

Archives nationales, Paris: Fonds des Colonies, série C¹¹ᴬ, vol. 91, fol. 121.

Photo Studio Littré.

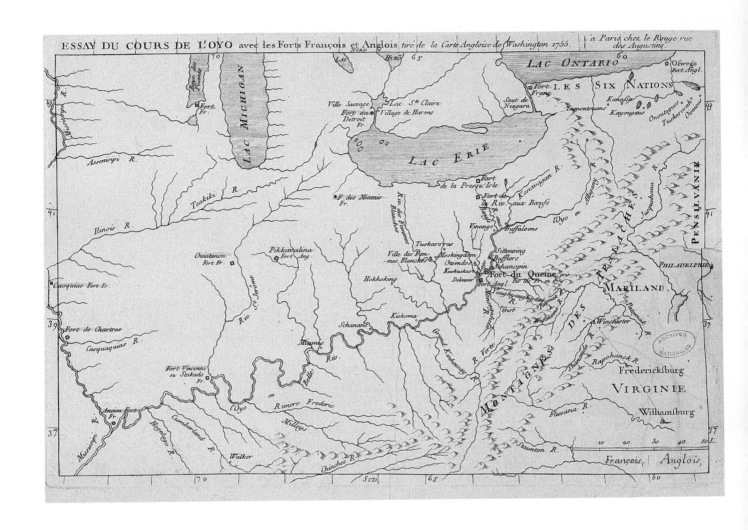

ESSAY DU COURS DE L'OYO avec les Forts François et Anglois tiré de la Carte Angloise de Washington 1755. [a Paris chez le Rouge rue des Augustins.]

Essay on the course of the OYO (Ohio), with the French and English forts . . . . George-Louis Le Rouge. Paris: chez Le Rouge, rue des Augustins, 1755. Map: hand coloured, 19.6 × 30.5 cm.

This map shows most of the forts or posts that had been built since 1713 in the Illinois country and the Ohio valley. The French posts helped consolidate trade with the Indians and the alliances with them, as well as check the expansion of the English in the West.

Archives nationales, Paris: Section des cartes et plans, NN 173, n° 46.

Photo Studio Littré.

Capitulation accordée par le Commandant des troupes de Sa Majesté très Chrétienne a celuy des troupes angloises actuellement dans le fort de necessité qui avoit été construit sur les terres du domaine du Roy. ce 3.e Juillet 1754 a huit heures du Soir.

Scavoir.

Comme notre intention n'a jamais été de troubler la paix et la bonne armonie qui régnoit entre les deux princes amis, mais seulement de venger l'assassin qui a été fait sur un de nos officiers porteur d'une Sommation et sur son Escorte, comme aussi d'empecher aucun Etablissement sur les terres du Domaine du Roy mon maitre.

a ces Considérations nous voulons bien accorder grace a toute les anglois qui sont dans le dit fort aux conditions cy apres.

article 1.r

nous accordons au commandant anglois de se retirer avec toute sa garnison pour s'en Retourner paisiblement dans son païs et luy promettons d'empecher qu'il luy soit fait aucun insulte par nos francois et de maintenir autant qu'il sera en notre pouvoir tous les sauvages qui sont avec nous.

2.o

il luy sera permis de sortir et d'emporter tout ce qui leur appartiendra a l'exception de l'artillerie et munitions de Guerre que nous nous Reservons.

3.o

que nous leur accordons les honneurs de la Guerre qu'ils sortiront tambour battant avec une piece de canon ...

The surrender of Fort Necessity, signed by George Washington and James Mackay, 3 July 1754.

In forcing Washington and his Virginia militiamen to surrender, Coulon de Villiers accomplished a double mission: "to avenge the assassination of one of our officers [his own brother, Jumonville] who was bearing an injunction, and of his escort, and also to prevent any establishment" of the English in the Ohio valley.

Archives nationales du Québec, Centre régional de Montréal.

Photo Diapolab.

IV

The Acadians' tragic fate

If Europe was still at peace, the war was already raging in North America, where the Ohio country, the Lake Champlain region and Acadia were being fought for. In this part of the French empire, Fort Beauséjour and Fort Gaspereau, on the Nova Scotia frontier, surrendered on 16 June and on 17 June 1755 respectively.

In Nova Scotia itself the Acadians' future was far from being assured, as a result of their constant refusal to take the oath of allegiance to England. Faced with the prospect of a general war in America, the authorities of the colony were worried about the so-called neutrality of these settlers who, in their very great majority, and because they had not taken the oath of allegiance, were not even British subjects.

The English also wanted to protect themselves against eventual attacks by the Acadians and their Indian allies. They did this by building forts at Les Mines and Pisiquid in 1749 and 1750, and by fortifying the new towns of Halifax, Lunenburg and Lawrencetown.

The idea of deporting the Acadians consequently resurfaced. It would fall to Governor Charles Lawrence to carry it out in 1755, when between 6,000 and 7,000 "French Neutrals" were dragged from their homes and scattered, most of them in the American colonies. The cruel operation went on until 1762, and after Louisbourg fell in 1758, the settlers on Île Royale and Île Saint-Jean did not escape it.

Not only were the Acadians deported, they were also dispersed. Too often even families were separated: children were taken from their parents, husbands from their wives, brothers from their sisters. Évangéline would spend a long time looking for Gabriel . . . .

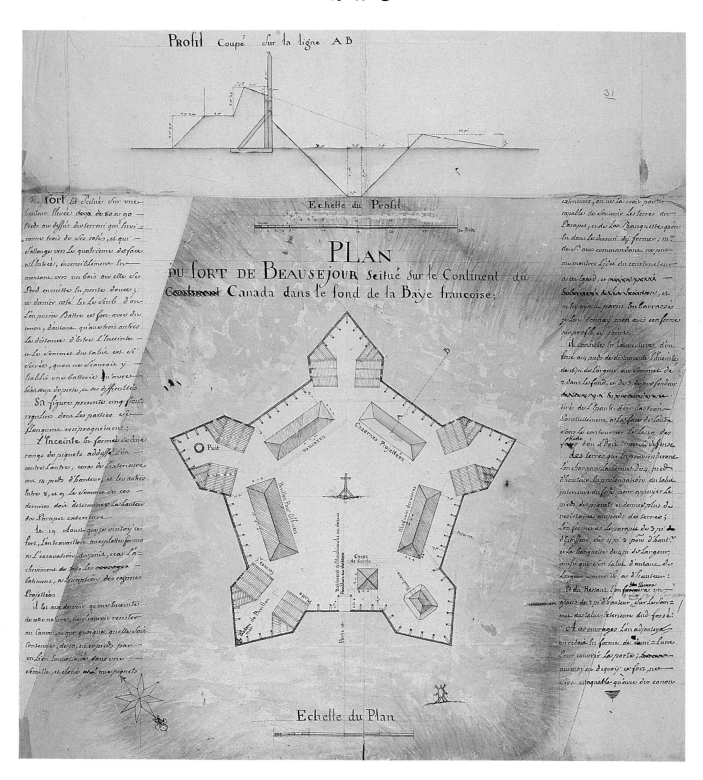

[Plan of Fort Beauséjour, on the Chignecto Isthmus. Louis Franquet. 1751]. Plan: col. ms.

In 1751 Fort Beauséjour and Fort Gaspereau were built on the border of Nova Scotia to prevent the British from spreading beyond the colony. By bringing them closer to Canada, such an expansion into present-day New Brunswick would enable them to cut the ground link between Québec and Louisbourg.

Public Archives of Canada, Ottawa: Manuscript Division, MG 18, K 5.

View of Fort Edward in PIZIGUIT RIVER, Nova Scotia taken in the year 1753 by Capn. John Hamilton of his Majestys 40th Reg.

View of Fort Edward. John Hamilton (known 1753–1777). Watercolour.

In 1749–1750, the English of Nova Scotia built forts at Mines and at Pisiquid (Fort Edward), which served to keep an eye on the Acadians. They erected Fort Lawrence (opposite Fort Beauséjour) to prevent the French from strengthening their positions in the Isthmus of Chignecto. The new settlements of Halifax, Lunenburg and Lawrencetown were likewise fortified, to protect the settlers from raids by Indians allied with the French.

Public Archives of Canada, Ottawa: Picture Division (Negative no. C-2708).

from the Governor, an assurance in Writing that they should not be called upon to bear Arms in the defence of the Province; and with this General Philipps did comply, of which step his Majesty has disapproved; and the Inhabitants pretending therefrom to be in a state of Neutrality between his Majesty and his Enemies, have continually furnished the French & Indians with intelligence, Quarters Provisions and assistance in annoying the Government; and while one part have abetted the French encroachments by their treachery, the other have countenanced them by open Rebellion, and three Hundred of them were ~~spanby~~ actually found in Arms, in the French Fort at Beausejour when it surrendered;

    Notwithstanding all their former bad behaviour, as his Majesty was

Letter from Charles Lawrence, Halifax, 11 August 1755.

Lawrence explains the reasons for the deportation of the Acadians: They "have continually furnished the French and Indians with intelligence, quarters, provisions and assistance in annoying the government"; it is necessary to "rid ourselves of a set of people, who would forever have been an obstruction to the intention of settling this colony."

Lands, and any further favour from the
Government; I called together his Majesty's
Council, (at which the Hon.ble Vice Admiral
Boscawen & Rear Admiral Mostyn assisted,) to
consider by what means we could with
the greatest security and effect, rid ourselves
of a set of People, who would forever have
been an obstruction to the intention of
settling this Colony, and that it was now
from their refusal of the Oath absolutely
incumbent upon us to remove.

As their numbers amount
to near Seven thousand persons the driving
them off with leave to go whither they please
would have doubtless strengthned Canada
with so considerable a number of Inhabit
ants, and as they have no cleared
Land to give them at present, such as

are

Public Archives of Canada, Ottawa:
Manuscript Division, MG 53, no. 71,
pp. 2,4.

donne de plus une vache, ou une
jument, ou deux truyes, ou cinq
brebis à chaque, et l'on
distribue un taureau et un
étalon par chaque certaine de
familles. Enfin la Colonie est
exempte de toutes impositions
pendant 30. ans. Cet établissement
sont coûteux, sans doute, mais
c'est une avance faite par le
Gouvernement dont les sujets
retirent tous les ans un intérêt
qui ne cesse d'augmenter, et
qui rentre au Gouvernement par
différentes formes par l'accroissement
de la population et de la consommation.

État des Acadiens.

En Angleterre	à Liverpool	224.	
	à Southampton	219.	
	à Penryn	159.	866.
	à Bristol	184.	
	Pris à bord des corsaires environ	80.	
En France	à Boulogne, St Malo Rochefort &c.		2,000.
En Amérique	Dans la nouvelle Angleterre, le Maryland, la Pensilvanie, la Caroline &c.		10,000.
	Total		**12,866.**

N. On ne garantit pas l'exactitude des deux
dernières évaluations que l'on ne tient que des rapports
d'Angleterre.

"État des Acadiens," February 1763.

From 1755 to 1762, several thousand Acadians were deported to the British colonies, to Britain and to France. Many took refuge in Canada, in Louisiana, in the islands of Saint-Pierre and Miquelon, and even in the West Indies. Some of them ended up staying "in their country" and others returned later.

Archives du ministère des Affaires étrangères, Paris: Correspondance politique, Angleterre, vol. 449, fol. 352v.

Photo Jean-Loup Charmet.

An indecisive struggle

In 1756 war broke out again in Europe; that same year the French besieged Oswego, on Lake Ontario. The fortress, which consisted of three forts, including Chouaguen, had to surrender in the face of the troops, superior in number, led by François-Pierre de Rigaud de Vaudreuil and Louis-Joseph, Marquis de Montcalm.

In the autumn of 1755 and after, the French, accompanied by Indian allies — when the latter were not virtually alone — multiplied their raids against the English settlements, some of them as far away as Carolina. In ordering these raids Governor General Pierre de Rigaud de Vaudreuil had two objectives in mind — tiring the English of the war, and keeping them so busy at home that they would be unable to go on the offensive against New France.

On 8 August 1757 Montcalm received the surrender of Fort William Henry. The following year, on 8 July, taking advantage of blunders by James Abercromby, even though the latter was leading larger troops, Montcalm won the celebrated victory of Carillon, a few kilometres from Lac Saint-Sacrement.

But in 1758 two defeats would offset these French victories: on 26 July Louisbourg surrendered after a sixty-day siege; and on 27 August Fort Frontenac, on Lake Ontario, also surrendered. Finally on 24 November, in the Ohio region, François-Marie Le Marchand de Lignery blew up Fort Duquesne to prevent it from falling into the hands of the English.

Medal with head of Louis XV commemorating the French victories, including the capture of Oswego. Struck in silver, 1758.

The capture of Oswego (Chouaguen), on Lake Ontario, marked the realization of an old dream on the part of the Canadians. For thirty years they had wanted to destroy this commercial centre that had been doing immense harm to their diplomatic and trading relations with the Indians.

Public Archives of Canada, Ottawa: Picture Division (Negative nos. C-62197 obverse and C-62198 reverse).

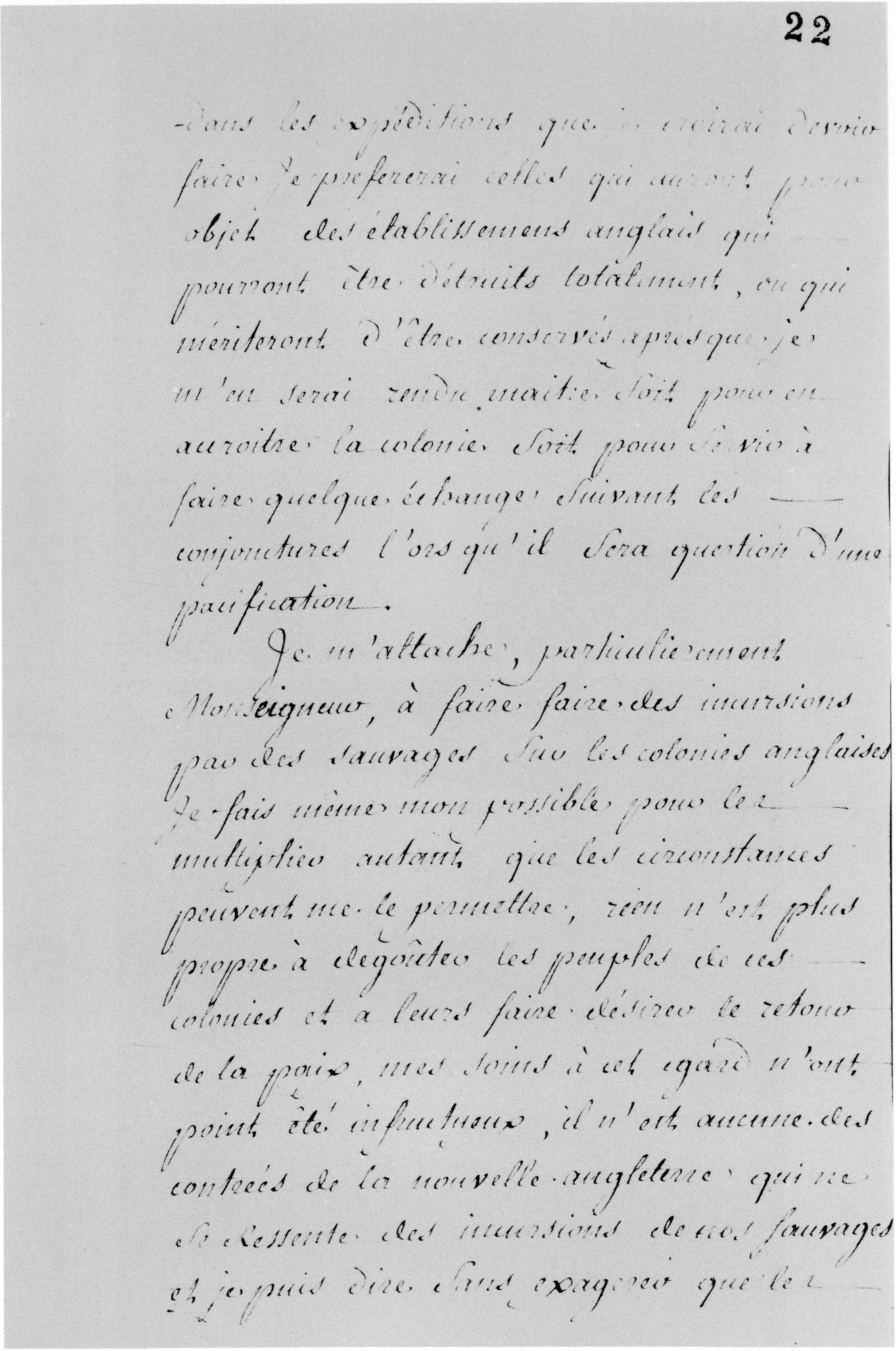
22

dans les expéditions que je croirai devoir
faire je préférerai celles qui auront pour
objet des établissemens anglais qui
pourront être détruits totalement, ou qui
mériteront d'être conservés après que je
m'en serai rendu maitre, soit pour en
accroitre la colonie, soit pour servir à
faire quelque échange suivant les
conjonctures lors qu'il sera question d'une
pacification.

Je m'attache, particulièrement
Monseigneur, à faire faire des incursions
par des sauvages sur les colonies anglaises
je fais même mon possible pour les
multiplier autant que les circonstances
peuvent me le permettre, rien n'est plus
propre à dégoûter les peuples de ces
colonies et à leurs faire désirer le retour
de la paix, mes soins à cet égard n'ont
point été infructueux, il n'est aucune des
contrées de la nouvelle angleterre qui ne
se ressente des incursions de nos sauvages
et je puis dire sans exagérer que les

Letter from Governor General de Vaudreuil to the minister, Montréal, 8 June 1756.

Vaudreuil was trying to increase the number of raids against the English colonies, for "nothing is more apt to disgust the populations of those colonies and make them wish for the return of peace."

anglais ont perdu cent têtes Contre
nous une, Je Sçais même que le peuple
en est grandement consterné et les anglais
ont bien de la peine à les faire mouvoir
parcequ'ils Sont penetrés de l'injustice
de leur prétantion), mais les colonies
anglaises Sont si peuplées qu'elles
fournissent aisément le nombre d'hommes
qui leur sont néćéssaires. Je Souhaitterois
fort découvrir quelque voye pour faire
sentir de plus en plus à ce peuple combien
il seroit leur avantage de ne se pas
prêter à des vûës si odieuses et dont
les suites peuvent être si funestes
pour eux même), mais la chose n'est
point aisée et je ne la mettroi en usage
qu'autant que je serai assuré de ne
rien compromettre.

Je Suis avec un très profond Respect

Monseigneur,

Vôtre très humble et
très obéissant serviteur.
Vaudreuil

Archives nationales, Paris: Fonds des
Colonies, série C¹¹A, vol. 101, fol. 22-
22v.

Photo Studio Littré.

Letter from Governor General de Vaudreuil to the minister, Montréal, 18 April 1757.

Since 1755 the French and their Indian bands had been relentlessly harassing the frontier settlements "from Carolina to New York," sowing death and destruction everywhere.

Archives nationales, Paris: Fonds des Colonies, série F³, vol. 15, fol. 18.

Photo Studio Littré.

Louisburg in North America, taken near the Light House when that city was besieg'd in 1758. Drawn by Capt Ince of th... Engraved by P. Canot. Louisbourg L'Amerique Sept... durant le dernier Si...

View of Louisbourg "seen from the lighthouse during the late siege of 1758." Captain Ince. Etching by P. Canot, printed by Thomas Jefferys, 1761.

In 1745 the English had good reasons for launching an offensive against Louisbourg: this fortress assured the predominance of the French fisheries in America; its privateers were attacking the New England merchant ships, and its troops had tried to capture Annapolis Royal, in Nova Scotia. In 1758 the capture of the fortress was a step towards the conquest of Canada.

Public Archives of Canada, Ottawa: Picture Division (Negative no. C-5907).

243.

Au Roy de Pologne

Le 12. Juillet 1758. de Carillon

Sire

Sur l'avis que nous receumes à Montreal que les ennemis s'avançoient à grands pas vers notre frontière du fort de Carillon et que M. le m.ie de Montcalm avoit été obligé de se replier sur ce fort. J'en partis avec toute la diligence qui me fut possible le 5. de juillet et j'y arrivai le 8. matin sur les trois heures; à midi l'ennemi parut sur les hauteurs ou nous nous étions retirés la veille et s'avança en bon ordre sur quatre colonnes : je Commandois notre droite, M. de — Bourlamaque la gauche, et M. de Montcalm le centre, nous étions deux mille neuf cents combattans de troupes de terre, et environ quatre cent hommes, tant des troupes de la marine que Canadiens. Les Ennemis au nombre de Vingt mille hommes de Milice de la nouvelle angleterre et cinq mille de troupes reglées de la Vielle, engagerent une affaire générale ou notre petit nombre a fait des prodiges de valeur et a obligé l'armée angloise à se retirer avec précipitation, et à neuf heures au matin le lendemain elle a — entierement évacué notre frontière et s'est retirée de l'autre côté du lac S. Sacrement, cette brillante victoire qui a Sauvé le Canada

Letter from François de Lévis, Second Commander of the Regular French troops, to the King of Poland, Carillon, 12 July 1758.

At Fort Carillon (south of Lake Champlain), the French forces were but "two thousand nine hundred French regulars and about four hundred others that included *troupes de la Marine* and Canadians. Nevertheless, this "small number worked wonders of valor and obliged the English [15,000 men] to beat a hasty retreat," leaving behind 2,000 dead and wounded.

Public Archives of Canada: Manuscript Division, MG 18, K 8, vol. 11, p. 243.

The London Gazette
EXTRAORDINARY.

Published by Authority.

TUESDAY, October 31, 1758.

Whitehall, October 31.

YESTERDAY a Mail arrived from New York, with Letters from Major General Abercromby to the Right Honourable Mr. Secretary Pitt, dated from the Camp at Lake George the 8th and 10th past, giving an Account, That Lieutenant Colonel Bradstreet, having proposed a Plan against Cadaraqui or Fort Frontenac, had been detached to make an Attempt on that Place, with a Body of Men consisting of 154 Regulars, 2491 Provincials, 27 of the Royal Regiment of Artillery, 61 Rangers, 300 Batteau-Men, and 70 Indians, in all 3103 Men, including Officers : And the following Copy of a Letter from Colonel Bradstreet to Major General Abercromby, dated Oswego, August 31, contains the Account of his Success in that very difficult and most important Enterprize.

" I Landed with the Troops within a
" Mile of Fort Frontenac, without
" Opposition, the 25th : The Garrison
" surrendered Prisoners of War the 27th,
" between Seven and Eight in the Morn-
" ing.—It was a square Fort of 100 Yards
" the exterior Side, and had in it 110
" Men, some Women, Children, and
" Indians; sixty Pieces of Cannon,
" (Half of which was mounted ;) Sixteen
" small Mortars ; with an immense Quan-
" tity of Provisions and Goods, to be
" sent to the Troops gone to oppose
" Brigadier General Forbes, their Western
" Garrisons, Indians, and to support the
" Army under the Command of M.
" Levy, on his intended Enterprize
" against the Mohawk River, valued by
" the French at 800,000 Livres.—We
" have likewise taken 9 Vessels from 8 to
" 18 Guns, which is all they have upon
" the Lake, two of which I have brought
" here; one richly laden ; and the rest
" and the Provisions I have burnt and
" destroyed, together with the Fort, Ar-
" tillery, Stores, &c. agreeable to your
" Excellency's Instructions, should I suc-
" ceed. The Garrison made no Scruple
" of saying, that their Troops to the
" Southward and Western Garrisons will
" suffer greatly, if not entirely starve,
" for Want of the Provisions and Vessels
" we have destroyed, as they have not
" any left to bring them Home from
" Niagara.
" The Terms on which the Garrison
" surrendered were Prisoners of War, un-
" til exchanged for equal Numbers and
" Rank."

(Price Two-pence Half-penny.)

Printed by *E. Owen* and *T. Harrison* in *Warwick Lane.* 1758.

The London Gazette, 31 October 1758.

According to Bradstreet, the capture of Fort Frontenac, on Lake Ontario, was a severe blow for the Canadians: "their troops to the southward and western garrisons will suffer greatly, if not entirely starve, for want of the provisions and vessels we have destroyed."

Queen's University Archives, Kingston.

Grenadier of the Régiment de Béarn carrying the regimental colour. Artist unknown. Watercolour: circa 1757–1762.

During the Seven Years' War the Ministry of the Marine increased its troops in the colonies. The Ministry of War supplied a certain number of battalions from the Régiment de Béarn and the Régiment du Languedoc, along with some from other provinces. French America could also count on its militiamen and its Indian allies.

Parks Canada, Ottawa.

IV

The conquest of Canada

The year 1759 marked the beginning of the end for the French in Canada. On 25 July Fort Niagara, on Lake Ontario, surrendered after vainly resisting for three weeks; the next day, in the Lake Champlain region, Louis-Philippe Le Dossu d'Hébécourt blew up the powder magazine at Fort Carillon; and on 31 July, in the face of Amherst's seemingly irresistible advance, François-Charles de Bourlamaque destroyed Fort Saint-Frédéric in the same way.

Now, since 23 June James Wolfe had been besieging Québec with a sizable fleet and army; he was applying a policy of pillaging the surrounding countryside and setting it afire; and from 12 July on he bombarded the town night and day, sowing death, destruction and confusion, without succeeding, however, in bringing the French troops out into the open as he was hoping. There seemed no way out of the situation, when he learned of the existence of a path by which he could ascend the cliff and take the town from the rear. During the night of 12–13 September he landed troops at Anse au Foulon and had them drawn up in battle order on the Plains of Abraham. In the morning the undue haste of the French resulted in a bitter defeat for them. On 18 September the town surrendered.

A few months after the brilliant but short-lived victory by François-Gaston, Chevalier de Lévis, at Sainte-Foy on 28 April 1760, Montréal, which was threatened by three army corps, surrendered on 8 September. The fall of this last centre of resistance led to the surrender of the whole colony and its occupation by the British army until 1764.

Portrait of William Pitt (1708–1778); William Hoare (1706–1792); oil on canvas; 1756.

Whereas France concentrated her forces in Europe, the British minister Pitt, who was in charge of conducting the war, directed the main effort to the colonies. According to him, taking America meant assuring Great Britain of supremacy on the sea and in trade, in other words supremacy world-wide.

Museum of Art, Carnegie Institute, Pittsburgh.

Donated by George Lauder.

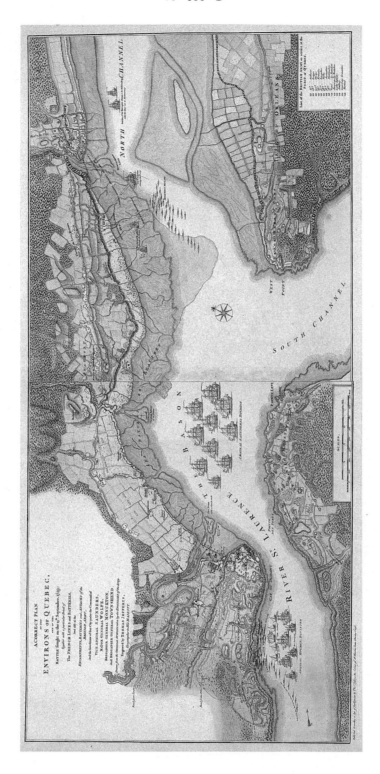

A Correct Plan of the Environs of Quebec . . . . Thomas Jefferys. London: Thomas Jefferys, [1760]. Map: hand coloured, 40.7 × 88.3 cm.

In Thomas Jefferys, *The American Atlas . . . .*, London: R. Sayer and J. Bennett, 1776.

This map shows the English and French positions on 13 September 1759, the day of the Battle of the Plains of Abraham. It serves to emphasize the importance of the forces who took part and the scale of the operations.

Public Archives of Canada, Ottawa: National Map Collection (NMC 54105).

Portrait of Louis-Joseph de Montcalm
(1712–1759), commander-in-chief of the
French forces during the siege of
Québec. Artist unknown. Oil on canvas.

Public Archives of Canada, Ottawa:
Picture Division (Negative no.
C-27665).

First and last pages of the terms of the
surrender of Québec signed by Charles
Saunders, George Townshend and Jean-
Baptiste-Nicolas-Roch de Ramezay,
Québec, 18 September 1759.

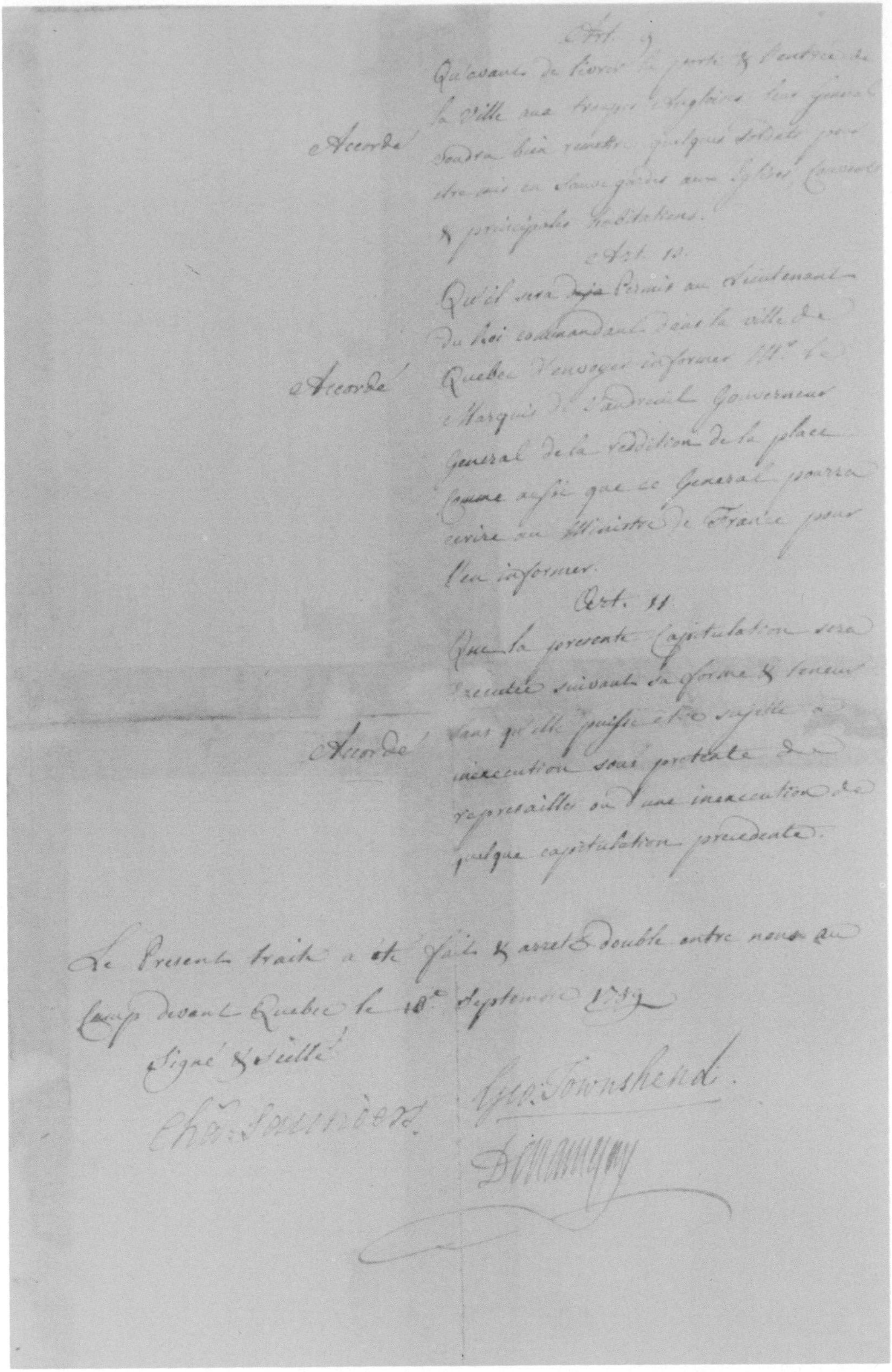

Accordé

Art. 9.
Qu'avant de livrer la porte & l'entrée de la ville aux troupes Anglaises leur général voudra bien remettre quelques soldats pour être mis en Sauvegardes aux Églises, Couvents & principales Habitations.

Art. 10.
Accordé

Qu'il sera permis au Lieutenant du Roi commandant dans la ville de Québec d'envoyer informer M^r le Marquis de Vaudreuil Gouverneur Général de la reddition de la place Comme aussi que ce Général pourra écrire au Ministre de France pour l'en informer.

Art. 11.
Accordé

Que la présente Capitulation sera exécutée suivant sa forme & teneur Sans qu'elle puisse être sujette à inexecution sous prétexte de représailles ou d'une inexécution de quelque capitulation précédente.

Le Présent traité a été fait & arrêté double entre nous au Camp devant Québec le 18e Septembre 1759.
Signé & scellé

Ch^s. Saunders.   Geo. Townshend.

De Ramzay

Archives nationales du Québec, Centre d'archives de Québec.

Photo Belvédère.

Portrait of James Wolfe (1727–1759), commander of the British expedition that took Québec in 1759. Attributed to Joseph Highmore (1692–1780). Oil on canvas, circa 1749.

Public Archives of Canada, Ottawa: Picture Division (Negative no. C-3916).

Copie /.

Articles de Capitulation Entre
Son Excellence Le General Amherst
Commandant en Chef Les Troupes &
forces de Sa Majesté Britanique En
L'Amerique Septentrionale, Et
Son Excellence Le Mis de Vaudreüil
Grand Croix de L'Ordre Royal, et
Militaire de S. Louis, Gouverneur et
Lieutenant Géneral pour Le Roy en
Canada.

Art: 1.er

Vingt quatre heures aprés La
Signature de la présente Capitulation,
Le Général Anglois fera prendre par
Les Troupes de Sa Majesté Britanique
possession des Portes de La Ville de
Montreal et La Garnison Angloise
ne poura y Entrer qu'aprés L'Evacua-
tion des Troupes Françoises.

Toute La Garnison de Montreal,
doit mettre bas les Armes, et ne
servira point pendant la presente
Guerre; immediatement aprés la
Signature de la presente, les Troupes
du Roy prendront possession des
Portes, et poseront les Gardes necessaires
pour maintenir le bon Ordre dans
La Ville.

Art: 2.

Les Troupes et les Milices qui seront
en Garnison dans La Ville de Montreal,
En Sortiront par la Porte de
avec tous les honeurs de la Guerre, Six
Pieces de Canon, et Un Mortier, qui
seront Chargés dans Le Vaisseau où
Le Marquis de Vaudreüil Embarquera
avec dix Coups à tirer par Piece.
Il En sera Usé de même pour la
Garnison des trois Rivieres pour les
honeurs de la Guerre.

Art

Terms of the surrender of Montréal
signed by Vaudreuil and Jeffery
Amherst, Montréal, 8 September 1760.

Public Record Office, London: Series
C.O. 5, vol. 58, pt. 3, p. 166.

aux délices 6 Septbre 1762

Lettres inédittes de Voltaire

Si je ne voulois que faire entendre ma voix
monseigneur, je me tairais dans la crise des
affaires ou vous etes. mais j'entends les voix de
beaucoup d'étrangers; touttes disent qu'on doit vous
bénir si vous faittes la paix a quelque prix que
ce soit. permettez moy donc monseigneur de
vous en faire mon compliment. je suis comme
le public, j'aime beaucoup mieux la paix
que le canada : et je crois que la france peut
etre heureuse sans quebec. vous nous donnez
précisément ce dont nous avons besoin. nous
vous devons des actions de grace. recevez
en attendant avec votre bonté ordinaire le
profond respect de voltaire —————

Letter from Voltaire, 6 September 1762.

"I am like the public. I much prefer peace to Canada, and I believe that France can be happy without Québec." Voltaire was right: the ceding to England of a colony that had a bad reputation throughout France (it was considered expensive and unproductive) would not give rise to many protests in the kingdom.

Public Archives of Canada, Ottawa: Manuscript Division, MG 18, A 3.

V

Economy

The king would one day explain to the colonial authorities the distinction between "special policy" and "general policy"; the latter, which rested with the governor general and the intendant, aimed at "increasing the population, the amount of land under cultivation and trade." But at the beginning of the eighteenth century this program might well have seemed extremely difficult to carry out.

To begin with, the War of the Spanish Succession exhausted France's financial resources and prompted the king and the minister to reduce expenditures in the colony; soon the State was incapable of paying for the goods and services that it obtained for itself in Canada; combined with the normal rise in shipping costs in time of war, this temporary insolvency caused uncontrollable inflation in the entire territory that was disastrous for trade, as well as a financial crisis that was only resolved in the period between 1716 and 1720. The State then withdrew playing-card money, which it redeemed at half its face value: the Canadians lost tidy sums of money in that operation.

The financial crisis was made still worse by the precarious nature of the fur trade: saturation of the European market had led the king to do away with fur-trading licences in 1696; it had also caused a drop in the prices offered for Canadian beaver, the elimination of *castor gras* and, naturally, a decided drop in demand. To keep their businesses going, Canadian tradesmen turned in large numbers to trading illegally with New England and New York, where Albany became an active smuggling centre. The result of all this was the bankruptcy of the Compagnie de la Colonie, which had been set up in the early years of the century.

After the War of the Spanish Succession had ended, and for a period of about thirty years, the colony would enjoy peace, which would bring it the security and stability needed for its economic growth, all the more so since, after the peace of Montréal in 1701, it no longer had to fear the Iroquois, who had held up settlement greatly in the previous century. Furthermore, the notable increase in population in those three decades was going to lead many enterprising men to give up agriculture (which was not very profitable) and the fur trade (which could not absorb all the available manpower) in favour of seeking other means of prospering, such as fishing, the lumbering industry, shipbuilding and trading among the colonies.

Besides, as early as 1714 and 1715 demand for Canadian beaver pelts — and gradually for other furs — increased with the result that little by little beaver lost its relative importance compared to that in the seventeenth century. No time was lost, therefore, in re-establishing the fur-trading licences. Two factors were going to work powerfully in favour of the fur trade: exploration in the Northwest, particularly by the La Vérendryes, who established numerous trading posts there; and the building of a network of military forts (which most often were also trading posts) intended to prevent economic and territorial expansion by the English into the Great Lakes region, the Upper Mississipi and the Ohio country.

Once the impetus had been given, the colony had the good luck to have at its head in the 1730s and 1740s an active and intelligent intendant, Gilles Hocquart, who endeavoured, supported by an enlightened minister, Jean-Frédéric Phélypeaux, Comte de Maurepas, to diversify the Canadian economy, and who was of great assistance to Canadians already engaged in the operation. Often under Hocquart's urging, Maurepas, for whom the colonies and sea-borne trade were a source of enrichment and power for France, facilitated trade between Canada, Île Royale and the West Indies; he gave subsidies to certain Canadian undertakings and granted privileges to Canadian traders and entrepreneurs, ordered the purchase on the king's account of Canadian products, had large warships built at Québec and agreed to the takeover by the State of the Forges du Saint-Maurice, ironworks that private interests had not been able to keep running at a profit.

Unfortunately the best of efforts were not always crowned with success in this colony, at grips with a certain number of chronic problems, among them lack of capital, scarcity and dearness of manpower, particularly of specialized manpower, the great distance from overseas markets, the closing of navigation for six months of the year, and the high costs of transport and of maritime insurance. In addition the home authorities, being overly sensitive to the kingdom's needs, sometimes made bad judgments concerning the colony's possibilities; in the shipbuilding area, for example, the kinds of wood found in Canada were hardly suitable for building large warships. To that was added the fact that not all Canadian merchants had a liking for adventure: the fur trade entailed few risks, while being profitable, and the majority preferred to stay with it. A similar attitude could be seen amongst the farmers: the smallness of the home market and the risks of overseas trade scarcely incited them to produce much more than what was sufficient for their own needs.

V

The resumption of war and some bad harvests one after another in the 1740s slowed down or suspended activity in several industrial and commercial undertakings. A peace economy was succeeded by a war economy in which the State greatly increased its expenditures for military purposes in the colony — particularly during the 1750s. Many entrepreneurs and tradesmen who were suppliers to the State, and even government officials and military officers, took advantage of this to make their fortune — often dishonestly — out of public funds.

In fact, despite some successes, on the economic level the period of French rule in Canada in the eighteenth century remains a striking illustration of the fundamental impotence of all the colonies in New France. Versailles wanted these colonies to serve the immediate interests of the mother country exclusively, whereas the colonies were often a prey to the greed of local government officials.

The Canadian merchants organize

At the beginning of the eighteenth century the merchants in the colony, becoming more and more aware of their common interests, began to organize themselves and take their affairs in hand.

At Québec for example, some 80 merchants and notables of the colony ratified on 10 October 1700 the transactions that had been concluded earlier in France by their delegate, Antoine Pascaud. This solemn deed, which the governor general, the intendant, the two bishops and the procurators of all the religious orders in Canada also signed, marked the creation of the Compagnie de la Colonie, which was mostly made up of merchants living in the colony.

In a political regime under which any public meeting that was not authorized by the governor and the intendant was considered a seditious act, the merchants nonetheless obtained in 1708 the creation at Québec of a *bourse*, an organism similar to our boards of trade, and in 1717 permission was granted merchants in Québec and Montréal to meet every day in a suitable place to carry on their business.

The new-found solidarity of these merchants, who unabashedly asserted themselves as Canadians, led them to fight against the competition of the non-resident merchants, who did not share the country's expenses but who came from La Rochelle, Bordeaux and other port cities in France every year, carrying off through their trading a good part of the profits realized in the colony.

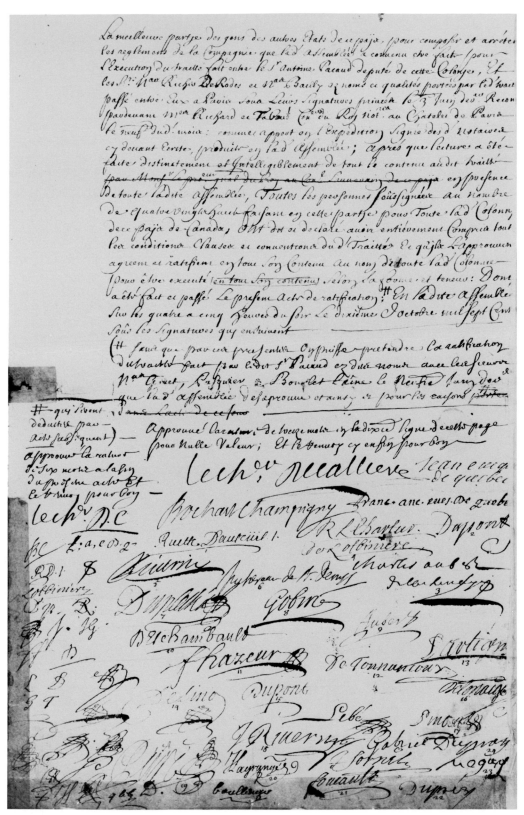

Ratification by the settlers in Canada of the conventions concluded in France between their representative Pascaud and the beaver tax-farmers, Québec, 10 October 1700.

The conventions with the beaver tax-farmers were approved by "the undersigned (governor general, intendant, bishop, merchants, etc.) to the number of eighty-eight acting on this part for all of the aforementioned colony of this country of Canada." The Canadians thus acquired the monopoly of the sale of beaver in France and Holland. Five days later they founded the Compagnie de la Colonie.

Public Archives of Canada, Ottawa: Manuscript Division, MG 18, C 3.

Letter from the Intendants Raudot to the minister, Québec, 15 November 1708.

"We have the honour to inform you that the merchants of this town [Québec] have established a *bourse*; they have clubbed together to pay for the house that they have rented for that purpose . . . ."

Archives nationales, Paris: Fonds des Colonies, série C[11A], vol. 28, fol. 300-300v.

Photo Studio Littré.

Decree from the king's Conseil d'État allowing the "merchants to meet every day . . . in each of the aforementioned towns of Québec and Montréal, there to conduct their trading business, and to appoint one of them in each of the aforementioned towns to make in the name of all of them the representations that will be necessary for the benefit of their trading," Paris, 11 May 1717.

The merchants had begun to meet well before this decree that authorized them to do so. On occasion they delegated one of their members to meet with the authorities, either in the colony or in the mother country, to defend their interests.

Archives nationales, Paris: Fonds des Colonies, série B, vol. 39, fol. 203.

Photo Studio Littré.

Troisième. POUR *accepté pourpan renvaller pour* 1331

A Québec, le *pr* Octobre 17 58.

EXERCICE 17 58. MONSIEUR, au *Dix huit avril prochain*

N.° 45. il vous plaira payer par cette troisième de Change, ma première ou

seconde ne l'étant, à l'ordre de M. *de Ramezay*

la somme de *sept cent vingt livres*

valeur reçûe en acquits. De laquelle somme je vous rendrai compte sur

les dépenses de la Marine de cette Colonie. Je suis,

Monsieur,

*VU par nous Intendant
de la nouvelle France.*

Votre très-humble & très-
obéissant serviteur,

A MONSIEUR

Monsieur *Perichon*
Trésorier général des Colonies.
rue Neuve S. Eustache
A PARIS.

Bill of exchange drawn on the "treasurer general of the Colonies" and payable "to the order of M. de Ramezay," signed Bigot and Imbert, Québec, 1 October 1758.

In New France there were numerous ways of making payment. There were, for example, bills of exchange, specie, playing-card money and letters of credit. Sometimes payment was also made in kind (grain, furs, goods) or in services.

Public Archives of Canada, Ottawa: Manuscript Division, MG 18, H 54, vol. 3, p. 1331.

V

Furs and fish

In the eighteenth century, as in the preceding one, furs — particularly beaver furs — were perceived as the most important exportable Canadian resource. If the fur trade were threatened, then the entire colony would be visibly rocked. Furs, the economic prize for the rival powers in North America, had also become through the years a military prize of prime importance.

The trade, which was conducted far from Québec and Montréal and which called for the services of the Indians, the coureurs de bois, and to a certain degree the garrison commanders, was very difficult to control, all the more so as the very people on whom the responsibility fell often manipulated situations for their own personal gain, in defiance of orders from the king and the minister.

Fish constituted another essential resource. If we are to believe the king himself, it was first of all to ensure her hold on this resource that France occupied and fortified Cap-Breton after the Treaty of Utrecht. Indeed, fishermen were able to keep on coming every year looking for cod, but also for seals, porpoises and walrus, in the gulf, which Canadian fishermen also frequented. Other Canadians fished closer to Québec, while others again worked fishing grounds on the Labrador coast; but the greatest concentration of fishermen in America was to be found on Île Royale and Newfoundland.

Des castors du Canada. Vignette taken from [Map of North and South America]. Nicolas de Fer, Paris: Chez l'auteur, 1698. Map: hand coloured, 90.9 × 118.0 cm.

More than two thirds of Canada's yearly exports consisted of skins and pelts: beaver, moose, bear, deer, otter, marten, fox, mink and others.

Public Archives of Canada, Ottawa: National Map Collection (NMC 26825).

pour eux et sans estre coupables ayans resolu de retablir
leurs vingt cinq congés qui se donnoient par le passé, mais en
mesme temps d'assujetir ceux a qui ils seront accordés de faire
la Traitte seulement dans les postes où ils auront permission
de monter afin qu'estant dans ces endroits sous leurs ordres
des Commandants ils ne puissent tomber dans les mesmes
desordres que par le passé, Nous avons resolu aussy
de faire distribuer ces congés aux pauvres familles, A
ces Causes et autres a ce nous mouvans, de l'avis de
nostre tres cher et tres amé Oncle, le Duc d'Orleans Regent,
de nostre tres cher et tres amé cousin le Duc de Bourbon,
de nostre tres cher et tres amé oncle le Duc du Maine, de nostre
tres cher et tres amé oncle Le Comte de Toulouse et autres
Pairs de France grands et Notables personnages de
nostre Royaume, et de nostre certaine Science pleine puissance
et autorité Royalles.

I

Nous avons dit Statué et ordonné, Disons Statuons et
ordonnons Voulons et nous Plaist qu'à l'avenir il soit accordé
tous les ans par nostre Gouverneur et Lieutenant general en
la nouvelle france Vingt cinq congés, pour aller faire la Traite
avec les Sauvages dans les Postes qui seront marqués par
leurs permissions.

2.

Ces Congés qui seront signés par l'Intendant audit pays seront
donnés par nostre dit Gouverneur et Lieutenant general aux pauvres
familles du Canada qu'il jugera en avoir le plus be
soin

Declaration by the king stating that every year the governor general would grant "twenty-five licences for going to trade with the Indians in the posts," Paris, 28 April 1716.

The recovery that was getting under way in the fur trade after a long period of saturation of the European market made possible the re-establishment of the trading licences, the re-opening of former trading posts and the creation of new ones. It was hoped that in this way relations could be restored with various Indian tribes in the West, and the expansion of the English checked.

Archives nationales, Paris: Fonds des Colonies, série B, vol. 38, fol. 236.

Photo Studio Littré.

les parties de l'amerique Septentrionale d'est —
aujourd'huy fort Eloigné de la Colonie peuplée —
ou il ne s'en trouve que peu — Les Postes —
d'ou il en vient une grande quantité sont ceux —
du Lac alepimigon, Cumunistigoya, la pointe
de Chagdamigon dans le Lac Superieur ; —
michilimakinac, la Baye, aux Sioux, le —
Poste de la mer d'Ouest, temiscamingue et les —
terres du Domaine de Tadoussac, Il en a esté
receu dans les Bureaux de la Compagnie des Indes —
en Canada pendant l'année derniere 185. Q.
Les anglois doivent tirer du Canada même —
une bien plus grande quantité de cette —
marchandise ; les Sauvages les plus Eloignez
la leur apportent a chouaguen ou ils sont
attirés par la distribution de l'eau de vie —
que les Anglois leur debitent Sans mesure. —
La Passion que les Sauvages ont pour cette —
boisson en connüe, cependant il faut convenir —
que ce n'est pas la le Seul motif qui les Engage
a aller chéz les anglois, ils y trouvent a —
bien meilleur Compte les Marchandises dont
ils ont besoin, et les anglois leur donnent —
un prix du Castor bien au dessus de celuy que
les francois leur donnent — La difference est
de plus d'un tiers en Sus. il Seroit a Souhaiter —
que la Compagnie des Indes püt augmenter le —
prix du Castor Si Elle y trouvoit Encor Son profit —

Report from Intendant Hocquart, 1737.

After mentioning several French posts from which came "a great quantity" of furs, Hocquart admitted that many Indians preferred to go to trade at Chouaguen (Oswego), on Lake Ontario: "They are drawn there by the distribution of spirits that the English sell them in unlimited quantities . . . they find the goods they need there at much lower prices, and the English offer them a price for beaver that is much above what the French give them . . . ."

Archives nationales, Paris: Fonds des Colonies, série C^{11A}, vol. 67, fol. 100v.

Photo Studio Littré.

Monsieur

Vous Etes Jnformé que quelques Négociants
dela Nouvelle angleterre prennent L'habitude
de venir toutes les années a Montréal munis
de Vos Passeports, mais je doûte que vous Soyés
jnstruits qu'ils n'y viennent que pour former
des Liaisons de Commerce auec les Marchands
françois qui y Sont Etablis; Malgré la bonne
jntelligence qui regne Entre les deux Couronnes,
jl n'a pas Encore plû a nos Maitres d'Etablir
Entre Elles vn Commerce réciproque, au
contraire jls le déffendent absolument, ainsy
pour obeïr aux ordres du Roy Mon Maitre
je ne puis me dispenser de Renvoyer les
Marchands Angloin qui se présenteront pour

Letter from Governor General de Beauharnois to the Governor of New England, Montréal, 20 June 1738.

Even if the authorities in the mother country "absolutely [forbade] it," the Canadians carried on a lot of trade with the British colonies. They brought furs there and returned with blankets, clothing, yard goods and various other products. Part of the trading was carried out through the mediation of the resident Indians. Moreover, "merchants from New England [and New York] made a habit of coming to Montreal every year," under various pretexts, but in fact "to form commercial ties with the French merchants."

Public Archives of Canada, Ottawa: Manuscript Division, MG 18, G 6.

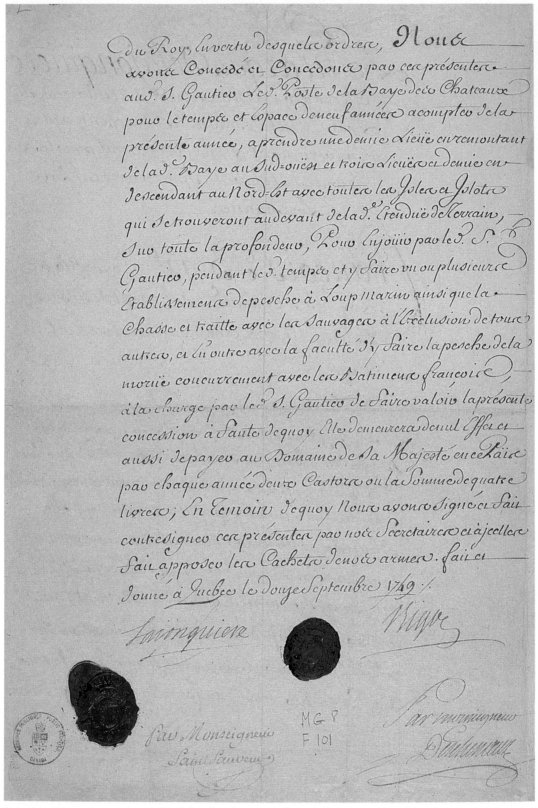

Grant of the Baie des Châteaux post in Labrador to Jean-François Gaultier, investing him with the right, to the exclusion of all others, to "fish for seals as well as to hunt and trade with the Indians, and furthermore with the right to fish for cod there," Québec, 12 September 1749.

In Labrador there were in certain years more than a thousand Frenchmen and Canadians who fished or engaged in trading with the Indians and Eskimoes.

Public Archives of Canada, Ottawa: Manuscript Division, MG 8, F 101.

33

cables et cordages necessaires et une manufacture
de toilles à Voiles dont on auroit besoin pour les
Vaisseaux de sa Majesté, qui s'y construiroient
y ayant actuellement une forge aux trois rivieres
pour le compte du Roy qui produit du fer qui est
aussi beau que celui d'Espagne, on n'auroit rien a
desirer pour l'accomplissement du service, et en cas
de guerre on ne seroit pas exposé à perdre les
agrès qui s'envoyent de France comme cela s'est
vû dans la derniere guerre.

Les Negotiants de Quebec Envoyent à la
pesche des Morues; dont ils font aussi un grand
Commerce, cette pesche se fait aux Environs de l'Isle
de terre Neuve dans le golfe du Canada, et dans
le bas du Fleuve St Laurent, comme il sera expliqué
cy aprés. dans les mêmes lieux se font les
pesches des marsouins et des loups marins qui
fournissent une grande quantité d'huile de Poissons
on y fait aussy la pesche des Vaches marines qui
ont deux dents ou crocs a la machoire superieure
gros environ comme le bras, et long d'un pied et
quelques pouces, elles s'en aident pour Grimper
Sur les rochers, on Employe ces dents comme

Report on "the present state of Canada," prepared by Nicolas-Gaspard Boucault, 1754.

"The Québec merchants send people off to the cod fishing, in which they also have a large trade. This fishing is done around the island of Newfoundland in the gulf of Canada and in the lower St. Lawrence . . . . fishing is carried on in the same places for porpoises and seals, which supply a large quantity of fish oils . . . ."

34

d'yvoire, on pesche aussi dans le golfe du Canada des
maquereaux qui sont fort bons ; on y faisoit autrefois
et dans le bas du fleuve la pesche des baleines, mais
on n'y en voit presque plus. les barques ont pourtant
recommencé cette pesche aux Sept Isles avec assé de
Succés depuis 1730. jusqu'en 1745. que la guerre les
a obligé de se retirer.

On fait dans le Fleuve jusqu'à 20 ou 30 lieues
au dessous de Quebec, une pesche très abondante
de harangs et de Sardines, pendant le printemts
et L'automne, on y pesche aussi et dans les rivieres
qui s'y dechargent, des Saumons, des Alozes, des
carpes, des brochets, des truittes, des Barbües, des
Eperlans, des poissons Dorés, des poissons blancs,
des bars, des Achigans, des masquinongés, des
Esturgeons et des Anguilles.

Le Pays est abondant en toute Espece de
Gibier a poil et a plume, a l'Exception du Lapin
n'y en ayant que de Domestiques ; les perdrix
qui sont une espece de gelinottes de bois et les
outardes y sont fort communs, outre les canards
ordinaires il y en a qui se branchent qu'on Nomme canards
branchus ; ils sont Excellents et d'un très beau
plumage. on trouve encore dans les pays d'enhaut

Public Archives of Canada, Ottawa:
Manuscript Division, MG 18, J 8,
pp. 33–34.

Factories and large-scale industries

The mercantilism practised by France had resulted in her always being opposed to the establishment in Canada of factories that would have competed with those in the mother country. Action was to be taken so that "everything that this country produce[d] [would be] taken to France for manufacturing there." In 1736, for example, it happened that the king forbade the making of "hats of any sort whatsoever" in the colony, and ordered in consequence the destruction of any "fulling benches" that might be found there.

Consequently the production was encouraged of raw materials, which were destined in part for the mother country, and also of materials (boards, joists, planks) for internal needs as well as for the overseas trade, and of products (tar, cordage, iron fittings) needed in shipbuilding.

For Canada, after all, had its large-scale industry in the 1730s: shipbuilding and the Forges du Saint-Maurice. But from 1740 on shipbuilding was almost completely a State monopoly, and it did not have the success that had been anticipated; large-scale industry, whose operation was at first entrusted to private interests, was saved from bankruptcy only after it had been taken over by the State in 1743.

Letter from Pontchartrain, minister of the Marine, to the Intendants Raudot, Versailles, 30 June 1707.

As every colony must first serve to make the kingdom wealthy, "it is not too advisable . . . that manufactories be established in Canada . . . . a course of action must be followed so that what that country produces is brought to France to be manufactured." The authorities in the mother country, however, favoured those industries that corresponded to the needs of the kingdom "without doing any harm" to its manufactories.

Archives nationales, Paris: Fonds des Colonies, série B, vol. 29, fol. 68v-69.

Photo Studio Littré.

Ordinance by Governor General de Beauharnois and Intendant Hocquart "to forbid all hat-making" in Canada and "as a consequence to have the fulling benches that exist in this country destroyed," Québec, 6 September 1736.

It was the king who insisted upon these measures "for the maintenance of the manufactories in the kingdom and for the good of trade in general."

Archives nationales, Paris: Fonds des Colonies, série C¹¹A, vol. 65, fol. 3.

Photo Studio Littré.

Portrait presumed to be that of Marie-Charlotte Denys de La Ronde (1668–1742), wife of Claude de Ramezay. Saint-Marc Moutillet. Oil on canvas.

Several Canadian women ran industrial or commercial firms. Among others we find Madame de Ramezay, who operated a sawmill, a brick factory and a tile works; her daughter Louise, who was the owner of a flour mill, a tannery and sawmills; Madame de Repentigny, who set up a factory for making canvases and fabrics; and Madame Fornel, who, in addition to operating the Tadoussac

trading posts, started a pottery works.

Musée du Château Ramezay, Montréal.

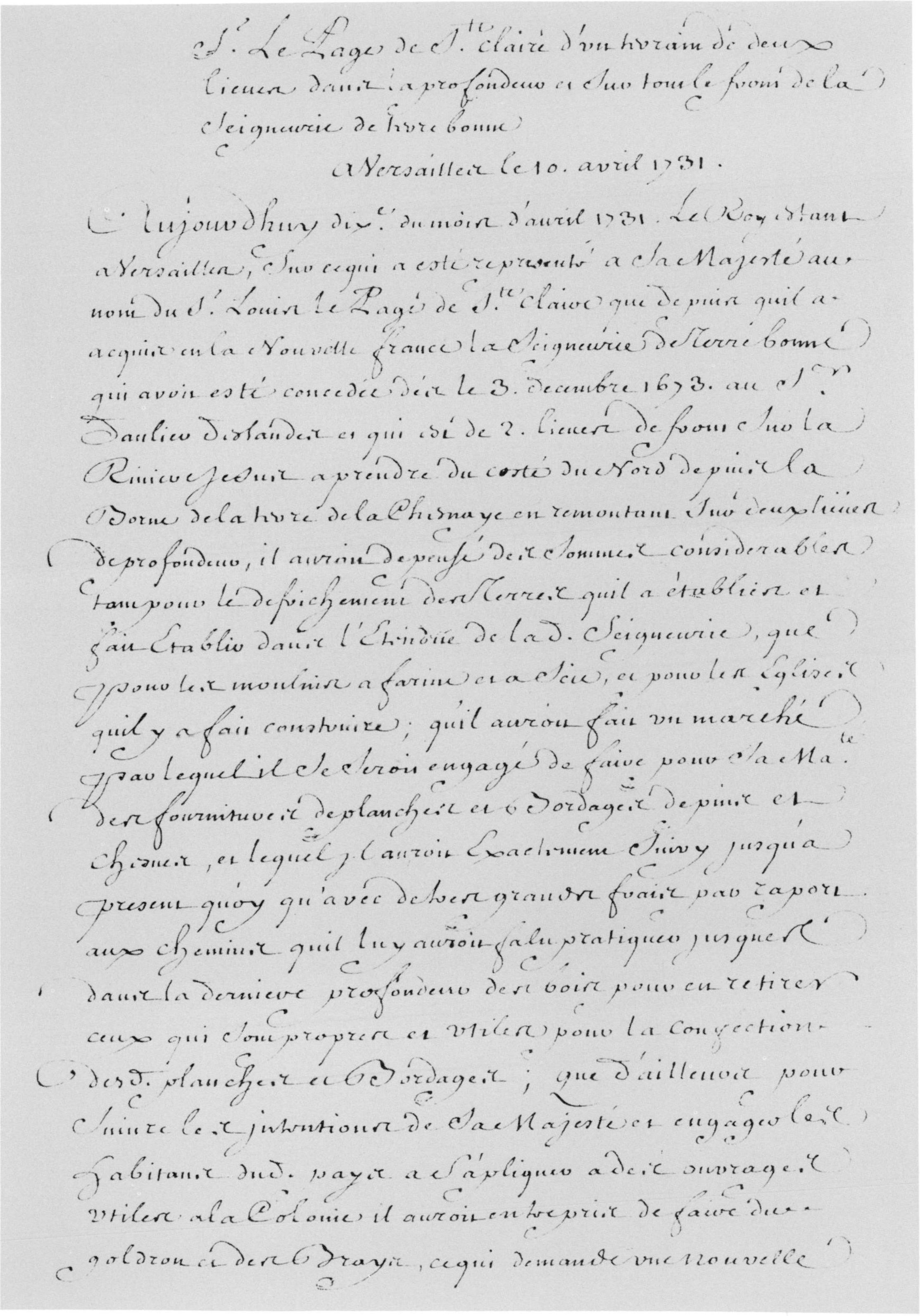

[Handwritten manuscript in 18th-century French cursive]

Sr Le Page de Ste Claire d'un terrain de deux
lieues dans la profondeur et sur tout le front de la
Seigneurie de Terrebonne

À Versailles le 10. avril 1731.

Aujourd'huy dix.e du mois d'avril 1731. Le Roy étant
à Versailles, Sur ce qui a esté representé à Sa Majesté au
nom du Sr Louis Le Page de Ste Claire que depuis qu'il a
acquis en la Nouvelle France la Seigneurie de Terrebonne
qui avoit esté concedée dès le 3. decembre 1673. au Sr
Daulier Deslandes et qui est de 2. lieues de front sur la
Riviere Jesus à prendre du costé du Nord depuis la
borne de la terre de la Chesnaye en remontant Sur deux lieues
de profondeur, il auroit depensé des Sommes considerables
tant pour le defrichement des Terres qu'il a établies et
fait établir dans l'Etendüe de la d. Seigneurie, que
pour les moulins à farine et à Scie, et pour les Eglises
qu'il y a fait construire; qu'il auroit fait un marché
par lequel il se seroit engagé de faire pour Sa Maté
des fournitures de planches et Bordages de pin et
chesne, et lequel il auroit Exactement Suivy jusqu'à
present quoy qu'avec de bien grands frais par raport
aux chemins qu'il luy auroit falu pratiquer jusques
dans la derniere profondeur des bois pour en retirer
ceux qui sont propres et utiles pour la Confection
des d. planches et Bordages; que d'ailleurs pour
Suivre les intentions de Sa Majesté et engager les
habitans dud. pays à S'appliquer à des ouvrages
utiles à la Colonie il auroit entrepris de faire du
goldron et des Brays, ce qui demande une nouvelle

Grant to Abbé Louis Lepage de Sainte-Claire of a piece of land adjoining his seigneury of Terrebonne, Versailles, 10 April 1731.

Lepage de Sainte-Claire was one of the most dynamic of Canadian entrepreneurs. He "has spent considerable sums on clearing the lands that he has settled and is having settled in the whole area of the aforementioned seigneury, as well as for the flour and saw mills and the churches that he has had built on it." He had "undertaken to supply His Majesty with supplies of pine and oak boards and planks."

Archives nationales, Paris: Fonds des Colonies, série B, vol. 55, fol. 546v.

Photo Studio Littré.

"Royal warrant as builder of the king's ships in Canada," granted to René-Nicolas Levasseur, 1 April 1743.

In the period from 1715 to 1738, private enterprise in the Government of Québec (the territory extending from Les Éboulements to Grondines and from Deschaillons to Rimouski) had built some forty merchant vessels "of between 50 and 300 tons burden." In the period from 1739 to 1759 the king had about fifteen warships built there, seven of them of more than 500 tons, and it was Levasseur who directed the operations.

Public Archives of Canada, Ottawa: Manuscript Division, MG 18, H 58.

luy remboursement pour l'ouverture et Exploitation desd.
hoirie non cultivées, comme aussy quil luy Soit permis
de faire tirer, prise et retirer d'Eaux necessaire &c.
alad. Entreprise dans les Endroits les plus commodes
aux offrir quil fait defaire ouvrir lesd. Mines dans
l'espace de deux années prochaines, et Sa Majesté
estant pleinement informée de la connoissance et experience
dud. Sr. Poulin defrancheville al'ouverture des
Mines et voulant legratiffier et traitter favorablement
Sa Majesté luy a accordé et accorde la permission tant
pour luy que pour Ses heritiers ou ayant cause de
faire l'ouverture desd. Mines de fer dans l'Etendue de
pays qui Se borne depuis et compris la Seigneurie
d'yamachiche jusques et compris la Seigneurie du Cap
delaMadelaine et deles faire fouiller et travailler a Son
proffit al'Exclusion detous autres et d'y faire construire
les forges, fourneaux et autres Ouvrages q. conviendra
pendant les. Temps de 20. années consecutives Seulement
a compter dujour del'ouverture desd. Mines quil Sera
tenu de faire dans l'espace de 2. Années prochaines
dujour del'Enregistrement dupresent brevet au Conseil
Superieur dequebec Sans queles proprietaires des
Terres Sur lesquelles lesd. Mines Seront ouvertes
puissent y rien pretendre ala charge deleur rembourser
Seulement le prix desd. hoirie qui Se Donneront.

King's warrant authorizing François Poulin de Francheville "to open up" some "iron mines" on his seigneury of Saint-Maurice and the surrounding area and "to have the ironworks, furnaces and other appropriate works built there," Versailles, 25 March 1730.

After they were taken over by the State in 1743, the Forges du Saint-Maurice enjoyed a certain period of rapid progress; various products were manufactured there: stoves, pots, cannons, cannonballs, iron fittings for ships, axes, nails and so on.

Archives nationales, Paris: Fonds des Colonies, série B, vol. 54, fol. 486v.

Photo Studio Littré.

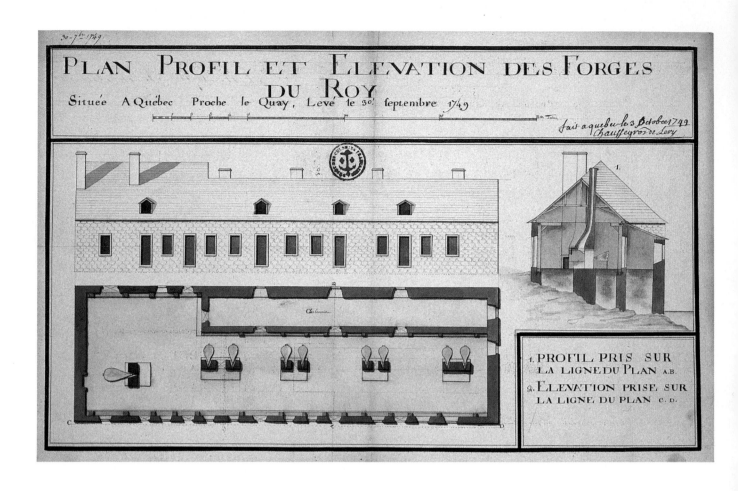

"Plan, profile and elevation of the Forges du Roi . . . ." Gaspard-Joseph Chaussegros de Léry. 3 October 1749. Plan: col. ms., 26.8 × 44.1 cm.

A furnace, in which would be cast the pieces needed for building the king's ships, was built at the Cul-de-Sac shipbuilding yard.

Archives nationales, Paris: Section Outre-Mer, Dépôt des fortifications des colonies, Amérique septentrionale, 427 C.

Photo Studio Littré.

53

de ces Endroits.

Il est vray que les habitans de cette colonie et laplûpart des négociants domiciliés se portent naturellement a la construction, mais lamain d'oeuvre y est si cherie, et les habitans sipeu opulens qu'ils ne peuvent pas faire de grandes Entreprises.

Nous avons l'honneur d'être avec un très profond respect;

Monseigneur.

Quebec ce 25.e Octobre 1729.

Vos très humbles et très obeïssants Serviteurs.

Beauharnois   Hocquart

Letter from Governor General de Beauharnois and the financial commissary, Hocquart, to the minister, Québec, 25 October 1729.

Two factors, among others, were often mentioned to explain the weakness of the Canadian economy: " . . . labour is so expensive and the settlers have so little money that they cannot build up big enterprises."

Archives nationales, Paris: Fonds des Colonies, série C¹¹ᴬ, vol. 51, fol. 53.

Photo Studio Littré.

V

Communication and transportation

During the entire French regime transportation was mainly by means of the St. Lawrence and its tributaries. While there were small roads linking up the seigneuries fairly early, it was not until the 1730s that a road 24 feet wide was built on the north shore between Québec and Montréal. In 1737 the journey was already being made on horseback in four days. Bridges were built over all the rivers less than 40 feet wide; the others were crossed on large rafts.

Once the first "king's road" had been finished, the chief road officer, Jean-Eustache Lanoullier de Boisclerc, went to work on a second one in 1739, this time on the south shore. Starting at Montréal, it ran along the St. Lawrence and the Richelieu, passed through Fort Saint-Jean, and ended at Fort Saint-Frédéric, which was reached in 1747.

Thanks in large measure to Lanoullier's energetic efforts, around 1740 towns and seigneuries were provided with streets, roads and bridges that greatly facilitated the traffic of cartage wagons. Although generally stony and sometimes muddy, as several travellers noted, these roads were of considerable influence on the economy of the country, while permitting new regions to be opened up to settlement.

Letter from the chief road officer Lanoullier de Boisclerc to the minister concerning the construction of a route between Québec and Montréal, Québec, 17 October 1733.

"This work establishes communication by land from Québec to as far as Montréal, and the distance can at the present time be covered in four days by the same horse . . . . next year carriages will come and go between Québec and Montréal. Since this piece of work several settlers have taken up new grants both around the lake [Saint-Pierre] and at the back of the neighbouring seigneuries."

Archives nationales, Paris: Fonds des Colonies, série C¹¹ᴬ, vol. 60, fol. 379-379v.

Photo Studio Littré.

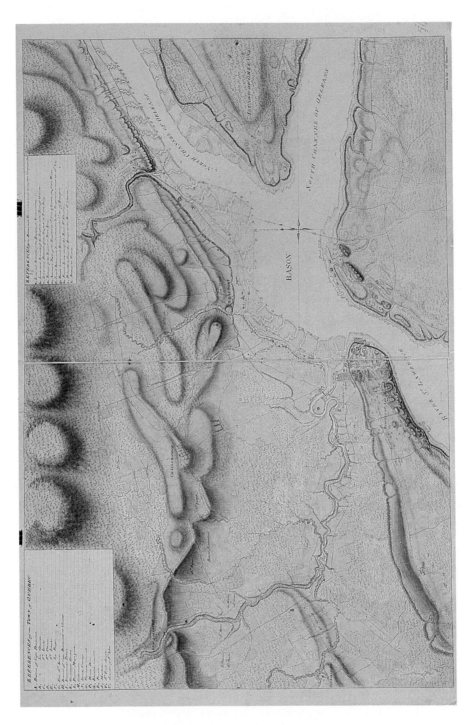

[Murray's map, the immediate region of Québec. 1761]. Map: col. ms., 94.6 × 62.3 cm.

In "Plan of Canada or the Province of Quebec from the uppermost Settlements to the Island of Coudre as survey'd by order of His Excellency Governor Murray in the year 1760. 61 & 62 . . . . " (Page EM).

In the middle of the eighteenth century, Canada had a good number of roads used by horses, carriages, wagons, sleighs and sleds. This map shows part of the road network in the Québec region. Roads are indicated by brown lines.

Public Archives of Canada, Ottawa: National Map Collection (NMC 10842).

V

Sea-borne trade

Every year many ships crossed the Atlantic laden with a wide variety of goods and products from the mother country and destined for local consumption or the fur trade, and cast anchor off Québec. Some of them returned directly to France with a full cargo of pelts, while others carried Canadian products to Île Royale or the West Indies.

Canada, however, did not export only furs; it supplied the garrison of Louisbourg and the settlers on Île Royale with flour and vegetables. But it also supplied the French West Indies not only with flour and peas, but also with salt and dried cod, fish oils, boards, planks, lathing and shingles, stave wood, tiles and bricks, and sometimes even horses. Most often, it is true, the Canadian exporters unloaded their cargoes at Île Royale, where local businessmen took charge of sending them to the West Indies, while pocketing the best part of the profits.

Although it was relatively small, this overseas trade nonetheless gave a stimulus to Canadian agriculture: production increased appreciably through the years, flour mills and sawmills multiplied, and above all, after having long been satisfied with subsistence farming, the Canadian habitant understood that it was to his interest to diversify his activities.

Letter from Intendant Hocquart to the minister, Québec, 15 October 1735.

Hocquart was sending to France "about 400 barrels of tar supplied by the settlers of Baie Saint-Paul, Rivière Oüelle and Chambly . . . 5,000 boards and 272 planks of pine and spruce . . . [and] 60 barrels of fish oil from the Tadoussac trading concession."

Archives nationales, Paris: Fonds des Colonies, série C¹¹ᴬ, vol. 64, fol. 87v.

Photo Studio Littré.

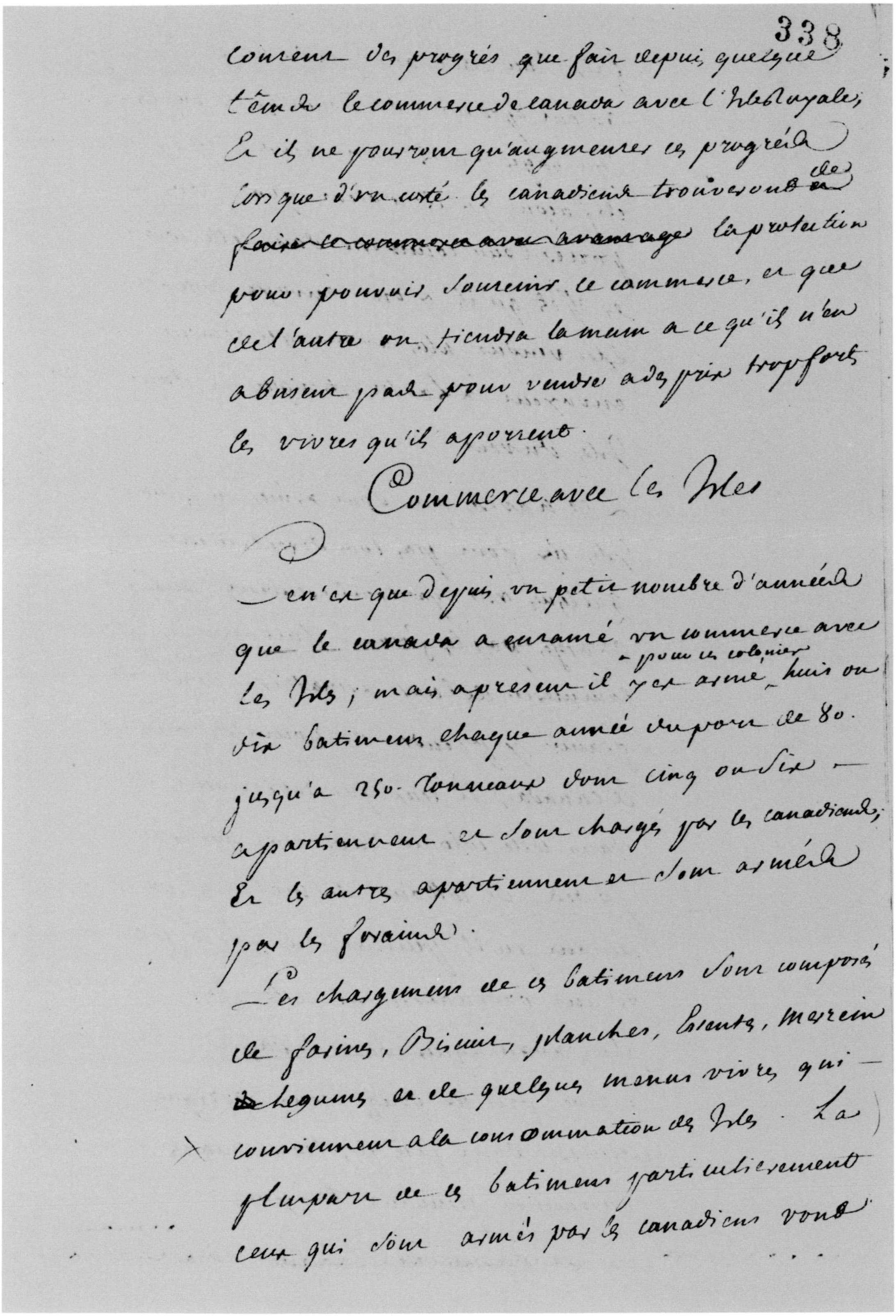
338

contenu des progrès que fait depuis quelque
tems le commerce de canada avec l'Isle Royale;
Et ils ne pourront qu'augmenter ces progrès
lorsque d'un costé les canadiens trouveront de
~~faire le commerce avec avantage~~ la protection
pour pouvoir soutenir le commerce, et que
de l'autre on tiendra la main a ce qu'ils n'en
abusent pas pour vendre a des prix trop forts
les vivres qu'ils aportent.

Commerce avec les Isles

Ce n'est que depuis un petit nombre d'années
que le canada a entamé un commerce avec
les Isles; mais apresent il y est armé pour ces colonies huit ou
dix batimens chaque année du port de 80.
jusqu'a 250. tonneaux dont cinq ou six
appartiennent et sont chargés par les canadiens;
Et les autres appartiennent et sont armés
par les forains.
Les chargemens de ces batimens sont composés
de farines, Biscuit, planches, Esentes, merrein
legumes et de quelques menus vivres qui
conviennent a la consommation des Isles. La
pluspart de ces batimens particulierement
ceux qui sont armés par les canadiens vont

"Memoir on Canada's trade," by Intendant Hocquart, 1741.

Canada was sending to the West Indies "eight or ten ships each year of 80 to 250 tons burden, of which five or six belong" to Canadians "and are loaded by [them] . . . . The cargoes of these ships consist of flour and various kinds of meal, biscuits, boards, shingles, stave wood, vegetables and some small items of food."

Archives nationales, Paris: Fonds des Colonies, série C[11A], vol. 76, fol. 338.

Photo Studio Littré.

Vous avez vû, Monseigneur, par
La Lettre de M Michel que le Commerce
Entre nous, L'jsle Royale et les jsles
de L'amerique a esté interrompu; qu'jl
Luy a esté impossible d'Envoyer a
L'jsle Royale La fourniture ord.re
de farines et de legumes ; jl a
feulement Envoyé au mois de
Juillet une partie des Legumes, Et
J'ay Envoyé le reste au mois de
Septembre dernier .

M Lenormant m'a'crû que
De concert avec M Des. Ovide jls
avoient détaché deux navires
de S.t Malo qui ont dû Estre de
retour le 20. Septembre dernier,
chargez de 4 a 5000. Quint.x de

Letter from Intendant Hocquart to the minister, Québec, 10 October 1738.

Periodical crises in agriculture disturbed the Canadian economy. In 1738, for example, because of the bad crops, trade with "Île Royale and the West Indies was interrupted," and "it was impossible to send to Île Royale the usual supply of flour and meals."

Archives nationales, Paris: Fonds des Colonies, série C¹¹A, vol. 70, fol. 12v.

Photo Studio Littré.

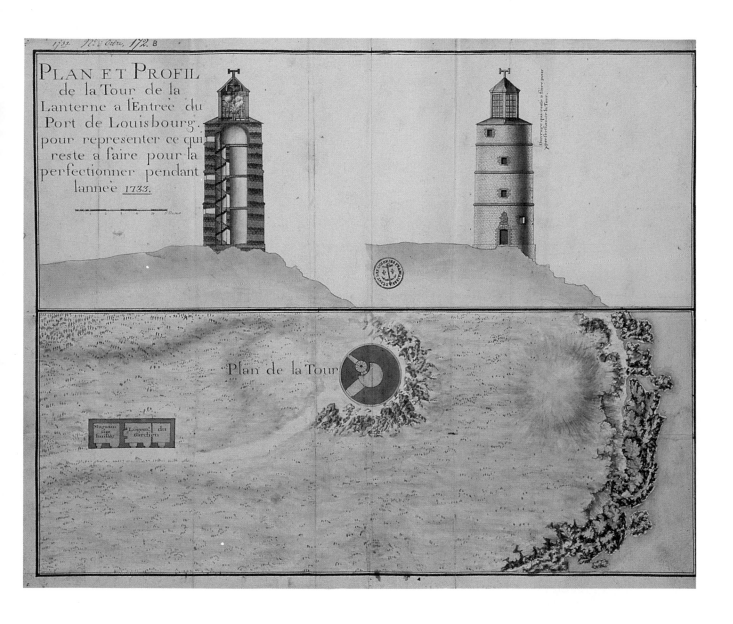

"Plan and profile of the lighthouse tower at the entrance to the port of Louisbourg . . . ." Étienne Verrier. [1733]. Plan: col. ms., 42.0 × 53.5 cm.

Louisbourg carried on trade with France, Canada, the West Indies, New England, and Nova Scotia. Through its location this town made it possible to increase exchanges between Canada and the West Indies by serving as a forwarding centre and trading warehouse for these two colonies.

Archives nationales, Paris: Section Outre-Mer, Dépôt des fortifications des colonies, Amérique septentrionale, 172 B.

Photo Studio Littré.

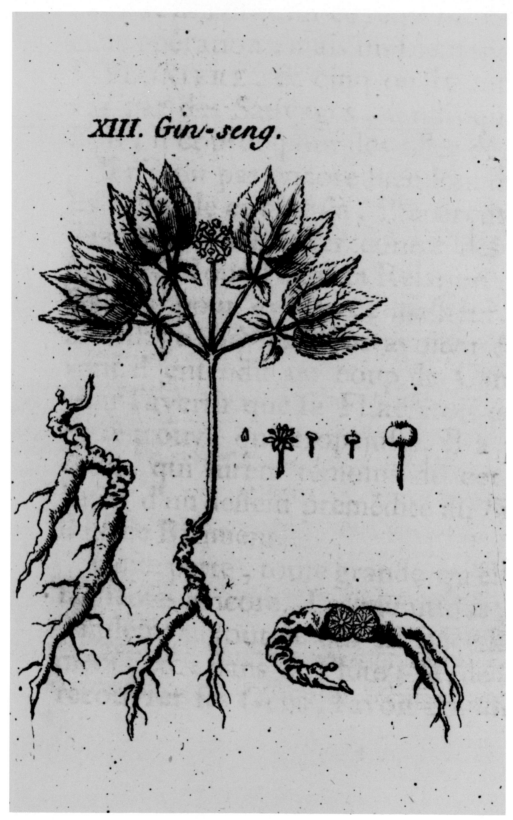

XIII. Gin-seng.

Ginseng. Etching.

In Pierre-François-Xavier de Charlevoix. *Histoire et description générale de la Nouvelle-France . . . .* Paris: chez Rolin fils, 1744. Vol. 2, p. 6.

For a certain period Canada exported ginseng, but from 1752 on the Chinese would not take any more of it: because their requirements concerning the season for picking and the drying of the roots were not complied with, they had lost all confidence in its aphrodisiac and curative properties.

Public Archives of Canada, Ottawa: Library.

Suite de la recapitulation

hommes au dessous	4994:		Moutons	20576:
hommes absents	276:		Cochons	24962:
femmes et Veuues	6631:		Armes a feu	6807:
Garcons au dessus de 15 ans	4067:		Epées	770:
Garcons au dessous	8841:			
filles au dessus de 15 ans	3863:			
filles au dessous	8599:			
Terres En valeur	164741: arpens			
Prairies	23563: idem			
Bled francois	669744: Minots			
Bled jnde	5215: idem			
Pois	70848: idem			
avoine	152681: idem			
Orge	3446: idem			
Tabac	195340: L			
Lin	92489: idem			
Chanure	9590: idem			
Cheuaux	8381:			
Bestes a Corne	36870:			

"Recapitulation of the census of the colony [Canada] for the year 1735–1736."

The number of acres brought into production tripled from 1721 to 1739. The main crop continued to be wheat, but production was fairly well diversified: oats, barley, rye, tobacco, flax, hemp, peas, carrots, turnips, onions, cabbage, beans, corn, lettuce, watermelon, pumpkin, etc.

Archives nationales, Paris: Section Outre-Mer, série G[1], vol. 460.

Photo Studio Littré.

The economy in the outlying regions

To the east of the Canadian colony trade was flourishing on a large scale. In 1733, for example, Île Royale was visited by 53 ships from France, 31 from Canada and 19 from the French West Indies; 55 were engaged in cabotage and trade at Île Royale itself. The previous year 193 ships of all sorts had visited the island. These figures are sufficient to justify on economic grounds the decision to occupy Cap-Breton after 1713.

There was no less fishing activity in Newfoundland, where 1,200 ships and small craft took 483,000 quintals of fish from the sea in 1748.

But in the Southwest, Louisiana did not begin to enjoy prosperity until the end of the 1740s. Her trade with France, the French West Indies and the Spanish colonies then increased prodigiously, thanks to the exportation of wood, indigo, wax, flax, pitch, tar and furs.

During the same period the Hudson's Bay Company continued to reap rich harvests of furs every year despite the presence of the La Vérendryes and their successors on the western rivers that emptied into the bay. In those northern regions, as in the South, the English were competing fiercely with the French for control of the fur trade. They had the advantage over their rivals of being able to offer the Indians better goods at a much lower cost.

1735.

Commerce.

Isle Royale.

Pêche et Commerce de l'année 1734. **13**

Suivant l'État qui en a été envoyé, Il paroît qu'il y a eu 158. Batiment qui ont fait la pêche et le Commerce en cette Isle

Savoir

Des ports de france po. la pêche ..... 19 ⎫ ... 53.
Et pour le Commerce .... 34 ⎭

Il y en avoit eu 70. en 1733, ainsy il y en a eu 17. de moins en 1734.

De Canada, pour le Commerce .... 31.

Il en avoit eu en 1733. que 17, ainsy il y a en 1734. une augmentation de 14.

Des Isles françoises po. le commerce .... 19.

Il y en avoit eu 25. en 1733, ainsy il y a une diminution de 6.

De l'Isle Royale même pour le Cabotage et le commerce .... 55.

Il y en avoit eu 81. en 1733. ainsy il se trouve en 1734. une diminution de 26.

_____

Total des Batiment ..... 158.

Il y en avoit eu 193. en 1733., ainsy il y a eu une diminution au total de 35. Batiment.

"Fishing and trade for the year 1734" at Île Royale.

"It seems that there were 158 ships that were engaged in fishing and in trade at this island" of Cap-Breton: 53 came from the French ports, 31 from Canada and 19 from the French West Indies.

Archives nationales, Paris: Fonds des Colonies, série C[11B], vol. 17, fol. 13.

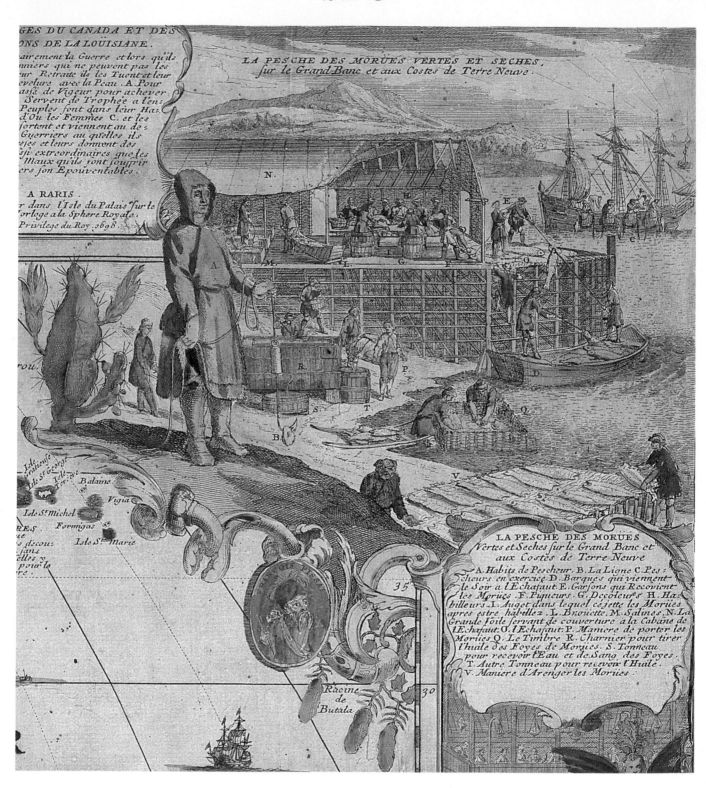

La Pesche des Morues . . . . Vignette taken from [Map of North and South America]. Nicolas de Fer, Paris; Chez l'auteur, 1698. Map: hand coloured, 90.9 × 118.0 cm.

Every year hundreds of ships from France and England came to Newfoundland to fish for cod. Europeans and North American settlers also fished in the area of Île Royale, Île Saint-Jean, Gaspé, Labrador, Chaleur Bay and Acadia (Nova Scotia).

Public Archives of Canada, Ottawa: National Map Collection (NMC 26825).

Newfoundland Fyshery for Three Years.

B 301

Years	Number of — Fishing Ships	Pack Ships	Ships frō America	Totals	Number of Men belonging to yͤ Ships	Number of — Fishing Ships	By Boats	Inhabitan Boats	Totals	Quintals of Fish made by — Fishing Ships	By Boats	Inhabitan Boats	Taken in Prizes	Totalls	Quintals of Fish carryed to Market	Tuns of Oyle made by — Fishing Ships	By Boats	Inhabitant Boats	Taken in Prizes	Totals	Number of Inhabitants — Men Mastᵉʳˢ & Servants	Women	Children	Totals
1708	49	33	15	97		170	*together* 356		526	40450	*together* 95484			135934		241	*together* 531			772	1807	114	253	2174
1709	35	57	5	97	985	130	*together* 258		388	19570	*together* 70794			90364	80600	124	*together* 379			503	1432	171	280	1883
1710	49	26	18	93	2802	153	51	314	518	34290	14068	91170	33000	172528	137226	162	65	373	92	692	1868	235	377	2480

Comparison

Number of ships	1708 and 1709 Exceeds 1710 Four Ships each Year.
Men	1710 Exceeds 1709 .. By 1817 Men.
Number of boats	1708 Exceeds 1709 ...... 138 Boats And / 1708 Exceeds 1710 .... 8 Boats.
Quintals	1708 Exceeds 1709 ...... 44570 Fish / 1710 Exceeds 1708 (Exclusive of the 33000 of Prize Fish) 3594 of Fish
Quintals carryed to Market	1710 Exceeds 1709 ...... 56626 Fish
Tuns	1708 Exceeds 1709 .... 296 Tuns / 1708 Exceeds 1710 .... 72 Tuns / But the 92 Tuns Prize Train is not included in 1710.
Inhabitants	1708 Exceeds 1709 ...... 291 Inhabitants / 1710 Exceeds 1708 ...... 306 Inhabitants

Report on fishing by the English at Newfoundland for the years 1708, 1709 and 1710.

Cod and salmon fishing, seal-hunting and the fur trade constituted the major part of the economic activity of the English at Newfoundland.

Public Record Office, London: Series C.O. 194, vol. 22, p. 301.

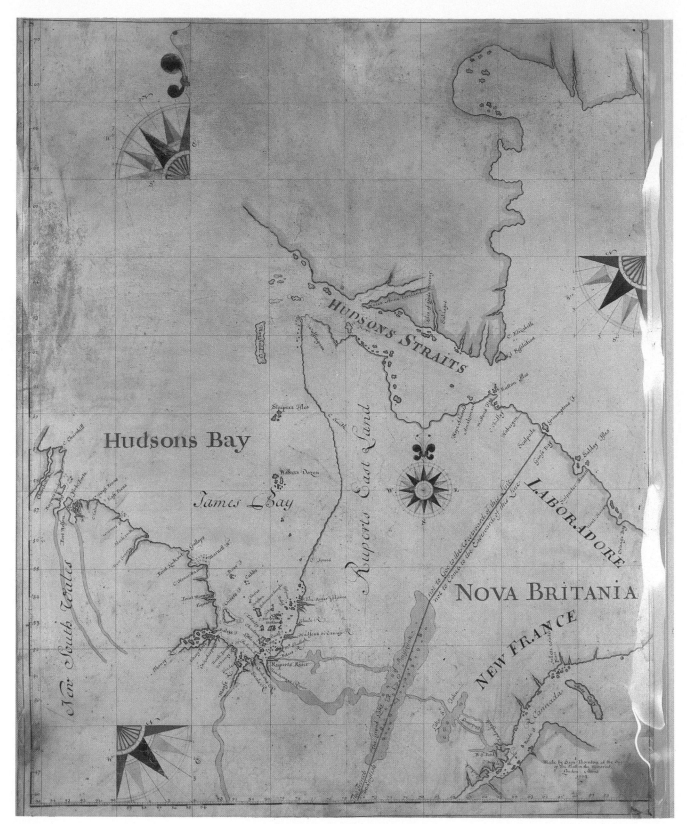

[Map of Hudson Bay and Hudson Strait]. Samuel Thornton. 1709. Map: col. ms., on parchment, 82.0 × 64.8 cm.

Up until 1713 the posts on Hudson Bay and James Bay were divided up between the English and the French. But after the Treaty of Utrecht the Hudson's Bay Company alone occupied this immense territory, profitably operating trading posts such as York Factory and Fort Churchill on Hudson Bay, and Moose Factory and Fort Albany on James Bay.

Archives of the Hudson's Bay Company, Provincial Archives of Manitoba, Winnipeg: G. 2/2.

VI

Society

In the period of 1701 until the conquest the State's grip on the colonies in New France, and more particularly on Canada, made itself felt even more, if possible, than in the preceding century. But the king's wish was that a form of paternal authority be exercised, one that was concerned with the well-being of every settler and was quick to correct injustices. At all costs situations had to be avoided in which the powerful took advantage of the weak and the rich left the poor without resources. Everyone in a position of power was constantly reminded of these principles. The king thus played the role of father to his people, which had a distinct effect on the quality of life in the French colonies in America.

The omnipresence of the State in Canada contributed greatly to the maintaining of aristocratic spirit and values, which were fostered as well within the colonial regular troops. Here one put his sword at the service of the monarch, from whom one expected in return promotions and rewards such as gratuities and pensions, perhaps even the prestigious cross of the Order of Saint-Louis.

Now, it was above all from among the nobility, real or self-styled, that the officers of the colonial regular troops were recruited in Canada. As in France, this social class generally saw no vocation for itself other than serving the king, and most often it did so through soldiering.

As for the bourgeoisie, which was composed mainly of merchants and entrepreneurs of rather modest means, it applied itself very seriously and very energetically to gaining recognition in the colony and becoming rich. Some amassed handsome fortunes, thanks often to their relations with military officers who commanded trading posts or else with some administrator in a position to grant or influence contracts for them. Besides, these Canadian merchants lacked neither dynamism nor ability and generally proved to be more inclined to be thrifty than to engage in ill-considered expenditures.

More than any other group, the Canadian merchants and businessmen, proud of the part they played in the country's growth, knew how to organize and work together. They were perhaps the only class that had a policy of their own on colonial matters, and they succeeded in having it applied. It is true that the economic interests of this class coincided with those of the colony, whose existence was based entirely on commercial exchanges with the mother country and the other French colonies. The fact remains that the merchants were successful in asserting their views, thanks in part to the relations that some of them maintained with the colonial administrators or with correspondents in France who, for their part, belonged to networks capable of extending their influence all the way to the court.

A fair number of those merchants, moreover, could not have done without the aid of the State, which, while strictly regulating their activities, was also their principal client in the colony and their source of subsidies for the development of natural resources.

Nevertheless, the fact remains that most of the trades-people were not much richer than the mass of farmers, craftsmen and workmen who made up the bulk of the population. Lacking capital, the Canadian settler displayed great resourcefulness; he built his own house, made his tools and furniture, worked at several crafts and took on the most varied tasks to ensure for himself a certain degree of comfort. Hard-working and inventive, he was also sturdy; he was said to be cheerful, hospitable, well-mannered and a good and courageous soldier, although sometimes arrogant and inclined to drinking bouts, and even to lasciviousness. The civil and ecclesiastical leaders were somewhat fearful of his "spirit of independence," and his "indocility," for he did not submit easily to orders when they were not to his liking. It must be added, perhaps, in his defence, that in most instances the Canadian was subject to the authority of Frenchmen, whom he considered somewhat as strangers despite their benevolent attitude towards him.

Indeed, conscious of their social responsibilities, the king and his representatives in the colony were anxious to meet the people's essential needs. The teaching establishments, primary schools, hospitals, charitable institutions and even the poor parishes subsisted in large measure thanks to the king's acts of generosity. In times of scarcity, for example, it was again the State that stepped in to alleviate the public's distress and prevent speculation on wheat.

The very obvious presence and role of the State did not prevent the settlers in New France from putting some distance between themselves and France and her American policy. They were conscious of having their roots in a new land that they knew and loved better than anyone else, and when the occasion arose they knew how to uphold their views openly and firmly. These settlers had become Acadians, Canadians and Louisianans.

Beginning as offshoots from the mother country, new social structures were born in New France.

VI

An aristocratic sort of society

In the eighteenth century noblemen were numerous in New France, particularly in Canada. As in France at the same period, many of them owned at least one seigneury; generally they placed their talents at the service of the State, either in the administration or in the army, where they were commissioned officers.

These government officials and military officers were attached to the aristocratic and military values of the mother country: a keen sense of hierarchy, studied elegance in manners and dress, a propensity for spending money for prestige, the aspiration to a higher social rank and the constant quest for honours.

Now, obtaining the promotions and honours that allowed one to rise in the social scale depended most often on the relationships and backing one had managed to acquire among the rulers of the colony as well as within an influential group overseas. But recommendations alone were not enough: one had to give proof of one's military valour or administrative competence, as the competition was keen, particularly among the military.

The pursuit of personal distinction and social prestige was not limited to the nobility, and was the source of incessant rivalries that showed up strikingly in the quarrels over precedence, which were even vented in church.

Letters of nobility granted the Canadian François Hertel, Paris, April 1716.

"We have ennobled and we ennoble the aforementioned François Hertel . . . together with his children and descendants . . . . " This ennoblement constituted an exception in New France in the eighteenth century. For the Canadians the most common ways to rise in society were through military promotions and through trade. Few of them succeeded in obtaining important posts in the civil administration.

Archives municipales, Rochefort, France.

Photo Studio Blain.

Portrait of Jean-Baptiste Hertel de Rouville (1668–1722). Artist unknown. Oil on canvas, circa 1710.

The Canadians were unequalled in the raiding warfare that was practised in America. The most meritorious received handsome promotions in the forces. For example, Hertel de Rouville, who distinguished himself in several raids against English settlements, was promoted successively to ensign, lieutenant and captain, and in 1721 received the cross of Saint-Louis.

McCord Museum, Montréal.

The Canadians

In Canada the top civil and religious positions were for the most part filled by native-born Frenchmen; in the colonial regular troops (troupes de la Marine), however, all the officers' positions were little by little entrusted to Canadians.

Because of the low rate of immigration, the proportion of the population born in Canada was very great. Through their dynamism the group consisting of the merchants and entrepreneurs succeeded in securing for themselves a certain degree of comfort and, on the social level, an unquestionable respectability; minor officers of the law and civil servants, craftsmen and even some workmen also reached a satisfactory living standard.

Three quarters of the Canadians, however, lived in the country; a good number of them were still at the stage of clearing new land and led a rather wretched existence; those who were established on cleared lands had an easier life: if some of them were content with simply satisfying their immediate needs, others (perhaps ten to twenty per cent of the farmers) produced large surpluses. All the same, on the whole the Canadian habitants enjoyed, according to observers of the period, a standard of living that was superior to that of the peasants in France, and they were less unhappy.

To be sure, adventuresome individuals, coureurs de bois or soldiers, were to be found among the population, but the majority of Canadians lived quietly on their lands.

Comme aux domiciliez du pays
L'on convient que le Commerce soit libre, mais
non pas de la Maniere que les formes se font au
prejudice des domiciliez, à la destruction et à la Ruine
d'une Colonie que le Roy a Intention de Conserver, ainsi
leurs objections sonfaites à Combatre par les raisons
Suivantes

Remarquez s'il vous plaît Nos
Seigneurs que les domiciliez ont lu en cette colon
trisayeulx, Bisayeulx, ayeulx, leurs peres, ou sont venus
Sy Establis qu'ils y ont leur famille dont la plus part
sont nombreuses, qu'ils ont contribué les premiers à l'étab-
qu'ils y ont ouvert et Cultivé les terres, Baty des Eglises
Arboré des Croix, maintenu la Religion, fait construire
de Belles maisons, Contribué à fortifier les villes,
Soustenu la Guerre tant contre les nations Sauvages
que Contre les autres Ennemis de l'Etat même aux
Suitez, qu'ils ont Estez sous les ordres qui leur
ont esté donnez, et Supportez toutes les fatigues
de la Guerre, les hivers nonobstant la rigueur des
Saisons aussy bien que l'Esté, et qu'ils n'ont Epargné ny
leurs Biens ny leurs vie, pour Seconder les Intentions
du Roy établis ce pays qui est un glorieux de sa
couronne puisque sa Grandeur se mesure pas
L'étendue de ses Etats et le nombre de ses Fideles serviteurs
et Sujets

Petition by the Canadian merchants to the governor general and the intendant, circa 1719.

The Canadians were more and more aware that they formed a distinct people with its own history, traditions and interests. The merchants pointed out that they "have had great-great-grandfathers, great-grandfathers, grandfathers, their fathers, in this colony, or they came to settle there, that they have their families there, most of which are large, that they were the first to contribute to establishing it, that they have opened up and farmed lands in it, built churches . . . had fine homes built, contributed to fortifying the towns, supported the war."

Archives nationales, Paris: Fonds des Colonies, série C¹¹A, vol. 40, fol. 264v.

Photo Studio Littré.

254 JOURNAL HISTORIQUE

l'exemple & la fréquentation de ses Habitans naturels, qui mettent tout leur bonheur dans la liberté & l'indépendance, sont plus que suffisans pour former ce caractere. On accuse encore nos Créoles d'une grande avidité pour amasser, & ils font véritablement pour cela des choses, qu'on ne peut croire, si on ne les a point vûës. Les courses, qu'ils entreprennent; les fatigues, qu'ils essuyent; les dangers, à quoi ils s'exposent; les efforts, qu'ils font, passent tout ce qu'on peut imaginer. Il est cependant peu d'Hommes moins intéressés, qui dissipent avec plus de facilité ce qui leur a coûté tant de peines à acquerir, & qui témoignent moins de regret de l'avoir perdu. Aussi n'y a-t-il aucun lieu de douter qu'ils n'entreprennent ordinairement par goût ces courses si pénibles & si dangéreuses. Ils aiment à respirer le grand air, ils se font accoûtumés de bonne heure à mener une vie errante; elle a pour eux des charmes, qui leur font oublier les périls & les fatigues passés, & ils mettent leur gloire à les affronter de nouveau. Ils ont beaucoup d'esprit, sur-tout les Personnes du Sexe, qui l'ont fort brillant, aisé, ferme, fécond en ressources, courageux, & capable de conduire les plus grandes affaires. Vous en avez connu, Madame, plus d'une de ce caractere, & vous m'en avez témoigné plus d'une fois votre étonnement. Je puis vous assûrer qu'elles font ici le plus grand nombre, & qu'on les trouve telles dans toutes les conditions.

Je ne sçai si je dois mettre parmi les défauts de nos Canadiens la bonne opinion, qu'ils ont d'eux-mêmes. Il est certain du moins

D'UN VOYAGE DE L'AMERIQ. LET. X. 255

qu'elle leur inspire une confiance, qui leur fait entreprendre & exécuter, ce qui ne paroîtroit pas possible à beaucoup d'autres. Il faut convenir d'ailleurs qu'ils ont d'excellentes qualités. Nous n'avons point dans le Royaume de Province, où le Sang soit communément si beau, la Taille plus avantageuse, & le Corps mieux proportionné. La force du tempéramment n'y répond pas toujours, & si les Canadiens vivent lontems, ils font vieux & usés de bonne heure. Ce n'est pas même uniquement leur faute; c'est aussi celle des Parens, qui, pour la plûpart, ne veillent pas assez sur leurs Enfans, pour les empêcher de ruiner leur santé dans un âge, où, quand elle se ruine, c'est sans ressource. Leur agilité & leur adresse font sans égales: les Sauvages les plus habiles ne conduisent pas mieux leurs Canots dans les Rapides les plus dangereux, & ne tirent pas plus juste.

Bien des Gens font persuadés qu'ils ne font pas propres aux Sciences, qui demandent beaucoup d'application, & une étude suivie. Je ne sçaurois vous dire si ce préjugé est bien ou mal fondé; car nous n'avons pas encore de Cananadien, qui ait entrepris de le combattre, il ne l'est peut être que sur la dissipation, dans laquelle on les éleve. Mais personne ne peut leur contester un génie rare pour les Méchaniques; ils n'ont presque pas besoin de Maîtres pour y exceller, & on en voit tous les jours, qui réussissent dans tous les Métiers, sans en avoir fait d'apprentissage.

Quelques-uns les taxent d'ingratitude, ils m'ont néanmoins paru avoir le cœur assez bon; mais leur légereté naturelle les empêche

Pierre-François-Xavier de Charlevoix. *Journal d'un voyage fait par ordre du roi dans l'Amérique septentrionnale* . . . . Paris: chez la veuve Ganeau, 1744, vol. 5, p. 254–255.

Even if he found certain faults in them, Father Charlevoix acknowledged that the Canadians also had some excellent qualities: "They have a great deal of intelligence, especially the persons of the (female) sex, who are brilliant, quick-witted, steadfast, resourceful, courageous . . . . We do not have any province in the kingdom where the race is generally so handsome, taller, or better proportioned . . . . Their nimbleness and dexterity are unequalled . . . . no one can dispute their rare genius in mechanical matters . . . ."

Public Archives of Canada, Ottawa: Library

aux intentions de Sa Majesté
excepté les habitants de la
Seigneurie de Longueüil, dans
lesquels Je ne trouvai pas d'abord
la même Soumission lorsque je
leur proposer les Corvées. Ils
etoient sous les armes pour me
recevoir en y arrivant, Je leur
parlai dans la maison de M.
de Longueüil et je leur dis tout ce
qui pouvoit être capable de les
engager ainsi les habitants
des autres cotes: mais ce fut
inutilement, parce qu'il se trouvou
parmi eux quelques mutins qui
gâtoient l'esprit des autres.
quelques uns de ces derniers m'aya
manqué de respect dans leurs reponse
furent poussez par ones gardes
ce qui allarma les autres, et tous
craignant d'être chargez, Ils se
Sortirent de la maison en foule

Letter from Governor General de Vaudreuil to the Conseil de Marine, Québec, 17 October 1717.

The settlers resisted in all sorts of ways orders they did not like. Their opposition could go so far as to look like a revolt: " . . . in the habitants of the seigneury of Longueuil I did not find the same submissiveness when I went to set out the corvées to them. They were under arms to receive me . . . some of the latter having been lacking in respect to me in their replies . . . ."

Archives nationales, Paris: Fonds des Colonies, série C[11A], vol. 38, fol. 121v.

Photo Studio Littré.

A View of the Orphan's or Urseline Nunnery, taken from the Ramparts.

Drawn on the SPOT by R. Short.   Engraved by James Mason.

Vue de l'Hopital des Orphelins desservi par les Ursulines, prise de dessus le Rampart.

Sept.r 1.1761. Published according to Act of Parliament by R. Short and Sold by T. Jefferys the Corner of St. Martins Lane Charing Cross.

View of the Ursuline convent. Richard Short (known 1759–1761). Etching by James Mason, printed by Thomas Jefferys, 1761.

In the foreground, we see some Canadians in a field. In the background is the convent, housing some 50 Ursulines, of whom a good number, according to a 1753 account, "see to the instruction of some sixty boarders and about 150 day-students."

Public Archives of Canada, Ottawa: Picture Division (Negative no. C-358).

VI

Entertainment

In Canada people knew how to enjoy themselves, as they did also on Île Royale and in Louisiana.

From time to time there were great festivities when all classes of society celebrated some important event together. These merrymakings were appreciated all the more because of their rarity.

High society could attend dinners and dance to the sound of music in the mansions of the governor and the intendant, and sometimes they could even applaud a minor theatrical entertainment there. Card games and games of chance were very much in fashion, and in Intendent François Bigot's circle, people gambled with abandon.

The common people also had their ways of enjoying themselves, which provoked a bishop of Québec, Pierre Herman Dosquet, to complain on at least one occasion. In particular the settlers liked to compose and sing satirical songs and to play tricks even during parish processions — practices that the intendant was frequently forced to forbid. Other songs of popular origin marked a happy event, such as the capture of Chouaguen (Oswego) in 1756.

Sleigh rides, outings "en calèche," skating, ninepins, bowls and billiards were also popular forms of entertainment.

48

ils chanterent une grande Messe en Musique, ou M.ᵉ Le Gouverneur general, Intendant, et toute La Noblesse assisterent, a L'issuë des Vêpres Le R.P. françois Xavier de la haye Religieux de leur ordre, prononça son discour, a L'occasion de la Naissance de M.ᵉʳ Le Dauphin qui fut universellement applaudy Le Te Deum y fut chanté en musique au bruit de toute L'artillerie.

e M.ᵉ Le Gouverneur general S'étant rendu chés M.ᵉ L'Intendant avec toute les Dames, les officiers et toutes les personnes de distinction. Le Signal fut donné pour tirer le feu d'artifice qui eut une Execution très reguliere. Le palais étoit Jlluminé: on Servit

"Account of what took place at Québec . . . on the occasion of the birth of His Royal Highness the Dauphin," 1730.

The Recollets "celebrated a High Mass; a member of their order delivered an address on the occasion of the birth of His Royal Highness the Dauphin that was universally applauded. The *Te Deum* was sung to music on that occasion, accompanied by the din of the entire artillery . . . . the signal was given to set off the fireworks, which was done in a very orderly manner."

Archives nationales, Paris: Fonds des Colonies, série C¹¹ᴬ, vol. 52, fol. 48.

Photo Studio Littré.

124

Au 31.

[manuscript text in French, Montcalm's diary]

*Ce M. le m.** de Vaudreuil est parti ce matin avec M.** le chev.** de Levis pour Quebec. M. de Langlade Enseigne reformé des troupes de la colonie est parti ce matin avec un detachement de 80 hommes Canadiens et Sauvages pour se rendre a Carrillon et dela aller en parti vers le fort George et le fort Lydius.*

*du 2 Jan.** 1757.*

Les chefs de guerre du Village du Sault S. Louis sont venus pour me complimenter et je suis parti le 3 pour me rendre a Quebec ou je suis arrivé le 6. M. L'Intendant y a tenu un tres grand Etat et y a donné deux tres beaux bals ou j'ay vu plus de 80 Dames ou dem.** tres aimables et tres bien mises. Quebec m'a paru une ville d'un fort bon ton et je ne crois pas que dans la france Il y en ait plus d'une douzaine au dessus de Quebec pour la société car d'ailleurs Il n'y a pas plus de 12000 ames...*

Extract from the Marquis de Montcalm's diary, 2 January 1757.

High society in the colony went in for the same worldly pleasures as did the nobility in the kingdom: gay parties, balls, delicate suppers and games of chance. On leaving "two very fine balls," where were present "more than 80 very agreeable and very well dressed ladies and young ladies," Montcalm wrote: "Québec struck me as a very elegant town . . . ."

Public Archives of Canada, Ottawa: Manuscript Division, MG 18, K 8, vol. 1.

Letter from Bishop Dosquet to the minister, Québec, 4 September 1731.

Many of the citizens liked to enjoy themselves in public places: "The lower-class people of both sexes meet right under my windows after their supper, they sing and engage in very free talk . . . . That is where the drunks come to sober up . . . . On feast days and Sundays the noise that the people make there playing ninepins and bowls is head-splitting."

Archives nationales, Paris: Fonds des Colonies, série C[11A], vol. 56, fol. 166v-167.

Photo Studio Littré.

View of the bishop's palace and its
ruins, as they looked on the top of the
height, seen from the lower town.
Richard Short (known 1759–1761).
Etching by A. Benoist, printed by
Thomas Jefferys, 1761.

The children enjoyed themselves, even
among the ruins.

Public Archives of Canada, Ottawa:
Picture Division (Negative no. C-350).

Song composed on the occasion of the capture of Chouaguen (Oswego), 1756.

By and large, the Canadians liked to sing. According to Kalm, many women saw to their household duties "while humming some ditty or other." Wits even composed songs to mark happy or comic events.

Bibliothèque nationale, Paris: Département des manuscrits, Fonds français, vol. 12506, fol. 3v.

VI

Education

Whether one was from nobility, the bourgeoisie, or the lower classes of craftsmen and farmers, theoretically one had equal access to the institutions in the colony that provided teaching for children and adolescents of both sexes.

Until the end of the French regime the Jesuit college in Québec furnished a classical education while at the same time conducting preparatory classes. Besides grammar, the humanities and philosophy, which formed part of the regular curriculum, hydrography and theology were also taught.

For some twenty years Attorney General Louis-Guillaume Verrier taught courses at Québec in law — a sort of initiation to ordinances, customary law and jurisprudence.

If boys could count upon the primary schools for acquiring their early education, and then on the Jesuit college, girls could count on the Ursuline convents at Québec and Trois-Rivières, and several establishments run by the sisters of the Congrégation de Notre-Dame both in the towns and in the country. At Louisbourg, the sisters of the Congrégation de Notre-Dame, and at Nouvelle-Orléans, the Ursulines also had schools.

There was also the Séminaire de Québec, a school for future priests whose students followed courses at the Jesuit college.

A View of the Jesuits College and Church.⎯ Vue de l'Eglise et du College des Jesuites.

Drawn on the SPOT by Richᵈ Short.   Engraved by C.Grignion.

London Published according to the Act of Parliament Sepʳ 1760 by Richᵈ Short & Sold by Thos Jefferys the Corner of St Martins Lane Charing Cross.

View of the Jesuit church and college. Richard Short (known 1759–1761). Etching by C. Grignion, printed by Thomas Jefferys, 1761.

According to Father Germain, at the Collège de Québec, "everything . . . is or is done as in our colleges in Europe, and perhaps with greater attention to rules and greater rigour and with better results than in many of our colleges in France."

Public Archives of Canada, Ottawa: Picture Division (Negative no. C-354).

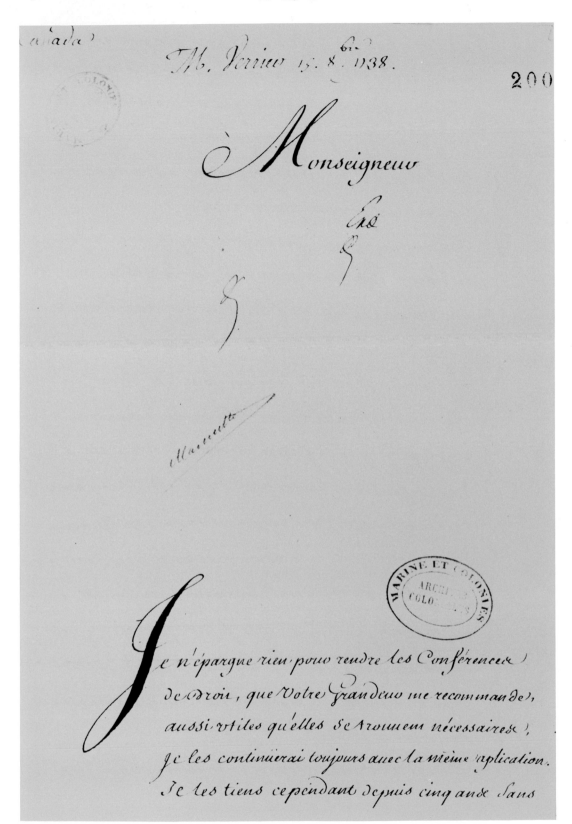

Letter from Louis-Guillaume Verrier, attorney general of the Conseil supérieur, to the minister, Québec, 15 October 1738.

"I spare no pains to make the lectures on law, which your Lordship advises me to give, as useful as they are necessary." These courses, which contributed towards training officers of the law, would continue until the 1750s.

Archives nationales, Paris: Fonds des Colonies, série C[11A], vol. 70, fol. 200.

Photo Studio Littré.

qui se tireroit de tous les evenemens qui pouroient
arriver au sujet des d'res terres, en ce cas ils commeteroient
le garde magasin de quebec qui se contenteroit de
tres peu de chose pour cette peine.

Les Religieuses de la congregation, Monseigneur e
sont toujours tres utiles a cette colonie par e
l'instruction qu'elles donnent a la jeunesse et dans e
les villes et dans les côtes ou elles sont établies, c'est
une communauté; ces filles sont des veux simples e
et M'rs Raudot sont persuadés qu'elles sont aussi e
des veux de stabilité comme font les freres e
charons ainsy qu'ils auront l'honneur de vous e
l'expliquer par la suitte de cette lettre, ils e
leurs deffendront de la part de Sa M. d'en faire
aucuns a l'avenir; cet ordre est tr favorable au
bien de cette colonie joint a ce qu'é vous leur a
faire l'honneur de leurs marquer que Sa M. e
ne soufrira jamais qu'elles soient eloignés, qu'ils
ne peuvent s'empecher de vous en rendre grace
et de vous prier en mesme tems, Monseigneur, de
ne le point changer.

Si ces filles étoient eloignés, les veux qu'on leurs

Letter from the Intendants Raudot to the minister, Québec, 23 October 1708.

The sisters of the Congrégation de Notre-Dame "are always very useful to this colony because of the schooling that they give the children in the towns and in the countryside." They had schools at Montréal, Québec, Lachine, Boucher-ville, Pointe-aux-Trembles and Champlain, among other places.

Archives nationales, Paris: Fonds des Colonies, série C[11A], vol. 28, fol. 259v.

Photo Studio Littré.

VI

Arts and science

Literature was virtually non-existent in New France. Except for travel accounts and a few plays in verse written for special occasions, one can scarcely mention anything for the eighteenth century other than the correspondence of Madame Bégon (Marie-Élisabeth Rocbert de La Morandière) and a certain number of funeral orations such as those by Abbé Joseph Serré de La Colombière.

On the other hand, the sciences were quite popular in New France: Jean François Gaultier, for example, and especially Michel Sarrazin did research that was carried to a fairly high level for the period in the area of natural science. They corresponded with scientists and scientific institutions in Europe. At the end of the 1740s the acting governor general, Roland-Michel Barrin de La Galissonière, would give considerable impetus to research throughout New France.

In the field of painting, sculpture and architecture, the number of artists and craftsmen born and trained in Canada increased greatly during the century. Some of their works are clearly distinguishable from their European models by their freshness, simplicity or naïvety. They are truly original examples of some of the earliest forms of expression by the Canadians.

New France had never had a newspaper, or even a printer. So it was an event for the land that is now Canada when a newspaper, *The Halifax Gazette*, which would run for many years, first came off the press in 1752.

Portrait of Marie-Élisabeth Rocbert de La Morandière (1696–1755), wife of Claude-Michel Bégon de La Cour. Oil on canvas.

This Canadian letterwriter reported virtually day by day the doings of Montréal society in the middle of the eighteenth century. Her letters were crammed with details of society life: festivities, society gatherings and other amusements. Her comments on the behaviour of her fellow citizens are often spicy.

Private collection, France.

Portrait of Abbé Joseph de La Colombière (1651–1723), canon, vicar general, archdeacon and ecclesiastical councillor on the Conseil supérieur. Artist unknown. Oil on canvas.

A gift for oratory was displayed by a few preachers, such as Abbé de La Colombière, several civil or military officers, and even some missionaries and interpreters.

Monastère des augustines de l'Hôtel-Dieu de Québec.

Photo W.B. Edwards.

Portrait of Michel Sarrazin (1659–1734), surgeon, doctor and naturalist. Pierre Mignard. Oil on canvas.

In New France, observations and research in fields such as astronomy, meteorology, botany, zoology and medicine increased. Two of the most active researchers were the doctors Michel Sarrazin and Jean-François Gaultier, who sent many reports and many specimens of animals, plants and minerals to members of the Académie royale des Sciences in Paris.

Musée de l'île Sainte-Hélène, Montréal.

Letter from Doctor Jean-François Gaultier to the minister, Québec, 1 November 1749.

" . . . I have handed over to Monsieur Bigot a considerable collection of fruits and tree and plant seeds for the Jardin royal des Plantes in Paris . . . . I shall not fail to give my attention to these areas of research and to everything that may concern natural history . . . ."

Archives nationales, Paris: Fonds des Colonies, série C¹¹ᴬ, vol. 94, fol. 44.

Ex-voto offered by the three shipwrecked persons from Lévis. Artist unknown. Oil, 1754.

It was particularly the Church that encouraged artistic creation in New France. Churches, hospitals and convents owned many works by Canadians: ex-votos commemorating miraculous events, portraits of religious and notables, carvings, silver plate, and so on.

Musée historial, Basilique de Sainte-Anne de Beaupré.

Photo Kedl.

VI

Charitable institutions

The three hospitals founded at Québec, Montréal and Trois-Rivières in the seventeenth century continued to play an indispensable role in the eighteenth century — to the great satisfaction of the governors and intendants — particularly during the great epidemics that periodically devastated the Canadian colony.

No less important was the role of the Hôpital Général in Québec and the Hôpital Général in Montréal. The two institutions took in the old, the chronically ill, the indigent and the mentally ill. In Montréal, towards the end of the French regime, the widowed Madame d'Youville, born Marie-Marguerite Dufrost de Lajemmerais, and her companions also took in prostitutes, whom they endeavoured to protect and rehabilitate.

Moral standards being less severe in the colony, care had to be provided for illegitimate children in the eighteenth century: the State committed them to the care of couples who promised before a notary to look after and bring up the children and treat them as if they were their own.

In Louisiana, Ursulines, who had arrived directly from France, ran a hospital in Nouvelle-Orléans, as did the Brothers of Charity at Louisbourg. In 1759, Halifax also benefited from charitable institutions.

Je dois aussy, Monseigneur,
Vous rendre compte du zéle
avec lequel Les Religieuses
hospitaliéres des trois Villes
decette Colonie se sont portez
au Soulagement des malades,
Leur charité et leurs soins ;—

n'ont point eû de bornes
à Quebec, et à Montreal, elles
ont eu pendant 4 mois plus
de 130 —— Malades a Soigner
continuellement ; Elles mériteroient
Monseigneur, que vous leur donnassiez
quelques marques de Satisfaction.

Letter from Intendant Hocquart to the minister, Québec, 3 October 1733.

The civil authorities regularly praised the hospital nuns. In this letter Hocquart describes "the zeal with which the nuns hospitallers in the three towns in this colony have gone to the relief of the sick; their charity and their cares have known no limits."

Archives nationales, Paris: Fonds des Colonies, série C[11A], vol. 60, fol. 42-42v.

Photo Studio Littré.

nous d'hopital General ne l'estoit point neanmoins, Et ceux qui avoient estés chargés de son administration servient toujours bornés a ny recevoir que des hommes et en avoient exclus les personnes du sexe; aujourd'huy l'un et l'autre y est reçu et on a fait et meublé exprés une salle pour les femmes; Les insensés, les incurables même y trouve un asile et la charité s'étend sur tous les affligés; elle n'a pas aussy oublié a pourvoir au salut et a la retraitte des filles et femmes débauchées qui corrompent la jeunesse, on a pratiqué plus de douze chambres pour servir de refuge où elles sont nouries et instruites.

Les biens de la campagne se sentent également de la vigilance qu'elles y apportent a les bien faire valoir et on y trouve desja un changement notable par les reparations qu'elles y ont fait faire;

Leur zele nos seigneurs n'est diminué en rien pour le service des pauvres dont elles se font gloire d'estre les servantes et elles sont actuellement dans des dispositions encore plus ardantes pour consacrer leur temps, leurs travaux et leur vie pour le soustien de cette maison.

Cependant par un revers imprevu après de si heureux commencemens et sans avoir, a ce qu'elles croyent donné aucun sujet de mécontentement elles apprenent d'une manière a n'en pouvoir doutter que vous pensés nos seigneurs a leur oster l'administration dud hopital et que vous y travaillés efficacement pour en transporter les biens et les revenus a celuy de québec ou a quelque autre communauté quelque bonne opinion qu'elles ayent de leur merite et de leur talens elles prennent neanmoins la liberté de vous representer avec Respect les suittes facheuses que produira necessairement un tel changem

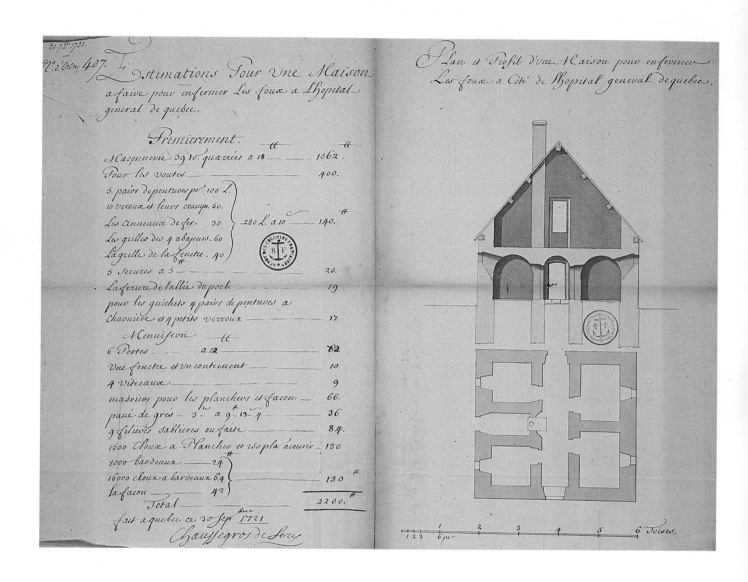

"Plan and profile of a building beside the Hôpital Général of Québec for locking up the insane." Gaspard-Joseph Chaussegros de Léry. 30 September 1721. Plan: col. ms., on a page 35.6×46.0 cm.

In addition to providing shelter for the aged, the insane and fallen women, the Hôpital Général of Québec began in 1725 to run a boarding school for girls.

Archives nationales, Paris: Section Outre-Mer, Dépôt des fortifications des colonies, Amérique septentrionale, 407 C.

Photo Studio Littré.

Agreement by which the deputy king's attorney put "into the hands of the aforementioned Fontene an illegitimate child" to "feed and keep him . . . bring him up and educate him" until he "reaches the age of eighteen," Montréal, 25 September 1730.

In 1736, 390 illegitimate children were brought up in Canada at the king's expense.

Archives nationales du Québec, Centre régional de Montréal: Minutes of the notary Joseph-Charles Raimbault.

Photo Diapolab.

manquants Tous de Travail. Ils continuent d'Estre à charge au Public, à M. Le General Et a moy. Et Encore plus au Roy. J'ay Esté Et je suis Toujours dans la nécessité de faire fournir régulièrement du pain, de la Viande et des Légumes des Magasins à Ces Indigents Et aux pauvres infirmes. M. Michel en a usé demême par mon ordre a Montréal, autrement Nous aurions Exposé Les sujets du Roy, des familles Entières à périr par La faim.

Vous aurez Esté informé, Monseigneur, même par d'autres

Letter from Intendant Hocquart to the minister, Québec, 12 May 1738.

When crops were very bad, the colonial administration found itself "in the necessity of having bread, meat and vegetables supplied regularly" to "the destitute and needy invalids," to avoid exposing "entire families to starvation."

Archives nationales, Paris: Fonds des Colonies, série C¹¹A, vol. 69, fol. 193v.

Photo Studio Littré.

Halifax. Richard Short (known 1759–1761). Etching by François-Antoine Aveline.

In 1759, Halifax had three churches, a hospital and an orphanage. Some school teachers taught the Protestant children. The Great Pontack Hotel was the centre of social life in this city.

Public Archives of Canada, Ottawa: Picture Division (Negative no. C-2482).

NOVA-SCOTIA. No. 175.

THE

Halifax GAZETTE.

SATURDAY, *August* 23, 1755.

From the London Magazine *for* May, 1755.

Number of the BRITISH SUBJECTS, *Men, Women, and Children, in the Colonies of North-America, taken from Militia-Rolls, Poll Taxes, Bills of Mortality, Returns from Governors, and other authentic Accounts.*

The Colonies of	Inhabitants.
Halifax & Lunenburg in Nova Scotia	5,000
New Hampshire	30,000
Massachusetts-Bay	240,000
Rhode Island and Providence	35,000
Connecticut	100,000
New York	100,000
The Jerseys	60,000
Pennsylvania	250,000
Maryland	85,000
Virginia	85,000
North Carolina	45,000
South Carolina	30,000
Georgia	6,000
Total Number	1,051,000

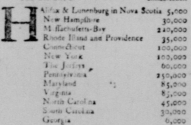

Exclusive of the Military Forces, in the Pay of the Government, and Negroes.

Number of the French *Inhabitants in* North-America, *exclusive of regular troops and Negroes.*

The Colonies of	Inhabitants.
Canada	45,000
Louisiana	7,000
Total Number	52,000

So that the English are more than in the Proportion of Twenty to One; but (in the Words of a Memorial quoted by the Author of *The State of the British and French Colonies in North America.*) Union, Situation, proper Management of the Indians, superior Knowledge of the Country, and constant Application to a Business will more than ballance divided Numbers, and will easily break a Rope of Sand.

From the BRITISH PRINTS.

FOREIGN ADVICES.

MADRID, April 21.

THE 27th of last Month Baron Wassanaer, Ambassador from the States General, received an Express from Alicant, with a Letter from several Masters of Dutch Vessels, importing, That having taken in their Ladings, they were ready to depart with the first fair Wind for Amsterdam, Rotterdam, Ostend, Hamburgh, &c. but durst not put to Sea, for fear of meeting with the Algerine Corsairs, and therefore they prayed his Excellency to procure them a Convoy of Dutch Men of War; or, if there were none at Hand, to use his Interest to get them convoyed by Spanish Men of War, if possible.

Baron Wassanaer being uncertain whether there was any Dutch Ships of War in the Ports of this Kingdom, and hearing the next Day that there was a Spanish Man of War at Carthagena ready to put to Sea, he went to Don Richard Wall, Secretary of State *del Dispatcho Universal*, and communicated to him the Petition of the Masters of the Dutch Merchantmen, desiring he would speak to the Minister of the Marine about it. M. Wall readily undertook to do it, went directly to the Office of M. d'Arriaga, returned in about a Quarter of an Hour, and said to Baron Wassanaer, "Your Business is done. They are already drawing up

the necessary Orders at the Admiralty-Office, and they will be sent away this Evening, so that you may write to your Captains, to make themselves easy, and that they may depend on the Protection of his Majesty's Ships."

The 29th the Baron Wassanaer went again to M. Wall's House, to thank him for the Orders dispatched the preceeding Evening, and having made use of Terms expressive of his lively Gratitude, M. Wall said to him, " Wave all Thanks; Humanity dictates such Assistance, and Friendship grants it." At the same Time he acquainted the Ambassador, that instead of one Ship two were ordered, one of 70 and the other of 60 Guns; and that after they had convoyed the Dutch Ships through the Streights of Gibraltar, they were to cruize upon the Algerines.

Rochfort, May 2. By a Letter from Cape Breton, we have certain Advice, that on the 10th of March a Party of 800 Men, and 12 Pieces of Artillery, were dispatched from Montreal, to reinforce the several Forts, &c. on the Ohio; these were followed on the 15th by a second Reinforcement from Quebec, to the Amount of 1500 Men; and on the 21st, by a third Detachment from the last Place of 300 Men, and 18 Pieces of Artillery. The same Advices add, that Supplies of every Kind are continually forwarding from Quebec up the River; and that 'tis not at all doubted, but that before the English, who, we hear, are in Motion on the Side of Virginia, can reach our Frontiers, we shall be able to form a Camp beyond the Erie, or employ, in what Manner is judged most aprop's, a Body of 10,000 Men, with a compleat Train of Artillery. In the mean Time Canada itself is not neglected; but all imaginable Precautions are taken to prevent a Surprize, as we have certain Assurances the English Colonies think themselves authorized to act against us on the Offensive, without waiting for the Ceremony of a War in Europe. We are therefore not exempt from the Suspicion of their making an Attack as well on those Parts, which will manifest a Violation of Treaty, as on the Side of our Frontiers, where their Pretensions call ours in Question.

PLANTATION-NEWS.

PHILADELPHIA, July 31.

Extract of a Letter from Berks-County, dated July 27.

" The People on the West Side of Susquehanna, in the New Purchase, are coming away, two Families having been murdered on Juniata; some are gathering together to defend themselves, others are coming on this Side the Mountains. The miserable Condition most of these People are in, I cannot express.

A Letter from Carlisle, of the 22d Instant, mentions, " That the Inhabitants of Juniata are entirely come away, and our People in general in great Trouble and Confusion."

In another Letter from Carlisle, of the same Date, there is the following Paragraph: " We are now in the utmost Confusion, not knowing what Hand to turn to, being more afraid of the Indians (whom we doubt not were the late Murderers on the new Road) than of the French. Our Back Settlers are in general fled, and are likely to be ruined for the Loss of their Crops and Summer's Labour; several of them on Juniata having left some Part of their Houshold Furniture in the Flight, and since, going back to fetch or hide it, have found every Thing broken and destroyed by the Indians, and their Horses in the Corn-fields."

NEW-YORK, Aug. 4.

The last Advices from Albany are, that Major Lyman, with a Detachment of 500 Men, were safe arrived at Still-Water, about 28 Miles from that Place, where they were conducted by a Number of the Inhabitants from Albany;
that

The Halifax Gazette, 23 August 1755.

In Nova Scotia, *The Halifax Gazette* had been appearing since 1752. One could find in it news of England and the British colonies, and some local news and announcements.

National Library of Canada, Ottawa.

VI

Indian society

There existed within the society of New France, whether in Acadia, Canada or Louisiana, several groups of Indians, whose presence seemed much more normal in the eighteenth century than in the previous one.

While continuing to live in their own way, these Indians did not completely escape the influence of the white men, some of whose ways they adopted, along with a great variety of their products; the reverse was equally true, however, and the settlers of New France seem to have been very strongly marked by their almost daily contacts with the original inhabitants of the country.

However, the Indians had not changed greatly; on the contrary, the closer their relations with the white man, the more they were conscious of their own identity. Consequently they maintained their traditions and attempted to protect themselves against a cultural assimilation that would have been irreversible.

In the eighteenth century the French in New France were also in contact with the Inuit (Eskimos), without, however, yet reaching with them the degree of familiarity that characterized their relations with the Indians.

"Method of making maple sugar."
Etching.

In Joseph-François Lafitau. *Moeurs des sauvages amériquains . . . .* Paris: Saugrain l'aîné et Charles Estienne Hochereau, 1724. Vol. 2, p. 154.

Father Lafitau described the method used by the squaws to make maple sugar and maple syrup: they "make transversal incisions with their axes on the trunk of these trees, from which a juice runs plentifully that they collect in big bark receptacles; then they boil this juice over a fire, which consumes all the phlegm in it and thickens what remains to the consistency of syrup, or even of loaf sugar."

Public Archives of Canada, Ottawa: Library.

Indian games. Etching.

In Joseph-François Lafitau. *Moeurs des sauvages amériquains . . . .* Paris: Saugrain l'aîné et Charles Estienne Hochereau, 1724. Vol. 2, p. 354.

The upper drawing shows Indians playing lacrosse. The lower one shows some Indians practising shooting with bows.

Public Archives of Canada, Ottawa: Library.

Eskimoes. Etching.

In Henry Ellis. *Voyage de la Baye de Hudson fait en 1746 et 1747, pour la découverte du passage de Nord-Ouest.* Paris: Chez Ballard fils, 1749. Vol. 2, p. 170.

At the beginning of the century, the Eskimoes from Labrador ventured into the Strait of Belle-Isle and along the north shore of the St. Lawrence to hunt seal and caribou. But the presence of the increasingly aggressive and hostile French and Canadian fishermen forced them to forsake these hunting grounds, and even to progressively retreat from southern Labrador.

Public Archives of Canada, Ottawa: Library.

Religion

If the Canadian Church had made rapid progress in the previous century, in the eighteenth century it would undergo a critical period in its growth and adaptation, if not its identity. This was complicated by the too frequent absence of a bishop and the equally frequent intervention of the State in its internal affairs.

The Church also suffered from the enormous size of the diocese of Québec and the difficulty of knowing exactly what was going on in the former Acadia and on Île Royale to the east, as well as in Louisiana and the Illinois country to the west; these two farthermost points of its jurisdiction were largely beyond the control of the bishop of Québec.

The Canadian colony continued to be served by the secular clergy, assigned mainly to parish work, by the Jesuits, who pursued their apostolic work with the Indian tribes while at the same time keeping up the college in Québec, by the Récollets (Grey Friars), who served as garrison chaplains and missionaries in certain parishes, and by the Sulpicians, who devoted themselves to service on Montréal Island.

A number of Sulpicians carried on their ministry in the former Acadia (Nova Scotia), some Récollets, who had recently come from France, established themselves on Île Royale and Île Saint-Jean, while some Capuchins landed in Louisiana. This latter colony was long racked by jurisdictional disputes between the Jesuits, who had arrived there first, and the priests who had been sent by the Séminaire de Québec (in particular to the Tamaroa country) at the beginning of the century, and between the Jesuits and Capuchins from 1720 onwards.

Even at the heart of the Canadian colony there were many worrisome problems. First, for nearly half a century there were difficulties concerning the status of the Séminaire de Québec, an institution which, because it was dependent on the Séminaire des Missions Étrangères in Paris, claimed that it did not come under the authority of the bishop of Québec — an interpretation that neither Bishop de Saint-Vallier nor his successors would accept. In addition the Cathedral Chapter, which by that time was composed mainly of Canadians, for a long time opposed the bishop, not even hesitating to bring its quarrel before the Conseil supérieur to have its rights confirmed and to obtain justice. This ill-considered step in a way furnished the State with justification to meddle in the Church's affairs, on the pretext that it was incapable of resolving its internal problems.

Again, immediately within the Chapter and the parish clergy there were subjects of discord, the Canadian canons and priests deeming it inadmissible for their Church to be entirely under the direction of French ecclesiastics. The lower clergy in particular showed its opposition so openly and displayed such an obvious spirit of independence that Bishop Dosquet considered setting up a flanking system of French priests for the Canadian priests so as to prevent them from communicating easily among themselves. Being in the majority, the Canadian members of the secular clergy finally saw certain of their members reach the top echelons in the diocese, which did not, however, change completely — nor permanently — the French character of the senior administration of the diocese.

These priests, spread about the colony's parishes, were poor, and most of them owed their subsistence entirely to the annual subsidies from the king. The parishes were too sprawling and too thinly populated; often the habitants, who were still at the stage of clearing the land, were as poor as their pastor; the tithes brought in scarcely anything, and the means were unavailable to build a church, much less a rectory. Consequently it was impossible to "fix" the parish charges, as the king and his representatives wanted. This problem of parish charges remained without a solution throughout the period of French rule in the eighteenth century, and at certain moments it antagonized relations between Church and State.

In the grip of internal problems, lacking priests, and in large measure living off the king's generosity, the Church withdrew somewhat into itself and lost some of its former enthusiasm for the Indian missions. To be sure, the Jesuits continued their work, but under different conditions, and less ostentatiously. In place of the long missionary expeditions of the previous century they often preferred the formula of "réductions," — villages where it was easier to keep the Indians faithful to Christianity and loyal to the French. The greatest successes of the century were perhaps the missions established within the populated area of the colony at Lorette, Saint-François and Sault Saint-Louis, where the Indians lived in parishes that had been created for them.

VII

The settlers probably had little knowledge of all the difficulties that faced their Church in the eighteenth century. Although they chafed at authority, even that of their priests, they were very much attached to their faith. Thus when the conquest came about, freedom of religion was a major concern for them, as it had been for the Acadians after 1713.

In 1760 another subject of anxiety tormented the Canadians: Bishop de Pontbriand having died in Montréal three months before the colony surrendered, they wondered whether the British would let them have a bishop if New France were to be ceded to them permanently.

Also, there was no doubt that the Protestant religion was establishing itself — at least provisionally — in the St. Lawrence valley, as it had not long ago in Nova Scotia. In this latter colony, which had been expanding at a great rate for the last ten years, the influence of the Anglicans, Lutherans and Methodists was evident, and churches and temples had been built at Halifax and Lunenburg.

What then would relations be like between the Catholics and Protestants in Canada?

VII

The bishops

In the eighteenth century the Church in New France too often found itself without a bishop, either because the see was vacant or the incumbent was in Europe. If we except Bishop François de Laval, who was retired and who died in 1708, and Bishop François-Louis de Pourroy de Lauberivière, who died a week after his arrival at Québec in 1740, over a period of sixty years only three bishops resided at Québec. Consequently the bishop's palace, which was falling into ruin because it was unoccupied, had to be repaired twice.

Bishop Jean-Baptiste de La Croix de Chevrières de Saint-Vallier distinguished himself through his pastoral work. In particular, in 1703 he published a catechism for the use of his diocese that is considered a model of religious pedagogy and that was well adapted to the character and mentality of the Canadian settlers.

Bishop Pierre-Herman Dosquet struggled in the midst of the Church's internal quarrels and finally returned to France in 1735; Bishop Henri-Marie Dubreil de Pontbriand, who came to Canada in 1741, found a Church that was relatively pacified, but he had to direct it during the critical period of the Seven Years' War.

The Canadian Church nevertheless continued slowly to progress: the number of parishes increased, and the religious communities grew in size, as did their charitable works — although the difficulties and problems were numerous.

Portrait of Bishop Pierre-Herman Dosquet (1691–1777), bishop of Québec from 1733 to 1739.

Bishop Dosquet and the other bishops of the eighteenth century, with the exception of Bishop Pontbriand, distinguished themselves by their long absences, intended or unintended. Various ills were attributed to this absenteeism: decline in moral standards, quarrels among the members of the clergy, the postponement of the ordination of priests and of Confirmations, and so on.

Société du Musée du Séminaire de Québec.

Photo Pierre Soulard.

Portrait of Bishop Henri-Marie Dubreil de Pontbriand (1708–1760), bishop of Québec from 1741 to 1760.

Société du Musée du Séminaire de Québec.

Photo Pierre Soulard.

A View of the Bishop's House with the Ruins as they appear in going down the Hill from the Upper to the Lower Town.   Drawn on the SPOT by Richᵈ Short.   Engraved by J. Fougeron.   Vue du Palais Episcopal et de ses Ruines, ainsi qu'elles paroissent en descendant a la Basse Ville.

London Published according to Act of Parliament Sepᵗ 25ᵗʰ 1761 by Richᵈ Short, & sold by Thoˢ Jefferys the Corner of St Martins Lane.

View of the bishop's palace and its ruins. Richard Short (known 1759–1761). Etching by J. Fougeron, printed by Thomas Jefferys, 1761.

Kalm described the bishop's palace as "a big, handsome building, with a large courtyard and a vegetable garden on one side of it, the whole being surrounded by a wall."

Public Archives of Canada, Ottawa: Picture Division (Negative no. C-352).

CATECHISME
DU DIOCESE
DE QUEBEC.
PAR MONSEIGNEUR
l'Illuſtriſſime & Reverendiſſime
Jean de la Croix de ſaint Valier,
Evêque de Quebec.

*En faveur des Curez & des Fideles de
ſon Diocêſe.*

A PARIS,

Chez URBAIN COUSTELIER,
ruë ſaint Jacques, au Cœur bon.

M. DCCII.

Jean-Baptiste de la Croix de Chevrières de Saint-Vallier. *Catéchisme du diocèse de Québec*. Paris: Chez Urbain Coustelier, 1702. Title page.

Bishop Saint-Vallier edited a catechism and a ritual of the diocese of Québec, because he wished "to see a uniform manner of teaching the Christian doctrine" and of celebrating religious worship. These works remained in use for a long time in Canada.

Société du Musée du Séminaire de Québec.

VII

The parishes

If the parishes in Canada had not sprung up entirely at random, they were generally so large that it was difficult and often arduous for a priest to serve them by himself, all the more so as he was sometimes responsible for more than one mission.

Consequently, at the king's request an inquiry was conducted in 1721 into the advantages and disadvantages of church locations with a view to effecting the necessary changes. This objective was achieved in 1722, with the intendant's assistance, through the creation of eighty-two parish districts.

Nevertheless, it remained virtually impossible to establish fixed parishes served by resident priests and supported by tithes levied in the parishes, which would have their own churches and rectories. The difficulty lay in the sparseness and poverty of the population in most of the parish districts. As late as 1742, Bishop de Pontbriand was still pointing this out to Maurepas.

Of the some 120 parishes or missions in Canada at the end of the French regime, perhaps about 40 could provide for the upkeep of their priest and church. Even at Québec Bishop de Pontbriand had to go heavily into debt in the 1740s to obtain the reconstruction of his cathedral church, which also served as the parish church: who in the rural areas could have done the same?

L'an mil sept cents vingt...

"Reports on expediency or inexpediency drawn up in each of the parishes of New France by Monsieur Collet, king's attorney general to the Conseil supérieur of Québec," 1721.

Collet inquired of the settlers everywhere about "the present size" of their parish and of the "number of heads of families that constitute it," and asked whether some of them "are hindered in attending divine service by the difficulty of the routes or the distance." The inquiry resulted in the ruling of 20 September 1721, delimiting 82 parish districts.

Archives nationales, Paris: Fonds des Colonies, série C11E, vol. 12, fol. 66.

Photo Studio Littré.

[Plan of an unidentified Canadian church]. Jean Maillou. [Circa 1715]. Plan: col. ms., 47.0 × 36.3 cm.

In addition to conducting his ministry, the parish priest might carry out many other duties, such as teaching the children, looking after the poor, visiting the sick, advising parishioners, keeping the registers of births, marriages and deaths, or even drawing up contracts when a notary was not available.

Société du Musée du Séminaire de Québec: Polygraphie 2, 77.

Photo Patrick Altman.

Letter from Bishop Pontbriand to the minister, 22 August 1742.

"It is not possible to make all the parish charges permanent [that is to say, to name parish priests with appointment for life], either because the parishes are not completely constituted, or because a single priest is serving several parishes, or because the income from some of them is too small . . . ." Furthermore, permanence of appointment would make the parish priests "independent" and would hinder the "making of the necessary partitionings."

Archives nationales, Paris: Fonds des Colonies, série C11A, vol. 78, fol. 403-403v.

Photo Studio Littré.

Paroisses qui peuvent se passer de suplémens

a Montreal.   190

La prairie de la Magdeleine

Boucherville.

Varennes.

Verchéres.

La pointe claire

La pointe aux trembles.

La chenayé

St Sulpices.

    a Quebec.

La pointe aux trembles.

Charlebourg.

Le Chateau Richer

St joachim

La ste famille

St pierre

St Laurent.

St jean

Le Cap St ignace.

List of the "parishes that can do without a supplement" in the Governments of Québec and Montréal, 1731.

Because of the small incomes coming from the tithes, most of the parishes could not do without the "supplement" granted by the king.

Archives nationales, Paris: Fonds des Colonies, série C[11A], vol. 56, fol. 190.

Photo Studio Littré.

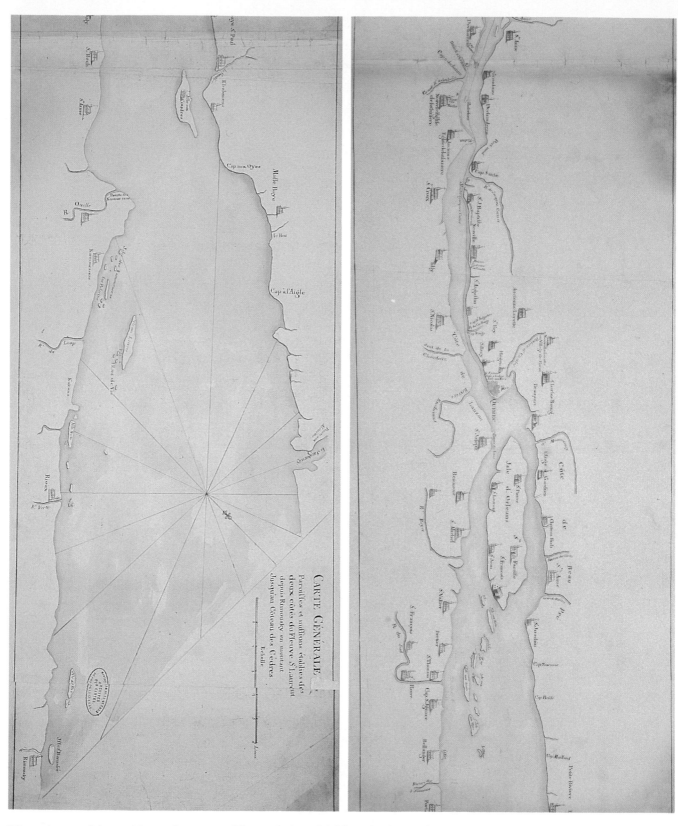

"General map of the parishes and missions established on both sides of the St. Lawrence River . . . ." [Anonymous, 1750]. Map: col. ms., 36.0 × 349.0 cm.

The settler's social life took place mainly within the parish. There he received the orders of the civil and religious authorities and took part in military exercises, corvées, festivities and ceremonies. The church became a centre for social gatherings and community activities.

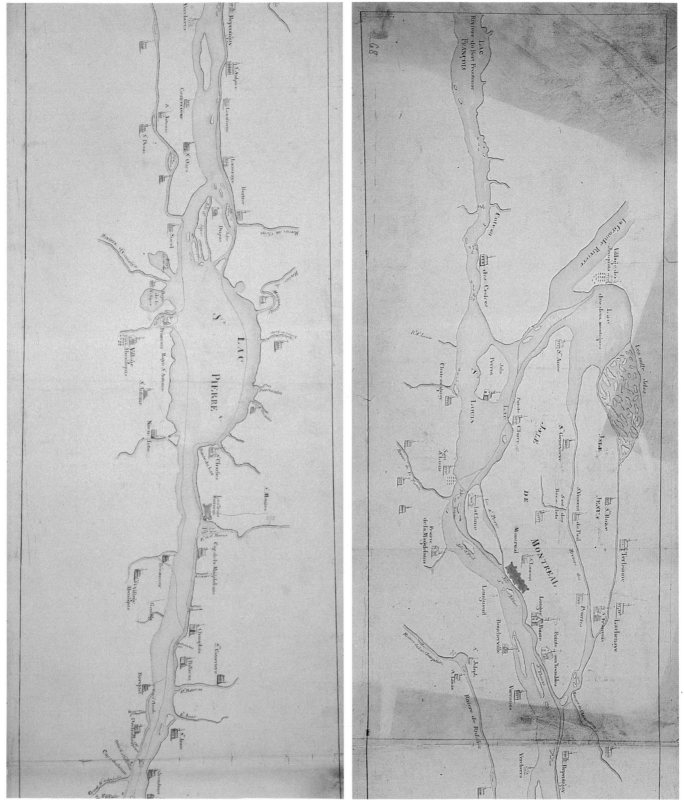

Service historique de l'Armée,
Vincennes, France: 7 B 68.

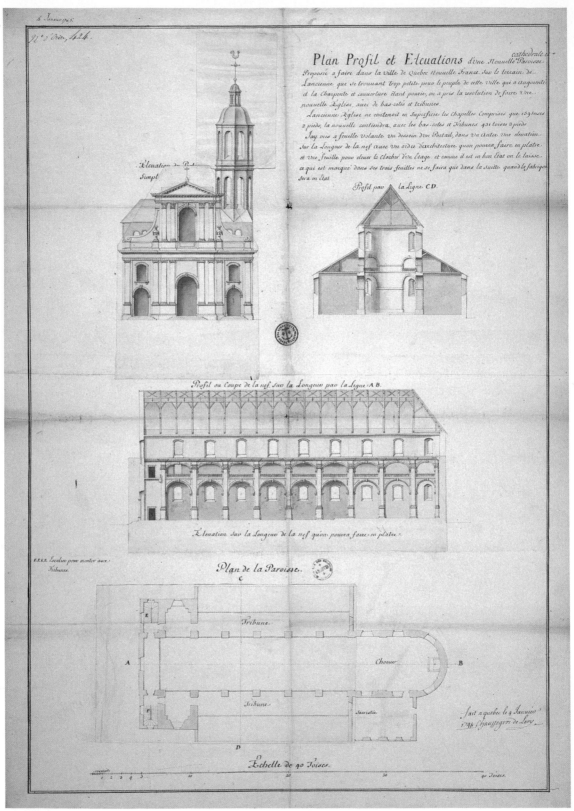

"Plan, profile and elevations of a new cathedral and parish church being proposed for the town of Québec . . . ." Gaspard-Joseph Chaussegros de Léry. 4 January 1745. Plan: col. ms., 83.5 × 56.0 cm.

Bishop Pontbriand decided to have his cathedral, which was too small and nearly in ruins, rebuilt. Work was begun in 1745, and four years later work was still going on "to decorate it."

Archives nationales, Paris: Section Outre-Mer, Dépôt des fortifications des colonies, Amerique septentrionale, 424 A.

Photo Studio Littré.

VII

Nationalism and the Canadian clergy

The Canadian priests who carried on their work in the colony had for the most part boarded at the Séminaire de Québec while following the courses given by the Jesuits at their college. They owed their training therefore to French priests and religious; now, around the 1720s, they became aware of the fact that their entire Church was still under the direction of the French.

With the spirit of independence and the inborn indocility that characterized them as much as their compatriots, these priests protested strongly against their subordinate status and caused the bishop great concern. Rather than giving in to demands that, after all, were legitimate, Bishop Dosquet sought a way to keep in check that part of the clergy of the diocese that was to his mind too turbulent.

The Chapter, in which Canadians were now in the majority, fought, sometimes fiercely, to have Canadian priests promoted; the canons attacked all the ecclesiastical leaders who were from France: the bishop, the superior of the Séminaire de Québec, the Jesuits and even their own dean. The situation changed somewhat: at the end of the 1730s the dean and the official of the Chapter, the vicar capitular and the vicar general in Montréal were Canadians. But in the 1740s, under Bishop de Pontbriand the French gradually resumed direction of the Church, and at the time of the conquest they held all the senior posts except within the Chapter and except for the office of vicar general at Trois-Rivières.

Petition from the Canadians addressed to Minister Maurepas, Québec, 18 October 1730.

The colony "feels particularly obliged to the Séminaire de Québec . . . for the care that it has taken to bring up the youth; it owes to it the number of priests, parish priests and missionaries who applied themselves zealously, as those at the present time apply themselves to ministering to the majority of its parishes and even of the missions to the Indians."

appliqués comme ceux d'apresent S'appliquent a deservir la plus grande partie de
Ses paroices et même des missions pour les sauvages elle doit par consequent
ressentir vivement la peine et l'embaras ou il Se trouve aujourd'huy acause des
Dettes que tout le monde en ce païs çait avoir été contractées en consequence des
mal heurs qui luy sont arrivés, ou des pertes considerables qu'il a Souffertes, Si
mieux on n'aime les attribuer a la trop grande, mais charitable generosité
des personnes qui l'ont gouverné jusqu'apresent. Cette communauté est
visiblement prête a Succomber Sous le poids des dtes Dettes qui l'accablent et qui
l'empeschent de faire actuelement au païs autant de bien qu'elle y en a fait
par le passé et qui cependant ne luy en otent point le desir ny la volonté ainsi
qu'évidemment il paroit par les efforts qu'elle fait tous les jours. C'est pour quoy
Monseigneur, les Soussignés vous prient tres humblement de vouloir bien
au pres du Roy nôtre Illustre Monarque, dont la nouvelle France éprouve
chaque jour les bontés et liberalités Royales, honorer d'une protection
speciale et particuliere cette dte communauté; c'est la grace, qu'en reconnoissance
de Ses services vous demandent tous les Suppliants avec confiance et avec
un tres profond respect.

a Quebec le 18e octobre 1730

Lachassaigne

[signatures]

Canada. Recapitulation du Recensement de la Colonie de l'année 1735: a 1736: Sçavoir

Eglises	99:
Curéa	79:
Chanoines et Eclesiastiq.s des Séminaires	81:
Jesuites	17:
Recolets	40:
Religieuses Vrsulines	79:
Religieuses des hôtels Dieu	86:
Religieuses de l'hopital general	80:
freres Charons	6:
filles de la Congregation	67:
Presbiteres	77:
Moulins a bled	118:
Moulins a scie	58:
familles	6758:
hommes au dessus de 50: ans	1790:

"Recapitulation of the census of the colony [Canada] for the year 1735–1736."

The Church had rapidly been Canadianized: in 1760, 50 per cent of the clergy was Canadian; as for the nuns, not one had been born in France.

Archives nationales, Paris: Section Outre-Mer, série G¹, vol. 460.

Photo Studio Littré.

Portrait of Eustache Chartier de Lotbinière (1688–1749). Artist unknown. Oil on canvas, 1725.

Chartier de Lotbinière, who was appointed in succession archdeacon, vicar general and dean of the chapter of the cathedral of Québec, was one of the few Canadians to hold a high post within the ecclesiastical hierarchy.

Public Archives of Canada, Ottawa: Picture Division (Negative no. C-100376).

Portrait of Mother Louise Soumande de Saint-Augustin (1664–1708), religious hospitaller, first superior of the Hôpital Général of Québec. Artist unknown. Oil on canvas, 1708.

Like Mother Saint-Augustin, several Canadian nuns would be elected superior of their communities in the eighteenth century.

Monastère des augustines de l'Hôpital-Général de Québec.

Photo Patrick Altman.

celles qui en ont besoin sont connuës par La

distribution qu'on en fait.

plusieurs seigneurs me demandent des prêtres pou

donner lieu à établir leurs terres. je ne puis leur en

donner parcequ'ils ne pourroïent y subsister &

parceque les prêtres nous manquent. il faudroi

en faire venir de france et je ne suis pas en

état de faire cette dépense qui seroit cependant

bien util en pais, non seulement pour l'établ

mais encore pour inspirer aux peuples La fidel

L'amour et le zéle que des sujets doivent à leur Ro

mon idée seroit de mettre un curé francois entre

deux paroisses gouvernées par des prêtres canadie

j'en dis hier les raisons à Mr de Beauharnois et

Letter from Bishop Dosquet to the minister, Québec, 11 September 1731.

Bishop Dosquet found that the Canadian priests were "of an unruly and independent mind." As the colony lacked priests, he suggested "bringing some from France" and "putting a Frenchman as parish priest in between two parishes governed by Canadian priests." That, he said, would be a good way "to inspire in the people the loyalty, love and zeal that subjects owe their king."

Archives nationales, Paris: Fonds des Colonies, série C11A, vol. 56, fol. 184v.

Photo Studio Littré.

Portrait of Father Emmanuel Crespel
(1703–1775), provincial commissioner
of the Récollets in Canada from 1750
on. Father François. Oil on canvas, circa
1755.

The Recollets carried on their work on
Île Royale, Île Saint-Jean, in Canada and
in certain distant posts. They might be
military chaplains, parish priests,
teachers or missionaries.

Musée du Québec, Québec.

The Canadians' religion

The Canadians were "devoted to their religion," and in their own way they held their bishops and priests in esteem, even though they sometimes had difficulty in submitting to their directives. The display of feeling by the people that followed Bishop de Laval's death clearly demonstrated the depth of their religious sentiments.

If on occasion they celebrated religious feast-days somewhat too irreverently, and if their pilgrimages, inspired as they were by piety, might nevertheless give rise to disturbances, the fact remains that the Canadians, moved by a sincere faith, liked to surround themselves with religious symbols, such as wayside shrines and holy pictures.

If one had escaped from any peril — particularly from shipwreck — after invoking the aid of a saint, he painted the scene in which his life had been threatened, or had it painted, and placed this *ex voto* in a church dedicated to the saint who had come to his aid.

The Canadians were pious, but they were not prudish for all that; Bishop de Saint-Vallier, with his greater austerity, certainly had reasons to reproach them on questions of vanity, excessive luxury, immodest dress, drunkenness and — the word keeps coming back constantly — indocility.

Letter from Intendant Raudot to the minister, Québec, 13 November 1708.

The great majority of religious led exemplary and devoted lives. Some, like Bishop Laval, had even acquired a reputation for saintliness. At the latter's death "the people canonized him, as it were, having had the same veneration for his body as for those of the saints. Having come in crowds from all parts . . . to touch him with their chaplets and prayer-books, they even cut off pieces of his robe."

Archives nationales, Paris: Fonds des Colonies, série C¹¹G, vol. 3, fol. 181v.

Photo Studio Littré.

Ex-voto offered by Louis Prat. Attributed to Michel Dessailliant, *dit* Richeterre (known 1700–1723). Oil on canvas, 1706.

The Canadians held in particular veneration the Blessed Virgin, Saint Joseph and Saint Louis. The devotion to Saint Anne was also very widespread, and several ex-votos were dedicated to her in recognition of favours received.

Musée historial, Basilique de Sainte-Anne-de-Beaupré.

Photo Kedl.

Pastoral letter from Bishop de Saint-Vallier denouncing "the bad habit . . . of appearing against decency in nothing but a shirt, without underpants or breeches during the summer to avoid the extreme heat," Montréal, 26 April 1719.

Rigid in its morality, the clergy regularly condemned certain weaknesses or ordinary occasions for sinning, such as dancing, games of chance, immodesty, drunkenness and fornication. But many settlers were more willing to submit to their inclinations than to the directives from the religious authorities.

Public Archives of Canada, Ottawa: Manuscript Division, MG 18, H 25.

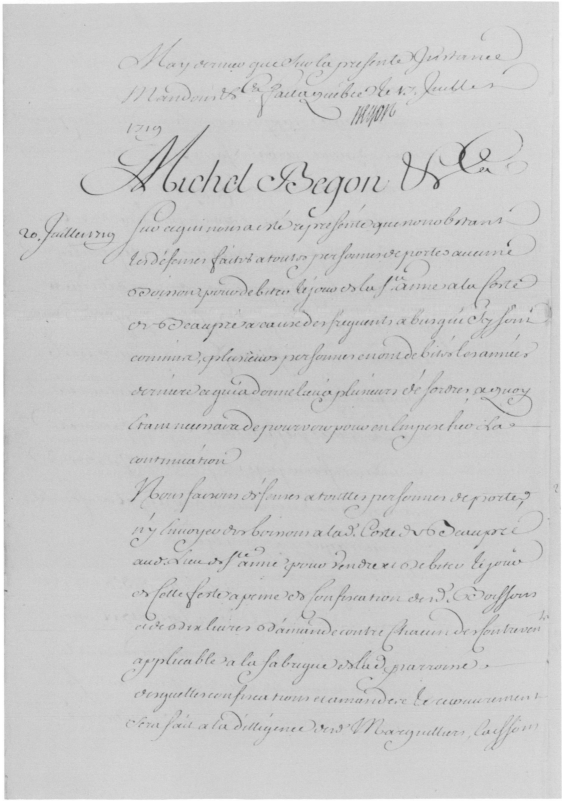

Ordinance by Intendant Bégon forbidding "taking or sending spirits to the aforementioned Côte de Beaupré in the aforementioned locality of Sainte-Anne to be sold and served to customers" on the feast day of Saint Anne, Québec, 20 July 1719.

The Church could count not only upon material aid from the State but also upon its support to enforce respect of its precepts and directives. In return it had to submit to the authority of the king and the minister, who sometimes intervened in its internal affairs.

Archives nationales du Québec, Centre d'archives de Québec: Ordonnances des intendants, cahier 6, fol. 344v.

Photo Belvédère.

The Indian missions

In the eighteenth century the Jesuits were still the main support of the missionary effort in New France. Their missions covered the entire territory: they were present in what are today Maine and the southern part of New Brunswick, at Tadoussac and Chicoutimi, Michillimakinac, and various Great Lake posts, and in the Kaskaskia and Chacta countries, among others, in Louisiana.

Certain Jesuits accompanied explorers such as La Vérendrye, but most of them preferred to carry on their work with the Indians who had already been converted and to evangelize the semi-sedentary tribes. The constant missionary expeditions of the preceding century therefore disappeared almost entirely in the eighteenth century.

On the Atlantic coast, on Île Royale, Île Saint-Jean, and in French Acadia (the southern part of New Brunswick), some secular priests and some Spiritains sent out by the Séminaire des Missions Étrangères succeeded in keeping the Micmacs loyal to the Church and the king.

Within the Canadian colony a certain number of missions were flourishing: at Lorette (Hurons), Saint-François and Bécancour (Abenakis), Sault Saint-Louis (Iroquois), and Lac des Deux-Montagnes (Algonkins, Nipissings and Iroquois).

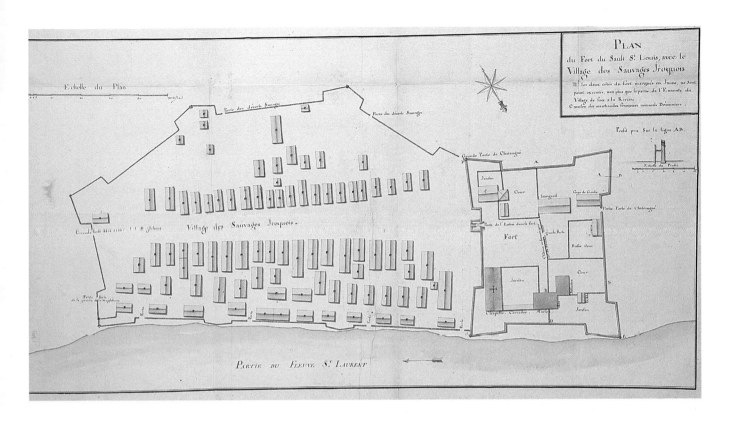

"Plan of the fort of Sault St. Louis, with the Iroquois Indian village." Louis Franquet. 1752. Plan: col. ms.

According to the engineer Franquet the Jesuit mission at Sault-Saint-Louis (Caughnawaga), near Montréal, had a population of about "200 warriors and 10 to 11 hundred souls."

Bibliothèque de l'Inspection du Génie, Paris: Ms f⁰ 210ᶜ, N⁰ 2.

Photo Studio Littré.

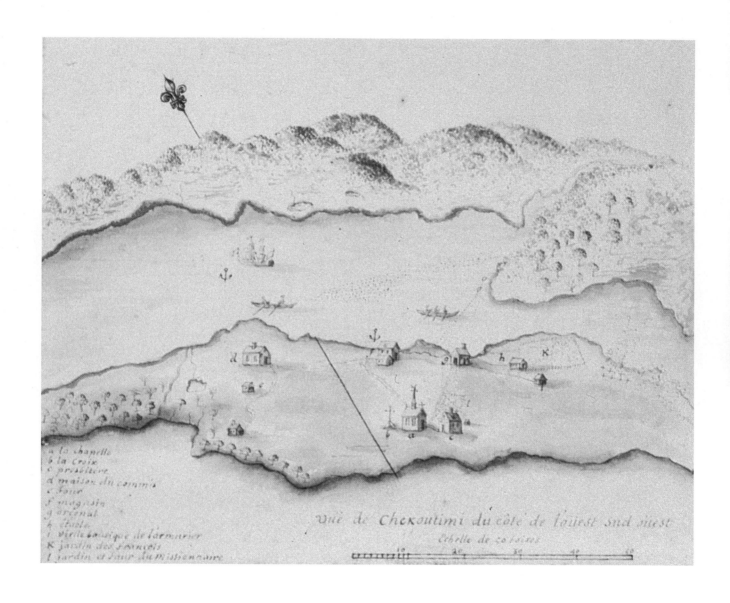

a la chapelle
b la Croix
c presbitère
d maison du commis
e four
f magasin
g arcenal
h etable
i vielle bastique de l'aemarier
K jardin des francois
l jardin et lair du missionnaire

Vüe de Chekoutimi du côté de l'oüest sud oüest

Echelle de 50 toises

"View of Chicoutimi from the West-South-West," taken from "The Saguenay River going upstream as far as Chicoutimi." [Anonymous. 1748]. Map: col. ms., 46.0 × 58.5 cm.

Chicoutimi was both a trading post belonging to the King's Domain and a Montagnais mission run by the Jesuits. The religious also ministered to other posts belonging to the Domain, such as Tadoussac and Sept-Îles.

Bibliothèque nationale, Paris: Département des cartes et plans, Service hydrographique de la Marine, portefeuille 127, 4, 5.

21

331

Cet accident acheva de deconcerter tous les habitans du pays,
qui n'avoit commencé cet ouvrage, qu'ils regardoient impossible,
que parceque le missionnaire l'avoit exigé d'eux: il sortoit de
chaire comme on vint luy apprendre cette facheuse nouvelle, et
et ne repondit autre chose, sinon qu'il falloit reprendre l'ouvrage,
les habitans eurent beau luy representer l'inutilité d'une nouvelle
tentative, il fallut mettre la main à l'oeuvre: et pour cela
commencer par gaigner adroitement les principaux, ce qu'il fit.
finalement au bout de deux ans cette digue immense a été
mise hors de marée, et tout ce qui restoit à faire à la prise
de beausejour, n'étoit tout au plus qu'un travail de 8 mois;
enfin le travail immense qui s'est fait sous la conduite de ce seul
missionnaire etoit en 1761 et 6 ans après que les anglois ont
pris cette partie, ce qu'il etoit lorsqu'on a été forcé de le quitter
suivant M. manach qui y a passé en la dite année plusieurs
fois. ainsi se multiplioit ce missionnaire, et toutes les oeuvres
qui partageoient, tendoient toujours à affermir la religion dans
le pays: il etoit persuadé comme on le doit être, qu'il falloit
avant toutes choses assurer la vie et la tranquilité aux habitans
pour en faire dans la suite de bons chretiens, et ainsi perpetuer
l'esprit de ferveur qui animoit les chretiens de l'acadie. pendant
tout le tems depuis son retour de france en 1753 dans l'îsle, jusqu'au
mois de juin 1755 les sauvages qu'il avoit confié aux soins de Monsieur
recevoient de tems à autre et 2 ou 3 fois l'année
il se joignoit à son confrere pour leur donner des retraites, les
affermir dans la foy et l'attachement au Roy leur pere: c'etoit
à luy à qui tous les ans on adressoit les presens que le Roy faisoit
à la nation, et pendant 3 ou 4 jours de duroit cette distribution
il y avoit deux discours chaque jours dont la substance etoit de
leur faire sentir l'obligation infinie qu'ils avoient au Roy,
surtout pour le bien inestimable du depot de la foy qu'il
leur avoit procuré: on leur mettoit devant les yeux d'une maniere
pathetique ce qu'ils etoient avant qu'ils fussent eclairés des lumieres de l'evangile,
et ce qu'ils seroient devenus s'ils etoient demeurés dans les tenebres
de l'idolatrie.

Report from the missionary Jean-Louis Le Loutre, circa 1763.

On the Atlantic coast (Maine and the present-day maritime provinces) the missionaries worked at "strengthening [the Indians] in the faith and in their attachment to the king their father." Some, such as the Abbé Le Loutre, even went so far as urging them to war against the British colonists: if they sided with the British, would these Indians not run the risk of losing the faith?

Séminaire des Missions étrangères, Paris.

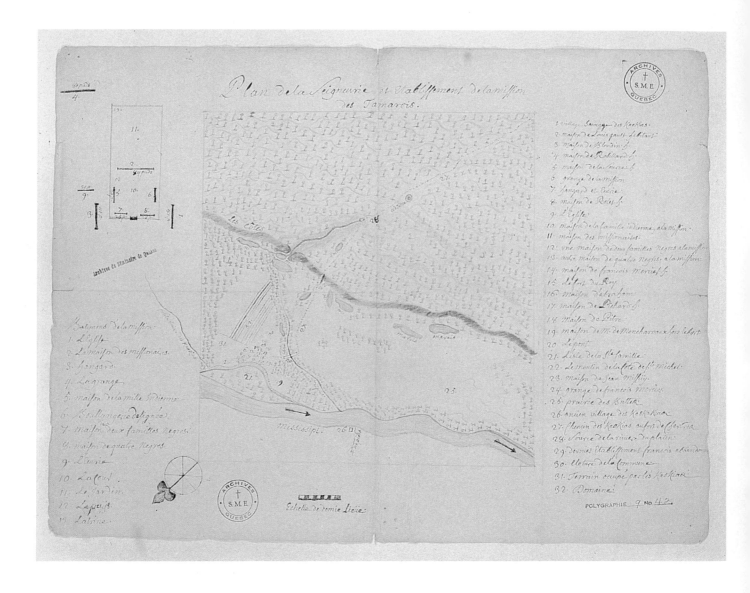

"Plan of the seigneury and the Tamaroa missionary establishment." J.P. Mercier, 1735. Map: col. ms., 24.7 × 25.4 cm.

Around 1740 there were a few Indian missions and five French parishes in the Illinois country (the Upper Mississippi valley) that were served by the Jesuits or by priests from the Séminaire des Missions Étrangères. The latter carried on their work at the Tamaroa mission, where they attended not only to the Indians but also to the Canadians who had created a village nearby.

Société du Musée du Séminaire de Québec: Polygraphie 9, 42.

Photo Pierre Soulard.

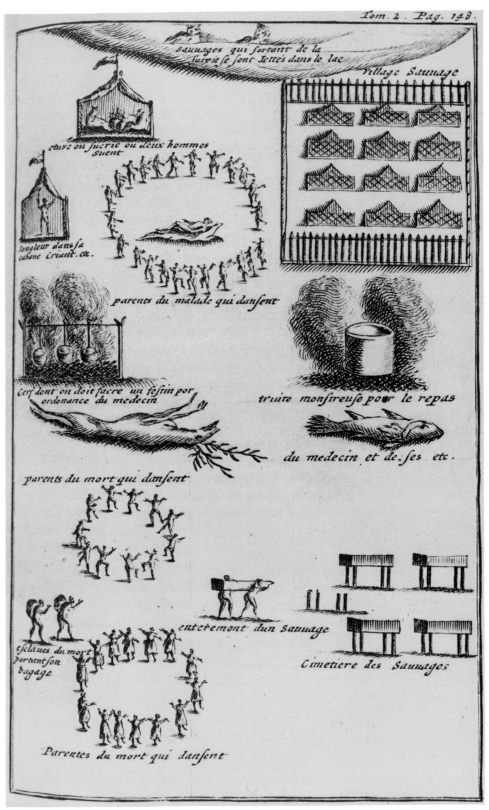

Indian practices. Etching with line engraving.

In Louis Armand de Lom d'Arce, Baron de Lahontan. *Mémoires de l'Amérique septentrionale* . . . . La Haye, Charles Delo, 1706. Vol. 2, p. 148.

The Indians believed that a multitude of spirits, good or bad, lived in men, animals and even objects. To win their good will they had recourse to various practices: sacrifices, sweating sessions, sacred dances, feasts, etc. Their medicine men, who were in a way intermediaries between men and the spirits, interpreted dreams, forecast the future and cured illnesses.

Public Archives of Canada, Ottawa: Library.

The Church in Acadia and Louisiana

At the beginning of the eighteenth century some Récollets exercised their ministry among the settlers in Acadia; after the territory had been ceded to England the Acadians were ministered to by secular priests, in particular Sulpicians. The situation of this greatly reduced clergy proved to be extremely delicate: if they succeeded in establishing good relations with the conqueror, the French authorities considered their conduct "not very patriotic"; if they displayed greater favour for the French cause, the English rulers then regarded them as hostile.

On Île Royale and Île Saint-Jean, Récollets from the provinces of Paris and Brittany were in charge of parishes until 1731, when "being unable to keep up these establishments," the Récollets from Paris withdrew, leaving the entire care of the ministry to the others. At Louisbourg the hospital was put in the hands of the Brothers of Charity, and teaching was entrusted to the sisters of the Congrégation de Notre-Dame.

In Louisiana, from the 1720s on it was mostly Capuchins who ministered to the capital city and the French territories along the Lower Mississippi; they often quarrelled with the Jesuits, who had charge mainly of the French posts in the North (in particular in the Illinois country), and who claimed wider jurisdiction to the South. In Nouvelle-Orléans Ursulines from France assumed responsibility for hospital care and education.

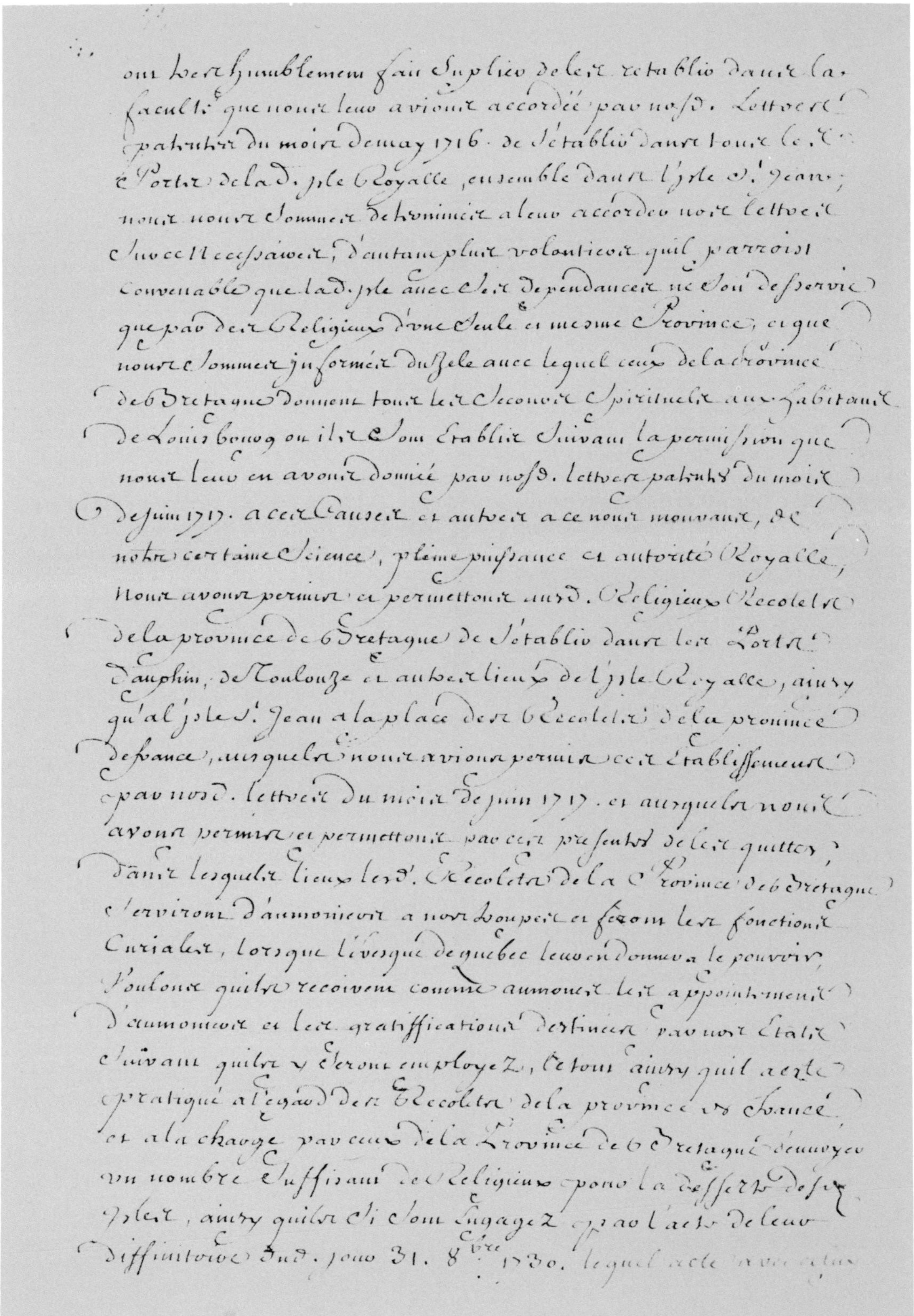
ont tres humblement fait supplier de les restablir dans la
faculté que nous leur avions accordée par nosd. Lettres
patentes du mois de may 1716. de s'establir dans tous les
Ports de lad. Isle Royalle, ensemble dans l'Isle St. Jean;
nous nous sommes determinés a leur accorder nos lettres
sur ce necessaires, d'autant plus volontiers qu'il paroist
convenable que lad. Isle avec ses dependances ne soit desservie
que par des Religieux d'une seule et mesme Province, et que
nous sommes informés du zele avec lequel ceux de la Province
de Bretagne donnent tous les secours spirituels aux habitans
de Louisbourg ou ils sont Etablis suivant la permission que
nous leur en avons donnée par nosd. lettres patentes du mois
de juin 1717. a ces causes et autres a ce nous mouvans, de
notre certaine science, pleine puissance et autorité Royalle,
nous avons permis et permettons ausd. Religieux Recolets
de la province de Bretagne de s'establir dans les Ports
Dauphin, de Toulouze et autres lieux de l'Isle Royalle, ainsy
qu'a l'Isle St. Jean a la place des Recolets de la province
de france, auxquels nous avions permis ces Etablissements
par nosd. lettres du mois de juin 1717. et auxquels nous
avons permis et permettons par ces presentes de les quitter;
dans lesquels lieux lesd. Recolets de la Province de Bretagne
serviront d'aumoniers a nos troupes et feront les fonctions
Curiales, lorsque l'evesque de quebec leur en donnera le pouvoir,
voulons qu'ils recoivent comme aumoniers les appointements
d'aumoniers et les gratiffications destinées par nos Etats
suivant qu'ils y seront employez, Ce tout ainsy qu'il a esté
pratiqué a l'egard des Recolets de la province de france.
et a la charge par ceux de la Province de Bretagne d'envoyer
un nombre suffisant de Religieux pour la desserte desd.
Isles, ainsy qu'ils s'y sont engagez par l'acte de leur
diffinitoire du 31. 8bre 1730. lequel acte avec celuy

Letters patent from the king permitting "the Récollets of the province of Brittany to establish themselves in the ports of Dauphin, Toulouse and other places on Île Royale, as well as at Île Saint-Jean, to replace the Récollets from the province of France," Fontainebleau, July 1731.

These Récollets "will serve as chaplains" to the troops "and perform certain functions of parish priests" in the French parishes.

Archives nationales, Paris: Fonds des Colonies, série B, vol. 55, fol. 583.

Photo Studio Littré.

1723.

rent rien de plus preſſé, que de remédier à un ſi grand déſordre. Ils jetterent les yeux ſur les PP. Capucins, & en ayant obtenu pluſieurs, ils les diſtribuerent dans les Quartiers, où il y avoit un plus grand nombre d'Habitations Françoiſes.

On penſe à donner des Miſſionnaires aux Sauvages.

Il n'étoit pas d'une moindre conſéquence d'avoir des Miſſionnaires parmi les Sauvages, au milieu deſquels nous nous étions établis. Nous avons vû que le ſalut de ces Peuples fut toujours le principal objet, que ſe propoſerent nos Rois par tout, où ils étendirent leur Domination dans le nouveau Monde, & l'experience de près de deux Siécles nous avoit fait comprendre que le moyen le plus ſûr de nous attacher les Naturels du Pays étoit de les gagner à JESUS-CHRIST. On ne pouvoit ignorer d'ailleurs qu'indépendamment même du fruit, que les Ouvriers évangéliques pouvoient faire parmi eux, la ſeule préſence d'un Homme, reſpectable par ſon caractere, qui entende leur langue, qui puiſſe obſerver leur démarches, & qui ſçache, en gagnant la confiance de quelques-uns, ſe faire inſtruire de leurs deſſeins, vaut ſouvent mieux qu'une Garniſon; ou peut du moins y ſuppléer, & donner le tems aux Gouverneurs de prendre des meſures pour déconcerter leurs intrigues. L'exemple des Illinois, qui depuis l'année 1717 étoient incorporés au Gouvernement de la Louyſiane, ſuffiſoit pour faire voir de quelle importance il étoit de ne point laiſſer plus lontems les autres Nations ſans Miſſionnaires.

On y envoye des Jeſuites.

La Compagnie des Indes le comprit, & dès l'année 1725 elle s'adreſſa aux Jeſuites, dont

1725.

un grand nombre s'offrit pour cette nouvelle Miſſion. Mais comme les Superieurs n'avoient pu accorder à tous la permiſſion de s'y conſacrer, & qu'il n'y en avoit pas aſſez pour en donner à toutes les Nations, le Commandant & les Directeurs crurent devoir placer ceux, qui arriverent les Premiers, dans les endroits, où il n'y avoit point de Capucins; d'où il arriva que les Natchez, ceux de tous les Peuples de la Louyſiane, qu'il étoit à propos d'éclairer de plus près, n'en eurent point, & l'on ne s'apperçut de la faute, qu'on avoit faite, que quand elle fut irréparable. On pourvut en même tems à l'éducation des jeunes Filles Françoiſes de la Capitale & des environs, en faiſant venir des Urſulines de France; & pour ne point multiplier les Etabliſſemens dans une Colonie, qui commençoit à peine à ſe former, ces mêmes Religieuſes furent chargées du ſoin de l'Hôpital.

M. Perrier Commandant Général de la Louyſiane,

Au mois d'Octobre de l'année 1726 M. PERRIER, Lieutenant de Vaiſſeau, fut nommé Commandant général de la Louyſiane à la place de M. de Bienville, qui repaſſa en France. Quoique tout parût aſſez tranquille dans le Pays, le nouveau Commandant comprit bientôt la néceſſité d'y avoir plus de Troupes, qu'il n'y en avoit trouvé. Plus il connut les Sauvages, & plus il ſe convainquit qu'on ne les fixeroit jamais dans notre alliance; qu'on ne s'aſſûreroit pas même de ne les point avoir pour Ennemis, & qu'on ne pourroit empêcher nos Voiſins de ſuccomber à la tentation de les engager à conſpirer contre nous, qu'en garniſſant tous les

1725.

1726.

Pierre-François-Xavier de Charlevoix. *Histoire et description générale de la Nouvelle-France . . . .* Paris: chez la veuve Ganeau, 1744, vol. 4, p. 238–239.

In Louisiana the Jesuits were responsible mainly for the French posts in the North and the Indian missions. Beginning in the 1720s Capuchins were assigned to "the regions [of the lower Mississippi] where there were a greater number of French settlements." "At the same time provision was made for the education of the French girls in the capital and the surrounding region by bringing in some Ursulines . . . . The same nuns were put in charge of running the hospital."

Public Archives of Canada, Ottawa: Library.

St. Paul's Church, Halifax. Richard Short (known, 1759–1761). Etching by J. Fougeron.

The settlers (English, German, Swiss, etc.) who colonised Nova Scotia around the 1750s were for the most part Protestant: Anglicans, Lutherans, Congregationalists, Calvinists and Presbyterians, among others. At Halifax, they built an Anglican church (St. Paul), a "Protestant Dissenter's Meeting House," and a little church (St. George) for the German Lutheran

community. At Lunenburg, the German and Swiss settlers built a temple (St. John), where an Anglican pastor practised his ministry.

Public Archives of Canada, Ottawa. Picture Division (Negative no. C-4293).

Sources of Illustrations

Canada

Archives des soeurs grises, Montréal
Document no. 171.

Archives nationales du Québec, Centre d'archives de Québec
20, 29, 30, 62, 64, 65, 113, 199.

Archives nationales du Québec, Centre régional de Montréal
98, 173.

Hudson's Bay Company Archives, Provincial Archives of Manitoba, Winnipeg
1, 2, 3, 15, 149.

McCord Museum, Montréal
151.

Monastère des augustines de l'Hôpital-Général de Québec
193.

Monastère des augustines de l'Hôtel-Dieu de Québec
166.

Musée de l'île Sainte-Hélène, Montréal
18, 57, 167.

Musée du château Ramezay, Montréal
132.

Musée du Québec, Québec
195.

Musée historial, Basilique de Sainte-Anne-de-Beaupré
169, 197.

Musée régional de Vaudreuil-Soulanges
68.

National Currency Collection, Bank of Canada, Ottawa
122.

National Gallery of Canada, Ottawa
27.

National Library of Canada, Ottawa
176.

Parks Canada, Fortress of Louisbourg
42.

Parks Canada, Ottawa
109.

Public Archives of Canada, Ottawa: Library
45, 81, 144, 154, 177, 178, 179, 204, 206.

Public Archives of Canada, Ottawa: Manuscript Division
36, 56, 95, 99, 101, 107, 116, 117, 123, 127, 128, 129, 134, 158, 198.

Public Archives of Canada, Ottawa: National Map Collection
4, 12, 13, 14, 28, 46, 66, 111, 124, 139, 147.

Public Archives of Canada, Ottawa: Picture Division
25, 44, 49, 52, 53, 59, 82, 89, 100, 103, 106, 112, 114, 156, 160, 162, 175, 182, 192, 207.

Queen's University Archives, Kingston
108.
Société du Musée du Séminaire de Québec
9, 63, 180, 181, 183, 185, 203.

Other Countries
Archives du ministère des Affaires étrangères, Paris
83, 102.
Archives municipales, Rochefort, France
150.
Archives nationales, Paris
5, 6, 17, 21, 23, 24, 33, 39, 40, 55, 58, 60, 61, 67, 69, 71, 73, 75, 77, 78, 80, 88, 90, 91, 93, 96, 97, 104, 105, 118, 119, 125, 126, 130, 131, 133, 135, 137, 138, 140, 141, 142, 146, 152, 153, 155, 157, 159, 163, 164, 168, 170, 174, 184, 186, 187, 190, 194, 196, 205.
Archives nationales, Paris: Section Outre-Mer
8, 31, 37, 38, 41, 47, 48, 72, 74, 84, 85, 86, 87, 92, 136, 143, 145, 172, 189, 191.
Bibliothèque de l'Inspection du Génie, Paris
34, 200.
Bibliothèque nationale, Paris
19, 32, 54, 76, 121, 161, 201.
British Library, London
10.
Musée de la Marine, Paris
22, 120.
Museum of Art, Carnegie Institute, Pittsburgh
110.
Newberry Library, Chicago
26.
Peabody Museum, Harvard University, Cambridge, Massachusetts
50, 51.
Public Record Office, London
43, 79, 115, 148.
Royal Library, Windsor Castle, England
16.
Séminaire des Missions étrangères, Paris
202.
Service historique de l'Armée, Vincennes, France
94, 188.
Service historique de la Marine, Vincennes, France
7, 35, 70.

Private Collections
Collection Le Moyne de Martigny, Rubelles, France
11.
Private collection, France
165.

Index

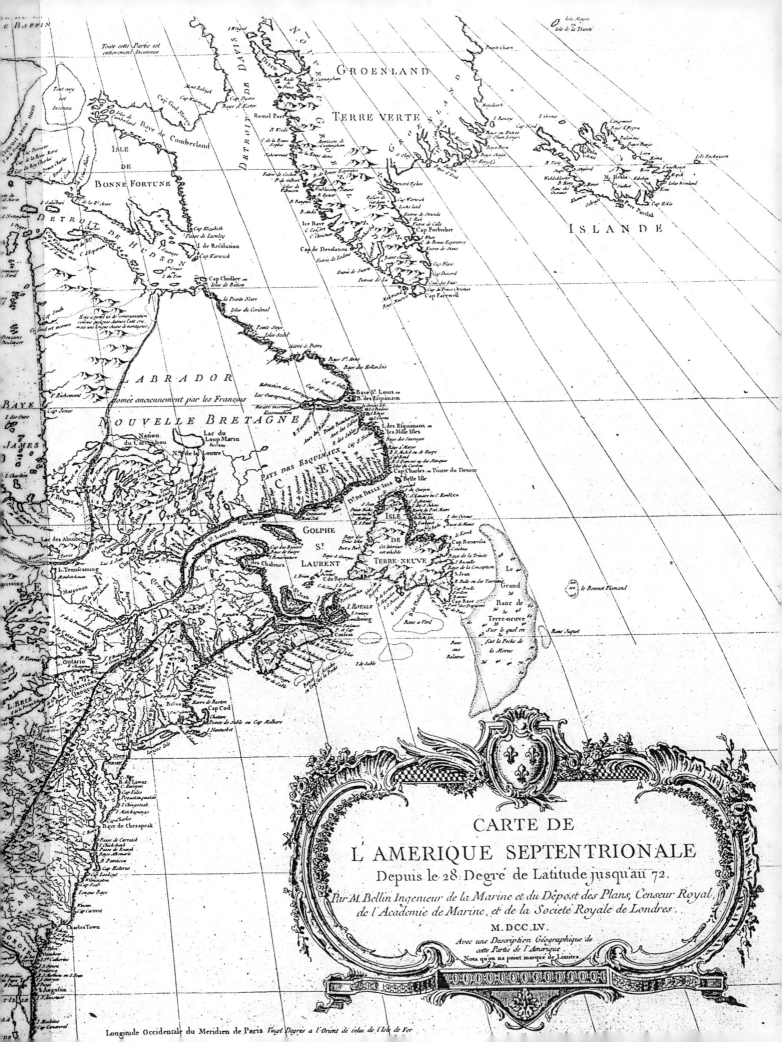

CARTE DE
L'AMERIQUE SEPTENTRIONALE
Depuis le 28 Degré de Latitude jusqu'au 72.

Par M. Bellin Ingenieur de la Marine et du Dépost des Plans, Censeur Royal,
de l'Académie de Marine, et de la Societé Royale de Londres.

M.DCC.LV.

Avec une Description Géographique de
cette Partie de l'Amerique.
Nota qu'on n'a point marqué de Limites.